THE INTERNATIONALIZATION
OF US WRITING PROGRAMS

THE INTERNATIONALIZATION OF US WRITING PROGRAMS

Edited by
SHIRLEY K ROSE
IRWIN WEISER

UTAH STATE UNIVERSITY PRESS
Logan

Published by Utah State University Press
An imprint of University Press of Colorado
245 Century Circle, Suite 202
Louisville, Colorado 80027

The University Press of Colorado is a proud member of
the Association of University Presses.

∞ This paper meets the requirements of the ANSI/NISO Z39.48-1992 (Permanence of
Paper)

The University Press of Colorado is a cooperative publishing enterprise supported,
in part, by Adams State University, Colorado State University, Fort Lewis College,
Metropolitan State University of Denver, Regis University, University of Colorado,
University of Northern Colorado, Utah State University, and Western State Colorado
University.

ISBN: 978-1-60732-675-5 (paperback)
ISBN: 978-1-60732-676-2 (ebook)
https://doi.org/10.7330/9781607326762

Library of Congress Cataloging-in-Publication Data

Names: Rose, Shirley K, editor. | Weiser, Irwin, editor.
Title: The internationalization of U.S. writing programs / edited by Shirley K Rose, Irwin
   Weiser.
Other titles: Internationalization of United States writing programs
Description: Logan: Utah State University Press, [2017] | Includes bibliographical
   references.
Identifiers: LCCN 2017037690| ISBN 9781607326755 (pbk.) | ISBN 9781607326762
   (ebook)
Subjects: LCSH: English language—Rhetoric—Study and teaching (Higher)—United
   States. | English language—Rhetoric—Study and teaching (Higher)—Foreign speakers.
   | Students, Foreign—Education (Higher)—United States. | Multilingual persons—
   Education (Higher)—United States.
Classification: LCC PE1405.U6 I58 2017 | DDC 808/.042071173—dc23
LC record available at https://lccn.loc.gov/2017037690

The University Press of Colorado gratefully acknowledges the generous support of
Purdue University's Office of Research and Partnerships and Department of English
toward the publication of this book.

Cover illustration © SuriyaPhoto/Shutterstock.

CONTENTS

THE INTERNATIONALIZATION OF US WRITING PROGRAMS

Introduction

INTERNATIONALIZED WRITING PROGRAMS IN THE TWENTY-FIRST-CENTURY UNITED STATES
Implications and Opportunities

Irwin Weiser and Shirley K Rose

SETTING THE CONTEXT

Universities in the United States are becoming increasingly attractive to undergraduate students from other countries. According to the 2016 *Open Doors* report from the Institute for International Education (released November 14, 2016, and the most recent at the time we are writing), there are 58 percent more international students in the United States now than there were a decade ago, and there have been ten consecutive years of steady increase (Institute for International Education 2016). The 7.1 percent increase between 2014–15 and 2015–16 represents sixty-nine thousand more students, bringing the total number of international students studying in the United States to over one million for the first time. While historically the majority of international degree-seeking students enrolling in US colleges and universities were pursuing graduate degrees, in 2015–16, for the fifth year in a row, there were more international undergraduate students than international graduate students in the United States (all statistics from *Open Doors* 2016)[1]

These increasing enrollments, as we have seen on our own campuses and as a number of our authors have noted, have come about for several often intertwined reasons. From the perspective of the students and the families of the students who come to the United States to study, the strong reputation of US higher education is an important draw. In many countries, having studied in the United States, and particularly earning a degree from a US college or university, carries with it prestige that enables returning students to get the most desirable jobs. Connected to the reputational and prestige attractiveness is the globalization of business, which not only makes it desirable for students from other countries to come to the United States but also is an important factor in

DOI: 10.7330/9781607326762.c000

the increasing emphasis on study-abroad experience for US students. Economic prosperity in their home countries is another factor contributing to increasing numbers of international undergraduate students coming to the United States to study, especially those from China who, despite a slowing of the rate of increase, constitute nearly one-third of the 1,043,839 international students in the United States. Put simply, there are not only more families in China who recognize the importance of an international educational experience for their children but there are also more families who can afford the cost of that experience. According to the *Open Doors* report, the primary source of funding for 66.5 percent of international students falls in the category of "Personal and Family" (Institute for International Education 2016).

Revenue plays an important part in the desire of US institutions to recruit and admit international students. These students typically pay full tuition. In public universities where there is a differential between in-state and out-of-state tuition, international students pay either out-of-state tuition or a higher tuition, as is the case at both our institutions. As several of our authors mention, revenue generation is a major motive for both public and private institutions, which are seeing traditional sources of revenue declining. There is, we believe, an element of charging what the market can bear, and as some of the authors note, these higher costs raise an ethical issue, particularly if there is no evidence that the increased tuition or special fees are being used to provide improved services, including writing and other language support, for international students.

A second reason US institutions seek international students is to globalize or internationalize or diversify their campuses. Just as globalization underlies the desire of many international students to come to the United States, many US institutions want to create opportunities for domestic students to become more globally aware and more prepared to live and work in what is often referred to as an *ever more interdependent world*. And, as Libby Miles points out in the final chapter of this collection, international students help institutions that have struggled to attract a more diverse domestic student population become more racially, ethnically, and culturally diverse.

The Internationalization of US Writing Programs contributes to a relatively recent conversation about writing program administration and second language writers. Of this recent work, David Martins's (2014) edited collection *Transnational Writing Program Administration* is most closely aligned with the work we present. However, with the exception of two chapters on writing programs on the US-Mexico border, *Transnational*

Writing Program Administration is concerned with the various ways writing is taught and administered in other countries, often as a version of a US-based writing program. *The Internationalization of US Writing Programs*, including a chapter by Martins and his coauthor Stan Van Horn, complements Martins's project by focusing on writing programs in US institutions and the way those programs respond to a student population that is both linguistically and culturally diverse. Other recent scholarship that has implications for the administrative and programmatic responsibilities of teaching nonnative speakers in mainstream postsecondary composition courses includes Bruce Horner, Min-Zhan Lu, and Paul Kei Matsuda's *Cross-Language Relations in Composition* (Horner, Lu, and Matsuda 2010) and Jay Jordan's *Redesigning Composition for Multilingual Realities* (Jordan 2012). In addition, Terry Myers Zawacki and Michelle Cox's *WAC and L2 Writers* (Zawacki and Cox 2014) serves to bring awareness of L2 student writers' perspectives to work in writing-across-the-curriculum pedagogy and curriculum. Each of these books represents important scholarship relevant to understanding the increasing diversity of college and university student populations and by extension the writing and writing-intensive courses those students take. This present collection focuses specifically on the evolving roles and responsibilities of writing program administrators who are leading efforts to provide all students on their campuses, regardless of nationality or first language, with competencies in writing that will serve them in the academy and beyond. By emphasizing the impact on writing programs of this multilingual, multicultural, multinational student population in US colleges and universities, *The Internationalization of US Writing Programs* offers an extended discussion that contributes to this increasingly important component of WPA preparation and work.

Our impetus for this collection came from our observations of the growth in the international student population at our own institutions. Currently, Arizona State University has the third largest international student enrollment in the United States and Purdue has the eighth largest (our institutions rank first and fourth in international student enrollments among public universities), so we have daily witnessed the quite literally changing faces of our campuses. We have participated in conversations, both informal and formal, about ways our campuses, and especially our writing programs, can better support international students and contribute to a positive campus culture. Further observations and conversations with colleagues at other institutions, articles in the higher education and popular press, and the examination of data from the Institute on International Education persuaded us we were not alone in thinking about how this demographic change affects our campuses and our writing programs. As the chapters in this collection demonstrate, writing program administrators and writing faculty across the country, in institutions of all kinds with large and with small international student enrollments, are conducting research, developing theories, and revising practices and are coming to similar conclusions. Most notable among those conclusions are

- that we must adopt and advocate for a perspective on language that acknowledges and respects the multi- and translinguality of both international and domestic L2 students,
- that we must better support our faculty who are committed to teaching all their students effectively, and
- that a review and revision of our practices motivated by the desire to respond to a changing student population can lead to improved practices for all students.

Our contributors discuss the role college and university writing programs have played in realizing the multiple reasons discussed earlier that are driving the increase in international students in US colleges and universities. Four key themes emerge in the discussion carried out in these chapters: productive change, seeing differently, supporting faculty, and language instruction versus writing instruction. In the following section, we will elaborate on each of these themes prior to our presenting a more detailed overview of the collection as a whole.

KEY THEMES

The Increase in International Students Motivates Productive Change.
Our premise for this collection is that the dramatic increase in international undergraduate students in US universities is changing—or should be changing—college writing programs because writing courses are among the first courses required of virtually every first-year student on every campus and writing plays an important role in students' success during and beyond that first year. While it may have been possible in the recent past either to offer a sufficient number of sections of second language writing (SLW) courses or to absorb a small number of nonnative speakers and writers of English (henceforward L2 students) into our composition courses, as the numbers of international undergraduate students attending US universities increase, in some institutions to as high as 20 percent of the total undergraduate population, writing programs and writing program administrators are having to—or will have to—consider how this changing demographic serves as a catalyst

for change throughout entire programs and alters conventional ways of seeing the presence of international students[2] on the campuses of US colleges and universities.

Change throughout programs is a consistent theme in the chapters in this collection. WPAs such as Christine Tardy and Susan Miller-Cochran, David Martins and Stan Van Horn, and Gail Shuck and Daniel Wilber emphasize that thinking about a changing student population has led them to recognize that revised administrative structures, curricular revisions, and new professional-development programs improve teaching and learning not just for international students but for all students. Such has been the case, as several authors including Christiane Donohue and Yu-Kyung Kang note, whenever major changes in student populations occur, from the increased number of veterans who attended college with support from the GI Bill after World War II to the open-admissions movement of the 1960s and 1970s and its continuing influences. And while such changes may bring about anxiety and sometimes even a sense of crisis (as was the case with the publication of *Why Johnny Can't Read* by Rudolph Flesch [1955] and *Newsweek*'s "Why Johnny Can't Write" cover story in 1977), contributors to this collection take this change in stride. They see the new reality of a much more linguistically, culturally, ethnically, geographically diverse student population as a challenging opportunity to review and revise their curriculum and pedagogy, the professional-development opportunities provided to their faculty, and their campus-wide collaborations. They reject the idea that addressing the needs of this growing student population lowers standards, as some on their campuses suggest, and instead consider benefits to all students, regardless of language background. Good pedagogy, they argue, is good pedagogy.

The chapters in this collection present the responses of writing program administrators (WPAs) and writing faculty as institutions of higher education become increasingly invested in recruiting undergraduate degree-seeking international students. These changes in the larger higher education landscape impact college and university writing programs and their administrators because, as mentioned above, these programs are expected to prepare students for academic and workplace writing through courses that are typically required for graduation and, in the case of first-year writing, that are assumed to provide the foundation for students' further academic coursework. In addition, as several authors point out, writing program administrators and writing faculty can do important cultural work in our universities. In their chapters, Jennifer Haan and Carolina Pelaez-Morales discuss how their research and experiences in faculty development across campus and within their own departments have not only revealed challenges under-prepared instructors face in working with international students but have also suggested that participation in research can be an impetus for self-reflection that leads to greater cultural awareness. Both Tarez Graban and Yu-Kyung Kang find that their responsibilities, as a coor-dinator for multilingual writing courses and an associate director of a writing center, respectively, involve them in interactions with academic staff and administrators from across campus that have the potential to increase support for writing instruction, enable new collaborations, and shape the way others think about international students and language difference. Perhaps most obviously, especially when international and domestic students are enrolled in the same courses, the kind of expo-sure to language and cultural differences that is an oft-stated reason for internationalizing our campuses benefits both groups of students, even if at times, as Heidi McKee points out, students both voice and must face stereotypes about one another.

Encountering Difference Helps Us See Differently.

Difference, especially language difference, emerges as another impor-tant theme for this collection, not unexpectedly. Authors make the case that increasing numbers of international students for whom English is not a first language (though it may be a frequently used second language or one of several languages these students use) draws our attention to questions about multi- and translinguality, about what English is, about what the appropriate goals of language instruction are, about what profi-ciency means, and so on. Indeed, it may be, as implied by both Margaret Willard-Traub and Carolina Pelaez-Morales, that increased numbers of international L2 students make us more conscious of the number of multilingual domestic students or domestic students whose home English differs from the traditional "standard" taught and expected in school. The obvious difference of having larger numbers of interna-tional students can make us more aware of other kinds of differences, even perhaps those invisible to us. The recognition of difference, lan-guage and otherwise, underlies the argument made by Jonathan Benda and his colleagues in their discussion of superdiversity, in which they argue that our conventional way of thinking about people as domestic or international, native speakers or L2, and so forth masks differences. While it is convenient to think in large categories such as these, the research, theoretical arguments, and experiences of our contributors remind us that recognizing difference is not some kind of misguided effort to be politically correct but rather is a challenge to see students, our most important stakeholders, as diverse individuals, not as a homogeneous group defined by their student status and our assumptions of what a college and university student is, should know, and so forth. Our authors point out that our international students have not a deficit but rather, as Margaret Willard-Traub put it, "a surplus of linguistic, cultural, and life knowledge that puts them at an advantage" (45). We must learn to recognize, appreciate, and tap into that surplus, knowing that doing so contributes to the understanding of others that a globalized university is supposed to support.

Faculty Want Professional-Development Support for
Working with Linguistically Diverse Students.

These chapters raise a number of points about the professional development of faculty who find themselves, generally with little or no background, teaching an increasingly linguistic and culturally diverse group of students. While some of these faculty are full time and some are on the tenure track or tenured, our authors point out that many, not surprisingly, are full time non-tenure track, part time, or graduate students. They are committed to teaching, including to teaching the new population of students who enroll in their courses, but they are also conscious that their lack of background in L2 theory and practice, and frequently in composition theory as well, has left them ill-prepared to work with diverse students. In their research at two different institutions, both Jennifer Haan and Carolina Pelaez-Morales found that faculty often try to compensate for what they perceive to be their own deficiencies and their students' needs by spending more time in individual conferences with international students or more time reading and responding to their writing. Stacey Sheriff and Paula Harrington explain that faculty want help, support, and professional-development opportunities, but as Pelaez-Morales points out, resources are frequently scarce. And as Katherine Daily O'Meara and Paul Matsuda remind us, building a community of faculty able to take advantage of such opportunities is difficult when many of them are part-time employees who may be teaching at several different institutions or may have other work and family responsibilities that make participation impossible.

While contributors offer a number of ideas about ways to support faculty through professional-development programs, one of the most compelling points raised in several chapters is that second language writing theory and practice must become part of every instructor's preparation and professionalization. Although scholarship by second language writing scholars has appeared in *WPA: Writing Program Administration,* including in the fall 2006 special issue "Second Language Writers and Writing Program Administrators," there must be further integration between second language writing scholarship and composition scholarship; and as Christine Tardy and Susan Miller-Cochran point out in their chapter, second language writing and ESL program administrators and composition program administrators must be active collaborators. The "CCCC Statement on Second Language Writing and Writers" (2009, reaffirmed November 2014) points out that second language writing scholarship and practice contribute to composition studies. The statement emphasizes that "second language writers have become an integral part of writing courses and programs" and urges "writing teachers and writing program administrators to [among other recommendations] recognize and take responsibility for the regular presence of second language writers in writing classes, to understand their characteristics, and to develop instructional and administrative practices that are sensitive to their linguistic and cultural needs."

Which Language(s)? or Writing Instruction Is Not the Same Thing as Language Instruction.

In the discussions of multilinguality and translinguality referred to above in our discussion of seeing differently, several authors point to ways that providing spaces for students to use their first language is beneficial. Yu-Kyung Kang writes about the single-language writing groups (SLWGs) she, a native speaker of Korean, facilitated for Korean students. She and the students frequently used Korean in their group work, even though they were discussing projects written in English. Stacey Sheriff and Paula Harrington discuss the benefits of recruiting international undergraduate tutors for the writing center Harrington directs. Heidi McKee notes the benefits of recruiting a Mandarin-speaking research assistant working with her and her Mandarin-speaking subjects. Jennifer Haan discusses the initial resistance of faculty to having students speak in Arabic and their eventual realization that the students were able to discuss their writing more easily and effectively when they used their first language. Their examples remind us that there is a distinction between writing instruction and English-language instruction and that the former may be facilitated by allowing or encouraging students to use their first language in situations where that is possible.

OVERVIEW OF THE COLLECTION

The essays in this collection present a variety of perspectives on the roles of writing programs and writing program administrators who recognize that approaches to defining program goals, curriculum, placement, assessment, and faculty development and teacher preparation must be responsive to an internationalized student population. The chapters demonstrate multiple approaches to theorizing the work of writing programs and/or illustrate a range of well-planned empirical writing program-based research projects, as we have advocated for and illustrated in our first two edited collections, *The Writing Program Administrator as Researcher* and *The Writing Program Administrator as Theorist* (Rose and Weiser 1999, 2002). Our contributors work in a wide range of institutions, from public to private, from urban to rural, and from liberal arts colleges to research universities, including the three public universities with the largest international enrollments in the United States and institutions with such small numbers of international undergraduate students that no specific programs exist to address their needs.

Following this introduction, the collection begins with three chapters that establish a global context, set out definitions, elaborate on the motivations for internationalization of US postsecondary institutions, and suggest a heuristic approach for thinking about the administration of internationalized writing programs that is exemplified implicitly in the chapters that follow. In chapter 1, "Writing Program Administrators in an Internationalizing Future: What's to Know?," Christiane Donahue addresses the question of what WPAs, and by extension the teachers with whom they work, need to know about global politics and economics, language and writing in higher education in other countries, and trends in internationalizing higher education in order to reimagine the local linguistic work of their programs in a global context. She also argues that *all* students, not only the traditional L2 students (some of whom are international but not all), will benefit from a differently imagined writing curriculum in our sure-to-be internationalized future. This argument is one that carries throughout the collection and is made explicitly by many of the contributors. The economic perspective raised by Donahue is continued by Margaret Willard-Traub in chapter 2, "Writing Programs and a New Ethos for 'Globalization.'" Using a feminist rhetorical lens, she offers a critique of the university-as-corporation and argues for a change toward (or perhaps return to) a feminist ethos of care in teaching and administration. In the final chapter of this introductory section, "Administrative Structures and Support for International L2 Writers: A Heuristic for WPAs," Christine Tardy and Susan Miller-Cochran explore the strengths and challenges of different models of writing program administrative structures with the goal of offering WPAs (broadly defined) a heuristic for assessing and revising structures that might best suit the needs and goals of their increasingly diverse student populations, programs, and institutions. Their heuristic, along with that offered by Libby Miles in the concluding chapter of this collection, provides WPAs with tools for reimagining their programs in response to changing student demographics.

We have grouped the next ten chapters according to their major focus: *program development*, which often requires collaboration with people outside the writing program (Benda, et al.; Graban, Sheriff and Harrington; and Kang); *curriculum development*, primarily within the specific writing program (Martins and Van Horn; Shuck and Wilber; McKee); and *faculty development* (O'Meara and Matsuda; Haan; and Pelaez-Morales.) In some ways, this grouping is artificial, implying a clear distinction among programs, curriculum, and faculty when in fact these three elements of writing program administration are intricately interrelated elements of what Edward White, Norbert Elliot, and Irvin Peckham have characterized as the "ecology" of a writing program (White, Elliot, and Peckham 2015, 7). We hope, however, that this structure guides readers to particular emphases within each section.

In the first of four chapters focusing on program development, the authorial team of Jonathan Benda, Michael Dedek, Chris Gallagher, Kristi Girdharry, Neal Lerner, and Matt Noonan from Northeastern University argues that their students exemplify what Jan Blommaert and Ben Rampton (Blommaert and Rampton 2011) describe as "superdiversity," characterized by an explosion of identity categories brought about by increased mobility in a globalizing world. The authors describe three initiatives they are taking to revise their writing program to better acknowledge superdiversity by becoming better attuned to the diverse language, literacy, and cultural experiences and practices of all their students. While Benda and his colleagues work primarily within their writing program, the next three chapters in this section offer insights into the strategies used by administrators to find collaborators and to work across their campuses to bring about changes in programs that serve multilingual writers. In chapter 5, "Contending with Difference: Points of Leverage for Intellectual Administration of the Multilingual FYC Course," Tarez Graban describes three "points of leverage" (Melzer 2013)—in the department, across disciplines, and in the institution—that enabled arguments for intellectual resources and pedagogical change during the five-year period she oversaw the multilingual composition curriculum at Indiana University. In chapter 6, "It's Not a Course, It's a Culture: Supporting International Student s' Writing at a Small Liberal Arts College," Stacey Sheriff and Paula Harrington focus on two central aspects of their work to build partnerships across campus to improve conditions for all students. The final chapter in this section examines the role writing centers can play in supporting international students. In "Expanding the Role of the Writing Center at the 'Global University,'" Yu-Kyung Kang explains how the rapid increase in the number of international students at the University of Illinois and the university's underpreparedness in supporting them heightened and altered the role of the writing center, making it a hub for international student support and a central source for administrator and teacher training.

The next section is comprised of three chapters that illustrate how WPAs employ research in their work to revise curriculum. The first two chapters in this section, by David Martins and Stan Van Horn and by Gail Shuck and Daniel Wilber, examine changes in first-year writing curriculums, while the third, Heidi McKee's "Intercultural Communication and Teamwork: Revising Business Writing for Global Networks," focuses on an upper-division business writing program. Martins and Van Horn describe an "internationalized curriculum" for first-year writing and offer preliminary findings of a research study on the redesigned curriculum. Following a brief description of the curriculum they designed, they discuss a pilot offering of the course and the findings of an assessment of that pilot. In "'Holding the Language in My Hand': A Multilingual Lens on Curricular Design," Gail Shuck and Daniel Wilber present research designed to address Ilona Leki's (2001) concern that student voices are rarely featured in research on second language writers. Shuck and Wilber's research complements recent studies of multilingual students' placement decisions by examining how such decisions play out within a curricular structure that does not offer parallel multilingual and mainstream tracks. In the final chapter of this section, Heidi McKee details the research methods and findings that led to the revision of the curriculum of Miami University's business writing program in response to changing student demographics. The new curriculum includes direct instruction in intercultural communication and teamwork in order to prepare all students for communicating in global networks. All three of these chapters describe programs in which domestic and international students enroll in the same courses and learn to work across language and cultural differences.

Faculty development is the concern of the next three chapters. Katherine Daily O'Meara and Paul Kei Matsuda, in "Building the Infrastructure of L2 Writing Support: The Case of Arizona State University," present an institutional case study of an effort to nurture the "culture of L2 writing" among instructors at Arizona State University, which, as we mentioned earlier, has one of the largest enrollments of international students in the United States. In contrast to the Arizona State context, the next two chapters are set in institutions where the numbers of international students are small in comparison with the overall student population and where there are limited resources to support faculty with little or no second language teaching preparation. In "Developing Faculty for the Multilingual Writing Classroom," Jennifer Haan describes a long-term study of faculty response to internationalization in a university writing program at a midsized private university that has experienced a 350 percent increase in international student enrollment over the last eight years and reports on the faculty-development approach that resulted from that research. Concluding this section, Carolina Pelaez-Morales describes research into the tensions faculty members with little or no background in second language writing experience in their work with L2 writers. Her discussion is particularly relevant to administrators looking to address small, gradual increases in L2 enrollment in institutions that do not offer ESL writing sections.

We conclude this collection with Libby Miles's "Infusing Multilingual Writers: A Heuristic for Moving Forward" because the chapter provides an exemplary case of how the use of a heuristic can help WPAs explore multiple perspectives as they grapple with changing conditions in their institution and writing programs. Miles explains how her use of Richard E. Young, Alton L. Becker, and Kenneth L. Pike's tagmemic heuristic for systematic inquiry (Young, Becker, and Pike 1970) helped her respond to the tripart exigency of how to support a rapidly increasing number of international students and their instructors while also developing a university culture enhanced by the differing perspectives, assumptions, backgrounds, and values a truly diverse campus affords. Thus, the chapter provides a strategy for other WPAs who are seeking a generative tool for analyzing the implications of change on their own campuses and investigating the options for developing workable approaches to supporting students, instructors, and institutional goals.

WHO SHOULD READ THIS BOOK?

As was the case with our three previous edited collections, *The WPA as Researcher*, *The WPA as Theorist*, and *Going Public: The WPA as Advocate for Engagement*, we have planned and developed this collection primarily for current administrators of a variety of college and university writing programs, including first-year composition, second language writing, ESL, writing across the curriculum, writing centers, and professional writing programs (Rose and Weiser 1999, 2002, 2010). As we point out early in this essay, each of these kinds of college and university writing programs is now enrolling significant numbers of international students who are second language writers. Our contributors demonstrate how serving these students is changing writing programs in positive ways.

With its emphasis on internationalization of writing programs, we anticipate that this collection will also be a valuable resource for colleagues who teach, for graduate students who take seminars on writing program administration, and for students writing dissertations focused on program leadership, curriculum, and professional development because it addresses a significant new demographic of writing students WPAs will need to consider.

In addition, we hope this collection will prove useful to the rapidly growing scholarly community of specialists in second language writing (SLW), particularly those who administer SLW courses and programs, those who teach graduate seminars on issues in second language writing, and those who are making SLW a focus of their graduate preparation and scholarship. We are particularly pleased that several of our contributors are scholars who are working at the intersections of writing program administration and second language writing.

Finally, because our contributors have provided extended discussions of concrete and specific examples of a variety of administrative configurations, curriculum designs, and program-based research, we recommend this collection to administrators including deans and provosts who find themselves seeking ways to provide academic support to the increasing number of international students on their campuses.

CONCLUDING OBSERVATIONS

While we have discussed at some length the responsibilities of people formally designated as WPAs, we have also observed that some faculty who are working with international students or who have responsibility or scholarly interest in the education of international students do not have official designations that identify them as being resources on their campuses. They may be the only faculty with training and expertise in L2 or second language writing. They and their work may be invisible to others on their campuses. But we urge administrators across campus to recognize and seek out their expertise and include them in discussions and initiatives about supporting internationalization efforts and international students.

We believe WPAs and writing faculty can help set a positive tone for campus discussions about internationalization of our colleges and universities. Our programs and courses are oriented toward serving students' educational needs, and we have learned to reject deficit models of literacy that often accompany changing student demographics. Our positive approach to difference benefits our students. Such an approach is especially important given the national and international xenophobia that characterizes much of the public discourse in late 2016. As we write, Britain has recently voted to exit the European Union, terrorist attacks based on religious ideology and killings by and of police officers are part of the daily news, and here and abroad politicians talk about ways to limit immigration, including the immigration of refugees seeking life-saving asylum. This context contributes to the experiences and consciousness of both our US and international students. Writing programs have the potential to teach and reinforce different values by recognizing and embracing linguistic, national, and cultural differences. The chapters in this collection offer suggestions about how we can do so, how we can contribute to the best purposes and goals of higher education, how we can be agents for public good.

Notes

1. Because the *Open Door* report is based on full-year data, its annual November release tells us about enrollments in the preceding years. We are aware, however, of some comments in the higher education press about a decline in the number of international students applying to and enrolling in US colleges and universities in the 2016–17 academic year. Varied reasons have been suggested for this decline. In a recent article in *Inside Higher Ed*, Elizabeth Redden explains that a change in the Saudi government's scholarship program has led to a significant decline in the numbers of Saudi students coming to the United States, especially those who are starting their studies in English-language programs rather than in degree programs (Redden 2016). Karen Fischer reports a dramatic decline in the number of Brazilian students studying in the United States, attributed to the cancellation of a government-sponsored scholarship program (Fischer 2016). She also cites a slowing of the Chinese economy, the improvement of Chinese universities, and "mixed messages" from the Chinese government about studying abroad as possible reasons for a decrease in the rate of growth of the number of Chinese students studying in the United States (Fischer 2016). In "The International Bubble," Rick Selzer mentions the impact of these changes in scholarship programs but also cites several other potential reasons for a decline, including a slowing economy in South Korea and the perception in both Japan and South Korea that it may be more advantageous to seek a degree from a top-ranked university in the student's home country than to study abroad (Selzer 2016). Selzer, whose article appeared prior to the 2016 US presidential election, is among journalists who cite concern about the outcome

of the election and anti-immigrant, anti-Muslim campaign statements by Donald J. Trump, now the president-elect (Fischer 2016; Selzer 2016). These economic and political considerations may have an impact in the upward trend of international students coming to the United States, but no one has suggested the likelihood of a dramatic drop from the record numbers in 2015–16.

There are additional reasons some universities may see changes in their international student populations, especially in regards to the numbers of students coming from the same country or a small number of countries. Some universities are realizing drawing most of their students from only one or two countries can counteract efforts to use international student enrollment to diversify and globalize the institution. Others are concerned about overdependence on students from a small number of countries to provide the much-needed revenue stream. At Purdue University, the number of international undergraduate students has declined slightly from a high of 5,251 in 2014 to 5,103 in fall 2016, but the decline is the result of a deliberate decision to diversify the international undergraduate student population and to hold the number of first-year international students to approximately 1,000 per year. Application data for the 2016–17 academic year show that the number of international students applying to Purdue for the first time has continued to increase, with 13,715 applications received (Pam T. Horne, e-mail message to Irwin Weiser, November 22, 2016; Brian Priester, e-mail message to Irwin Weiser, November 15, 2016; Purdue University 2016).

We believe that while the numbers of international students from any given country may fluctuate due to any or a combination of the reasons cited above, US colleges and universities will continue to enroll large numbers of international undergraduate students, and writing program administrators and writing faculty will continue to be attentive to the challenges and opportunities such diversity brings. Though their numbers may decrease, their impact on our writing programs will not.

2. While we recognize that the second language writers in our classes who are immigrants or US citizens present many of the same challenges and benefits as these international students, our focus is on ways writing programs are changing in order to meet the needs of second language writers who are in the United States specifically and primarily for the purpose of college-level study.

References

Blommaert, Jan, and Ben Rampton. 2011. "Language and Superdiversity." *Diversities* 13 (2): 1–21. http://www.unesco.org/new/en/social-and-human-sciences/resources/periodicals/diversities/past-issues/vol-13-no-2-2011/language-and-superdiversity/.

CCCC Statement on Second Language Writing and Writers. 2009 (reaffirmed Nov. 2014). Conference on College Composition and Communication.

Fischer, Karen. 2016. "A History Lesson on the Future of Foreign Enrollments." *Chronicle of Higher Education* 14 (November). http://www.chronicle.com/article/A-History-Lesson-on-on-the-Future/238372.

Flesch, Rudolph. 1955. *Why Johnny Can't Read, and What You Can Do About It.* New York: Harper & Brothers.

Horner, Bruce, Min-Zhan Lu, and Paul Kei Matsuda. 2010. *Cross-Language Relations in Composition.* Carbondale: Southern Illinois University Press.

Institute for International Education. 2016. *Open Doors 2016.* https://www.iie.org/Research-and-Publications/Open-Doors#.WCnbX0fqVbr.

Jordan, Jay. 2012. *Redesigning Composition for Multilingual Realities.* Carbondale: Southern Illinois University Press.

Leki, Ilona. 2001. "Hearing Voices: L2 Students' Experiences in L2 Writing Courses."
    In *On Second Language Writing*, edited by Tony Silva and Paul Kei Matsuda, 17–28.
    Mahwah, NJ: Lawrence Erlbaum.

Martins, David. 2014. *Transnational Writing Program Administration*. Logan: Utah State
    University Press.

Melzer, Dan. 2013. "Using Systems Thinking to Transform Writing Programs." *WPA:
    Writing Program Administration* 36 (2): 75–94.

Purdue University. 2016. *Data Digest*. https://www.purdue.edu/datadigest/.

Redden, Elizabeth. 2016. "Saudi Enrollment Declines." *Inside Higher Ed* 18 (July).
    https://www.insidehighered.com/news/2016/07/18/saudi-student-numbers-fall
    -many-campuses.

Rose, Shirley K, and Irwin Weiser. 1999. *The Writing Program Administrator as Researcher:
    Inquiry in Action and Reflection*. Portsmouth, NH: Heinemann.

Rose, Shirley K, and Irwin Weiser. 2002. *The Writing Program Administrator as Theorist:
    Making Knowledge Work*. Portsmouth, NH: Heinemann.

Rose, Shirley K, and Irwin Weiser. 2010. *Going Public: What Writing Programs Learn from
    Engagement*. Logan: Utah State University Press. https://doi.org/10.2307/j.ctt4cgpfh.

Selzer, Rick. 2016. "The International Bubble." *Inside Higher Ed* 26 (September).
    https://www.insidehighered.com/news/2016/09/26/panelists-warn-international-
    student-bubble.

White, Edward M., Norbert Elliot, and Irvin Peckham. 2015. *Very Like a Whale: The
    Assessment of Writing Programs*. Logan: Utah State University Press.

Young, Richard E., Alton L. Becker, and Kenneth L. Pike. 1970. *Rhetoric Discovery and
    Change*. New York: Harcourt.

Zawacki, Terry Myers, and Michelle Cox. 2014. *WAC and Second Language Writers*.
    Anderson, SC: Parlor.

PART I

Contexts, Definitions, and Heuristics

1

WRITING PROGRAM ADMINISTRATORS IN AN INTERNATIONALIZING FUTURE
What's to Know?

Christiane Donahue

INTRODUCTION

There is no doubt that the student population in US higher education is rapidly changing—a change that, it turns out, is shared around the globe. European institutions are seeing high rates of international enrollees, from across Europe (encouraged by the Bologna Process) but also from Asia, South America, and Africa; Korean colleagues report high numbers of students from China seeking to complete their education in Korean universities; and so on. But this change within our classrooms is only part of the picture. The multdirectional movement suggests change in the world in which graduates will do their work, live their lives.

My title asks, for today's WPA, "What's to know?" Put simply, my reply is, "We need to know that while we do great things in US writing programs, and have a rich and strong history, the world is changing. We are sending students out into that world and we want them to be as prepared as possible." We need to know that (1) we are not alone—other work on higher education writing can help us sharply articulate our own strengths and challenges—and (2) all students must grapple with questions of language and English if they are to be truly and fully prepared. We, and our students, are part of a new ecology, a new ground and new air: an overall organic system of relationships among individuals, institutions, and environments that demands interdependence. As Mary Jo Reiff, Anis Bawarshi, Michelle Baliff, and Christian Weisser note in *Writing Program Ecologies* (Reiff et al. 2015), in an ecology model, "the system provides the site of meaning," (3) and the complex relationships and dynamic connections among participants occur within "a network, a system, a web: an ecology" (3).

DOI: 10.7330/9781607326762.c001

New modes of interaction in that ecology entail changes in the way institutions respond to students generally and in how they respond to student writing specifically. This chapter explores what WPAs, and by extension the teachers with whom they work, need to know about these issues in order to think through new demands in the local work of their programs in a global context. In terms of our purposes in higher education overall, I will argue that a metacritical, internationalized awareness of writing research and teaching in higher education is essential to helping our culture, our attitudes, and our self-awareness evolve in new directions. It can inform our programmatic decisions, raise questions about components of writing and writing instruction that we have naturalized, and call us to better understand the role of language in that writing.

In terms of the implications for language, I argue that all students, not only the traditional range of L2 students, will benefit from a differently imagined writing curriculum in our sure-to-be internationalized future. Ultimately, WPAs' understanding of English is at the heart of students' future work in a superdiverse world: English as both not inherently tied to writing and no longer seeable as a single normed entity. I hope WPAs will find this thought piece a provocation and a useful tool. What readers will not find is an article about language diversity in our US classrooms today as a way to improve or broaden our attention to L2 learners, though I will be treating questions of superdiversity, globalization, and mobility that clearly also impact that issue. What I hope to share is a sense of the value of changing our collective consciousness about our enterprise.

PART ONE: HIGHER EDUCATION: INTERNATIONAL, GLOBAL, MOBILE, SUPERDIVERSE . . . ?

The terms *international* and *global* are sometimes used interchangeably. Perspectives from fields as diverse as sociology, economics, education, and international politics suggest that internationalizing is built from the starting point of *nations* and then imagines *inter*-nation interactions. *Internationalizing higher education* tends toward the idea that US colleges might expand their reach, establish campuses overseas, or draw additional students in from other countries. *Globalization* generally draws on questions concerning, for example, increasing economic interdependence, the "shrinking" of the world stage, driven in part by social media and the Internet, lower travel costs, and the rehierarchizing of multinational corporations over nation-states. With no *nation* in its root, it focuses our attention on common experiences driven by something other than nation-state configurations.

Globalization and internationalization affect higher education in overlapping ways. The global and international aspects can in fact take quite different shapes, despite the shared terminology. Higher education's internationalization has been defined by Jane Knight in "Internationalisation of Higher Education: A Conceptual Framework" (cited in Ninnes and Hellsten 2005), as "the process of integrating international and intercultural dimensions into the teaching, research, and service functions of higher education institutions" (215). The globalization of higher education engages with commodification of brands of teaching and pedagogy and with market forces (215) driving, for example, competition for student populations, a phenomenon intensified by the evolution of MOOCs or distance-learning models or even the opening of US campuses abroad.

Social geography, a human geography that serves to make sense of the geographical nature of being-in-the-world (Verstraete and Cresswell 2002, 12), deepens our understanding of internationalization and globalization by offering mobility as the framing concept for twenty-first-century societal dynamics.[1] Ginette Verstraete and Tim Cresswell note that the concepts of place and roots were long valued over mobility; we've had a humanistic engagement with place as a site of authentic roots (11). A mobility perspective considers place as radically open and permeable (12), and the stability we seem to have counted on becomes less foundational, replaced by an expectation that people will move, travel, engage, whether virtually or in person, whether in real time or asynchronously, in every lived context. Mobility is more focused on the individual in relation to these broader phenomena, exploring how and why people move, in what ways, with what contours and consequences.

A related term more recently taken up by writing scholars is *transnationalism*, a frame grounded in anthropology, sociology, economics, and geography. It emphasizes *trans* activity but still works from a *nations* starting point, while indicating a fluid relationship among those nations. The social scholarship defines transnationalism as "immigrants who stay connected with the source country and use current modes of communication to do so," much like what is described in social network theory more broadly (Vertovec 2007, 1044); migrants, through daily-life activity, create social fields that cross nation-state boundaries (Basch, Schiller, and Blanc 1994; Gonzalez 2013). Transnational contexts are often driven by a tension between integration into the new culture or country and maintaining ties to a home context. For student populations, this "anchored mobility" influences how they prioritize their learning choices. For our purposes, the new social fields and interconnections created transnationally deeply influence communication and text construction.

This is a new moving world, moving into, out of, across, or within countries. Steven Vertovec (2007) suggests that while "managing multiculturalism" isn't new, we have entered an era of "superdiversity" in which it isn't that the variables and the correlations are new, it's the sheer scale of things, the "coalescence of factors which condition people's lives" (1025). He suggests the key to superdiversity is not only the increased international mobility of peoples for an increasing range of reasons but also the internal diversity within populations on the move—workers, students, new citizens, spouses and families, refugees, illegal or undocumented workers—which means that country of origin is simply a less relevant variable (1030, 1039). Of course, schools in particular are sites of these diversities.

In terms of language, writing, and higher education, the idea of superdiversity helps us see the language-specific ways globalization and mobility can impact US writing classrooms, writing instruction, writing research, and our choices about what to value, what to teach, and how to support writing faculty. Certainly L2 teaching and scholarship have worked long and hard to highlight these challenges and to support multilingual students in these ranges of populations. WPAs cannot avoid encountering multilingual writing questions in their work, and language diversity has been increasingly broadly acknowledged, though these questions can look quite different in different institutions. But the writing question is not only about multilingual student needs and repertoires.

Writing Research and Instruction Internationally

Attention to writing outside US contexts offers insight into the prioritization of writing as a construction of meaning in diverse disciplinary contexts. The myths that there is no writing instruction outside our known US contexts and that there has been no research about higher education writing until recently are patent examples of our misreading of the world through a US lens, one that can be refocused via growth in our awareness of other traditions. I believe this awareness does unsettle our clean narratives about world dominance in this development, but that unsettling is not a negative.

Our US narrative is our own, after all. We have, from the 1960s on, established a unique path with our situated approaches to pedagogy, our institutional and programmatic trends, and our own traditions of research, all with clear strengths and clear limitations that are them-selves often the subject of intense debate within the field. We can point to the early work in the City University of New York system, often cited as the birthplace of composition. The "constellation of people and ideas" (Brereton 2011) at that time in that system set a path via the attention to ordinary student writing as something worth reading as carefully as literature (Trimbur 2011). The Dartmouth Seminar of 1966, whose work with personal growth and expressive writing controlled the field for quite some time afterwards, established the focus on writing as a process that has remained one of the single most important elements of writing instruction today.

These and other important events should not lead us to feeling first but simply to contextualizing our work within the specificities of US higher education, just as other countries do for their contexts. Certainly, worldwide, teachers and scholars have thought about students' needs, studied writing in a population beyond grammar school, and developed support programs. Some US work is helpful to these contexts, some is not, just as some work outside US contexts is helpful to the United States and some is not. I think the contact with other traditions, much like the contact described in superdiversity studies, offers alternative ways of growing writing studies and multiple opportunities for WPAs to broaden their knowledge and understanding.

The work on writing in higher education around the world is rich and deep: writing centers, writing programs, publications, conferences drawing on writing research and how it works, develops, is best taught and learned, is situated—across all levels, in a variety of cultural and institutional contexts, sometimes focused on students learning aca-demic English but more often focused on writing in languages of the countries in question as students move through higher education. We must be open to radically different grounds and approaches across international lines that do constitute writing program work (see for example Martins 2015), even as shared motivations and approaches also emerge. New frames of writing research from around the globe also interrogate our assumptions.

I offer two cases that can highlight these issues. I draw a very broad-brush overview to give a sense of both intersections and divergences with US priorities, as well as histories of and possible misperceptions about the work in and through these cases: Australia and the francophone cluster of France, Belgium, and Canada. I hope to show the degree to which writing instruction and research have a history we will recognize and different insights from which we can benefit.

Australia

Australia's forty-some-year history with writing in higher education, starting in the early 1980s, has evolved in key domains: identifying challenges for students in higher education writing; supporting writing instruction through the disciplines; eschewing "generic" writing education; grounding the theory of writing education through diverse fields including education and applied linguistics; developing support for students in higher education writing. I spend some time developing what has happened in Australia because it serves well the question of what has developed outside the United States more generally and because it offers intriguing, useful insights in comparison to US developments. In addition, Australia's history avoids treating the complicated question of whether writing instruction outside the United States has been attached to writing in English or writing in languages of particular countries or regions, a question I'll take up separately. Here I am particularly indebted to Australian scholars like Kate Chanock for their recent historical overviews of these developments on which I am drawing. Chanock, in "Academic Writing Instruction in Australian Tertiary Education: The Early Years" (Chanock 2012), notes, "I read every publication in this field that I could obtain from the eighties, often in the form of non-refereed conference papers" (7), thus offering a comprehensive overview not available to every reader.

Chanock notes that early development of attention to higher education writing was in part in response to the politics of "wider participation in higher education," a phenomenon that has been called "massification" by scholars and journalists in Australian and European contexts since the 1980s, with its accompanying worry about underprepared students (7; see also Skillen 2006). She suggests that these concerns predated the "wider participation" era of the late 1980s but were highlighted by it (9). One response in the 1980s to this perceived need was the development of "learning centers" staffed by learning advisors (Ballard 1984; Beasley 1988; Skillen 2006). The learning advisors, who worked largely one on one with students, believed students' challenges grew out of encountering new communities of practice and new (academic) dialects, not deficiencies in their abilities (Chanock 2012, 10).

These challenges have also been described by Iris Vardi (2000), citing research from the 1990s, as difficulty working out "the hidden rules governing what could be said and how it needed to be said" (2), as if academic discourse were a new language with new underlying understandings, both in students' transition from secondary to higher education and in their moves across disciplines. Jan Maree Maher and Jennifer Mitchell later explored this transition from students' points of view.

They gathered student perceptions in the humanities and the social sciences, via focus groups, and identified key student uncertainties as well as mismatches between student and faculty perspectives in the areas of purpose ("what am I doing here?"), reading strategy ("what and how much should I be reading?"), and writing assessments as students were faced with complex new tasks and genres (Maher and Mitchell 2010).

The learning advisors of the 1980s and 1990s, whose roles were not limited to writing, demonstrated that student writers could in fact succeed in most contexts if they responded to the assignment and used strong conventional argument techniques, regardless of factors such as error (Chanock 2012, 10). In a study of peer-review effectiveness, Vardi (2009) identified the challenges students face as primarily in terms of "voice in relation to authorities" and being able to evaluate textual materials in discipline-appropriate ways (350), noting that disciplines themselves are internally diverse with respect to discursive and rhetorical patterns.

These concerns had been evident in the 1970s and 80s in Australia's history and resulted in the development, by the 1980s, first of "remedial" writing classes or "generic" approaches and then of writing attention embedded in disciplinary contexts. The generic approaches—approaches that try to teach writing as skill, separate from disciplinary context—were fairly quickly deemed inadequate, a determination we find echoed across various national contexts and time periods outside the United States. Brigid Ballard (1984), for example, "found instruction in grammar or ideal structures of essays . . . to be of marginal value . . . if [students] are approaching their materials in a manner inappropriate to the academic culture of which they are a part" (52).

In fact, if there is a unifying theme across cultural contexts, it is the different iterations of the same tension between generic and context-specific questions of writing—one we have been experiencing fairly acutely in the United States as first-year writing is called into question in various ways. Sharon Crowley aggressively made the case in her 1998 work, *Composition in the University*, that US composition is not grounded in the content of the field and its methods as are other disciplines (Crowley 1998); David Smit (2004) famously argued for the "end of composition studies," as he titled his book. Others have pointed to the nongeneralizable knowledge that can be acquired in a generic first-year course, as for example David Russell (1995) describing the nature of balls and ball-ness as compared to the huge variety of ball games one might play, drawing on significantly different perceptions and abilities. The growing body of scholarship on writing-knowledge transfer and adaptation has been building some empirical evidence for a lack of connection between first-year composition in most of the relatively generic ways it is commonly taught and the needs and demands of later specific contexts. This work extends what we had already learned in earlier reports from longitudinal studies such as Lucille McCarthy's (1987) or Marilyn Sternglass's (1997) about some of the issues with a generic approach to first-year writing.

For Chanock (2012), "A consensus has been building that little of value can be said about writing at the generic level" (15). Jan Skillen et al. (1998), in reviewing the 1970s and 1980s, had already identified one of the learning models they rejected as the "remedial" model that cited the lack of preparation of some students arriving at the university and positioned students as those who needed help or did not, when in fact all students need to develop writing ability, in particular in the various specific contexts they will encounter (3). This approach had "marginalize[d] learning development by keeping it on the 'fringe' of academic study instead of being situated as an integral part of all students' development" (4). Maintaining that writing instruction can and must be generic in content "isolate[s] it from other disciplines and their curricula" (Skillen 2006, 141).

The 1990s, according to Skillen et al. (1998), saw the beginning of "integrated" models of writing instruction that positioned literacy and language learning as part and parcel of disciplinary learning. The modes grew out of substantial research about writing and disciplinarity, from both student and faculty perspectives as well as theoretically. The studies targeted specific connections, for example, between thinking in a discipline and what writing in that discipline performs and enables, or key discourse patterns and linguistic features in different disciplinary contexts, including within disciplines in subfields (Vardi 2000). The argument for "explicit instruction in, and development of, academic literacies [as] integrated into the curriculum of each discipline" surfaced (Chanock 2012, 15).

These models suggested that "students need to acquire new sets of literacy and learning skills pertinent to academia in general and to their fields of study in particular" (Skillen 2006, 142). They moved the work on writing into the content curriculum and created problems for the learning advisors who had initially worked with students on writing outside their curricular work. But in some models, such as the one Skillen (2006) describes for the University of Wollongang, university faculty in the disciplines were able to partner with academic developers to enable deep-level learning support for student writers in the disciplines and to help faculty understand that part of their responsibility is indeed to help students enter into the discourses of their disciplines. This model had the additional benefit of more generally improving faculty teaching, making it more student centered and more intentional. Monash University's "transition to tertiary education" model focuses on "not just a vertical [transition], school/previous study to university, but also a lateral one, moving from one discipline specialization to another" (Clerehan 2003, 79). It has centered its work on developing textual practices, discursive practices, and institutional practices with students as part of their disciplinary work. These models go far in "escaping the remedial tag" (Skillen 2006, 141) by engaging directly with the curriculum and its faculty, though not without escaping the problem WID programs everywhere encounter: the writing experts can be marginalized because they don't know the content, but the disciplinary faculty are not always convinced of either the value of writing or their own ability to support students in these ways.

Francophone Writing Work in France and Belgium

The evolution in these francophone settings has been equally varied in terms of contributing disciplines, from "didactics" and education to linguistics and psychology. As in Australia, francophone scholars and teachers were fairly quick to try and to reject, in the 1960s, a national skills-based generic curriculum intended to offer acontextual instruction in basic abilities (Donahue 2009). But in France, where this kind of program was near universal, the rejection resulted in decades of little development. In the past twenty years, a renewed, contextual interest has evolved via research about polyphony and intertextuality in college students' writing, difficulties students face entering new discourse communities, cognitive processes of writing, writing in professional and professionalizing contexts, and the development of a new domain, "university literacies" (Donahue 2009).

In Belgium, on the other hand, the rejection of generic skills-based writing instruction resulted in some more local signature programs focused on deep learning embedded in the disciplines and cotaught by language and disciplinary experts. The Center for University Methodology at l'Université Libre de Bruxelles is an outstanding example. Recently celebrating its thirtieth anniversary, it has worked with students and faculty across the university. It began with a focus on skills and grammar and normative approaches but evolved over time, through a phase of attention to the discourse-community model, to its current framework of acculturation and competence-based attention to student writing in disciplinary contexts and from a "remedial" focus to a focus on student growth and development (Pollet 2012). Center faculty work with faculty across the disciplines in tight partnership, developing curricula for disciplinary courses as well as offering independent courses. We see in this work some intersections with US writing-in-the-disciplines initiatives, faculty-development initiatives, and a marriage of language and writing "didactics" with disciplinary knowledge. We see as well both echoes of and differences from the two Australian models of learning advisors and academic developers.

Emergent interests, research, and programming in other countries around the globe raise different kinds of questions for us as we and our students become highly mobile. For example, francophone Canada's research into higher education writing has been strongly influenced by demands at the professional level that have filtered down into college settings (Beaudet and Rey 2012). Decades of respected and substantive empirical research on *preuniversity* writing around the world could prove to be an unparalleled resource for US writing scholars. For example, while recent work in Latin America appears to be young, as depicted in the innovative metawork of Charles Bazerman, Natiliz Avila, Ana Valeria Bork, Francinia Cristofia Poliseli-Correa, Vera Lucia Cristovao, Monica Ladino, and E. Narvaez, the focus on reading alongside writing in the Latin American research is particularly exciting and encouraging. It shows a deeper approach to literacy as both reading and writing from the start. This kind of insight might allow for what Bazerman et al. hope for, "approaches from outside the region entering into a complex, multi-sided discussion, in which Latin American scholars as equals are contributing new perspectives and fresh research, even as they are learning from what has gone on in other parts of the world." (Bazerman et al., forthcoming, 18).

Writing instruction and writing research have been thriving in sites outside the United States and beyond US institutions implanted outside the United States, sometimes with a thirty- or forty-year history (see Martins 2015). But, while these sites have some threads in common with each other or with our US priorities, they also have specific, concrete differences that can prompt deep questioning in our US programs, questioning specifically relevant to current attention to writing-knowledge adaptation across contexts. The unilateral rejection, over time, of a generic or autonomous model of literacy in favor of a disciplinary one is a strong common thread: interest in disciplinary writing has been the driving force of much, though not all, of the writing scholarship and research elsewhere, in contrast to FYC in the United States.

Other Histories

The deep valuing of writing in the disciplines in these other traditions is solidly shared with the United States. But here as well, perhaps, developments are more complicated than we might think. WID has a more recent history in the United States than does first-year composition, dating back to the mid-1970s, and at least some other countries began to focus on writing and disciplinarity sooner than the United States did, especially in graduate-student contexts where the research about student writing continues to be much more developed today than in the United States. The single most striking example of an early history is described by Otto Kruse (2006), who traces the origins of writing in the disciplines to the early 1800s in the Humboldtian university in Germany, citing explicit regulations and writing-to-learn pedagogies in place. Another example is the history of attention to writing in Western Canada. Kevin Alfred Brooks (1997) firmly establishes a strong, deep history of higher education writing instruction in the *first* half of the twentieth century, delivered by English departments as a part of nation-building and influenced by the United States. That attention ended in Western Canada in the mid-1950s in large part, Brooks notes, because of Cold War effects there on the idea of nation building, which allowed the discipline of English to move away from writing instruction; the attention to writing instruction only recently returned. It is difficult in any case to make sweeping claims about global writing-in-the-disciplines development or traditions without an exhaustive review of publications and institutional documentation written in languages other than English.

PART TWO: LOCAL *LINGUISTIC* WORK IN A GLOBAL CONTEXT

In all of this international development, the question of language often lurks—or looms. In every context, the writing is tied up in international questions about English: Should students work in English (only)? What should be taught about English? Which English? What linguistic competencies do student writers need? L2 scholarship around the globe provides, already, a significant part of the answer to these questions. In the United States, translingual scholarship can provide another part of the answer, in particular in terms of what writing programs must take up regarding these questions, including how to think usefully about linguistic repertoires for *all* student writers.

Linguistic theories inform several of the international approaches to writing far more than they do in the United States. And language teaching and learning are (my earlier comments notwithstanding) often part of the writing landscape, for instruction and for research, in ways that "flip"—ideologically, politically, and rhetorically—the attention to language paid in US contexts. These differences can inform US WPAs about the language questions they might be engaging in their local contexts.

In the US context, many have tended to think that because of rapid globalization and internationalization, English as the language of shared communication will only grow. This indeed makes sense in some ways—statistics abound in terms of English as a lingua franca worldwide. But a closer look at the nature of that "English" raises other questions (see also Donahue, forthcoming). Language is the stuff of writing, at least insofar as we work with words (because of course we work with other semiotic resources). Superdiversity, mobility as the new order, in any of the forms mentioned, means encountering the international and knowing what shapes not only the students who come to us but also the ones we send out into that superdiverse world. What do these students need to know? What do they need to know how to do? That shift from inward looking (how we work with multilingual and multinational students in our institutions) to outward looking (how we best prepare all students for a translingual, superdiverse world) is the core reason for WPAs to ask themselves new questions.

International trends as described in the first section directly impact language. Mobility and superdiversity are at the heart of increasing language diversity around the globe, not just in the United States, and have also in part provoked the need for a language of communication, whether in the sciences or the local marketplace. If we see that communication as meaning coconstruction and not transparent transmission, though, we can imagine the significant implications. Understanding these language effects is useful to us both for rethinking what our role and responsibility is re: English(es) and for understanding that role in terms of our students' language resources.

The language in our classrooms has been deeply treated by scholars in the fields of second language acquisition, second language writing, and so forth (noting again that SLA and SLW are not about English but about any "second" language; worldwide scholarship on multiple languages is available). As Dana Ferris (2014) reminds us, questions of ideology and English have been studied by applied linguistics scholars for decades, generally under the "language-policy" rubric (74). Every WPA is aware of questions of language and international or multilingual students. Most WPAs are also aware of recent developments in scholarship focused on the way language intersects with writing and have long been responding to local linguistic questions with programs and courses.

Chris Tardy (2011) reiterates what Paul Kei Matsuda and Bruce Horner and John Trimbur have argued: we recognize the classroom is already multilingual and has been diverse for most of our history. As Trimbur notes, "Monolingualism is not a pre-fall state of linguistic innocence, unmarked by difference" (Trimbur 2016, 219); indeed, monolingualism as a linguistic reality isn't even possible. What is possible is a monolingual *ideology* that "endows mainstream English a sense of inevitability and historical destiny, erases other languages, and associates language differences, both within and across languages, with subaltern groups of unnaturalized strangers" (219).

Ellen Cushman (2016) suggests that teachers and scholars must "move beyond the presumption that English is the only language of knowledge-making and learning" (234). Ideology, she reminds us, is always present, in any linguistic tool chosen for meaning making, and certainly writing in "standard" English is never neutral (260). "What might our classrooms and scholarship be like if teachers and students spoke, read, wrote, and listened to more than one language?" she asks (236). This perspective is complemented by Xiaoye You in *Writing in the Devil's Tongue: A History of Composition in China* (cited in Ferris 2014, 77) among others, who note that English does not belong to the standard-bearers (among them, the United States) but to *all* users of the language; standards are always up for negotiation in what is ultimately a democratizing understanding, one that offers a condensed version of the kinds of language evolution linguistics has long studied (Donahue 2008). For WPAs perhaps the important takeaways thus include that English is not owned by the traditional standard-bearers, that writing competence is not specifically linked to English, and that multilingualism is a resource.

A monolingual ideology is not restricted to English, of course. But it's our relationship with English that is my focus here. Internationalization has been raising the question of English both directly and indirectly. As noted earlier, the common lore is that English has become the lingua franca of the world and of education, leading to our thinking that (1) writing students must learn English and (2) English is becoming the language of writing in higher education around the globe. English, Tardy notes, is always assumed; if it isn't discussed, people will work from myths about its place and function (Tardy 2011, 651; see also Matsuda 2006).

These questions of monolingualism, of English-only implicit policies and pedagogies, and of myths of linguistic homogeneity in US classrooms have already prodded US scholars and teachers to question the ways in which we have structured and designed our writing curricula in the United States. In current structures, a "deep-seated assumption of homogeneity [has permeated] every aspect of writing instruction, from placement models to the language of writing prompts to the texts chosen to grading rubrics and assessment standards" (Ferris 2014, 75). As language has become more and more explicitly considered in writing work around the world, for some scholars, questioning monolingualism and arguing for multilingualism has simply not been sufficient "since both conceptions emerge from the same context of European-based thinking about language" with its colonial-modernist epistemological framework (Pennycook 2008, 301) and its views of languages as discrete entities (hence the *multi*) and speakers or writers "having" more than one such discrete code.[2] A *trans*lingual model has emerged.

In a 2011 study, Tardy learned that the belief is widespread that Standard English is indeed the key to academic and professional success and thus centrally important to first-year writing (648). Understanding and potentially changing that belief is thus an essential WPA challenge. My purpose here is not to promote a translingual model in that context but to see how translingualism might illuminate US WPA challenges and how it might help provoke that same meta-awareness and change in the ecology of our ground and air I mentioned earlier.

The translingual model has been discussed frequently in relation to L2 writing research and teaching models. But perhaps the discipline of L2 writing and the translingual model don't so much intersect as run parallel; to entwine L2 writing with translingual discussions is to misunderstand both L2 work and the translingual model. I believe the translingual model is a rhetorical model important to the work of composition but not a model destined to supersede L2 writing (its "next phase") or to redirect current transformative, essential models of L2 writing instruction. It's actually the flip side of L2 writing, the side about multilingual repertoires an L2 writer might already have more than would a monolingual writer. This contribution is not arguing to replace that work, those courses and programs, though in the long run, a paradigm shift might make that work easier.

Translingual Models

Because translingualism has been a subject of much recent discussion and is potentially so illuminating in terms of the challenges WPAs face and the new demands placed on writers worldwide today, I highlight briefly some ways of thinking about it before returning to how we might think about our WPA responsibilities to research and teaching in light of it.

Translingualism invites us to move beyond thinking about language in national or geographic terms (Pennycook 2008, 301). In terms of English, for example, Alastair Pennycook suggests that when we look at the diversity of Englishes across domains, we simply can't justify English as tied to nations—we're in a "post-geographic" language era (Allan James 2008, cited in Pennycook 2008, 302). Rather than considering whether there is an English or Englishes, Pennycook argues for a focus on "the interconnectedness of all English use" (307) and the fact that "in its emerging role as a world language, English has *no native speakers*" (Kanavillil Rajagopalan 2004, cited in Pennycook 2008, 307; emphasis mine). This does represent a radical shift for US writing faculty, courses, and students. It suggests a quite different kind of competence for twenty-first-century students of writing who will of necessity be "out in the world" (see Donahue, forthcoming). It suggests by extension that "activist" WPA work, in terms of English and language, may be a pressing need if we are to fully prepare students. This is not a short order; Tardy (2011, 637) cites A. Suresh Canagarajah's point, for example, that while some writing faculty now acknowledge world Englishes, they rarely move to not requiring standard US English in all composition (Canagarajah 2013).

Translingualism has been shaping and reshaping its focus over time. It serves well for WPAs as a model for thinking about curricular decisions, in a superdiverse and mobile context, that will impact all students and target all students' competencies. Early definitions of translingualism coalesced around some key principles, some of which are shared with other scholarly work on college writing and languages: language diversity should be understood as a resource (Horner et al. 2011); any language is always in the presence of other languages (Pennycook 2008) and always internally heterogeneous; writers need today the ability to merge and transform their linguistic resources (Molina 2011), to flexibly mix, mesh, and negotiate (Canagarajah 2013). For Pennycook (2008), "translingual" is "an attempt to move away from nation-based models of English" and to ask what the practices are "across communities other than those defined along national criteria: language resources, local language practices, and language users' relationship to language varieties" (304).

These initial descriptions shared a key tenet: start with assumed difference as the norm in language in use, the linguistically "unmarked" condition (Pennycook 2008) Trimbur (2016) reminds us has always been the case, certainly as early as the CUNY days (219). Our job, he notes, is to study how composition "works" with English. The evolving translingual attention has grounded itself in an understanding of "language in use," a thread developed in the 1960s in linguistics as the key to describing language function in both speech and writing.

Current definitions of translingualism draw out different key potentialities and new layers. As Min Zhan Lu and Bruce Horner (Lu and Horner 2016) note in the introduction to the 2016 special issue of *College English*, the concept of "translingualism" is itself diverse (207) and slippery. They offer a set of principles that might be seen as the current culmination of their work on translingualism, including that language is "not something we have but something we do," that users of language actively form and transform conventions and contexts; that communicative practices are always embedded in various asymmetrical power relations and cannot be neutral; that "difference is the norm of all utterances, conceived of as acts of translation" across languages, modes, and media and by all speakers and writers (208). The special issue itself highlights the evolving nature of our understanding of translingualism and its ways of being: its deep critical awareness (Guerra 2016), its specific orientation to difference and to meaning making (Bawarshi 2016; Canagarajah 2013), and its nature as situated literacy practice (Canagarajah 2013), decolonizing force (Cushman 2016), and role in agency and flexibility (Lorimer Leonard and Nowacek 2016).

What Does This All Mean for Language Knowledge in Our Writing Classrooms?

The notion of language knowledge does change in important ways. Bilingual scholars have argued for some time that bilinguals develop particular strengths in terms of, for example, flexibility, originality, or divergent thinking (Aparici 2015; Hall, Cheng, and Carlson 2006). The kind of competence—for Joan Kelly Hall, An Cheng, and Matthew Carlson, "multicompetence"—that evolves in a multilingual context resists some of the assumptions we had been making about the way language might function: that different languages are discrete different systems and that language knowledge is homogeneous across speakers and contexts (222). This multicompetence is not only needed in the *now* (via anything from physical migration/immigration to online gaming to tweets); it defines *the future* of our students' lives. That is, we are not just imagining their lived contact now; we see they will negotiate contact in every part of their futures. So, we can reinvigorate what we see as our core WPA responsibility.

WPA Roles and Responsibilities

These changes in understanding of linguistic realities offer something specifically to WPAs and to writing faculty. They create challenges and raise concerns, but they offer a productive return to attention to language and the role of language in writing. Most notably, they offer a different understanding of competence that connects to our rethinking of the curriculum in terms of design, strategy, frameworks for success, threshold concepts, and so on. They give us a chance to recover competence from the more instrumental ways that term has been used. They also connect to rethinking "language": when we know we are all working on writing, everywhere, we know writing competence is not about English. In the context of a globalized world, linguistic and discursive "competence" is simply evolving. Student writers need, according to Cynthia Selfe (2009), a "full quiver of the cultural, linguistic, and semiotic resources," a dexterity and an agility in the face of any meaning-making challenge or demand (cited in Guerra 2012, 38). That "full quiver" should underlie all we try to develop in first-year writing and writing in every other domain beyond the first year.

The sweeping change introduced to writing studies scholarship and practice by multimodality—to our thinking about the design of compositions and the rhetorical flexibility demanded of writers—is being matched by demands for linguistic flexibility in writing, demands foretold by the New London Group in the 1990s, demands arising out of contact and heterogeneous superdiversity, both now and in our students' futures (New London Group 1996). Language knowledge becomes a repertoire that supports thinking about language resources as part of rhetorical flexibility and design, broadening approaches for all students in the twenty-first century.

PART 3: WHEN "WHAT'S TO KNOW" BECOMES "WHAT'S TO DO?"

What can WPAs draw from other practices, other contexts (national and disciplinary)? What practices might WPAs use to foreground the complex language questions we have raised in ways that support our teaching goals and our research strands? What general principles can help in considering new practices? New approaches must, as Tardy (2011) highlights, encourage change by faculty and students on the ground (635). Many writing faculty do not have the luxury of attending conferences, reading or producing research, and so on; Tardy notes they are more likely and more often in the trenches of teaching. WPAs must do the work of making space to think about the issues of internationalization and globalization and their very relevant impacts on every classroom with every profile of diversity we can imagine.

But, that work must be interpreted locally at each institution. New policies must develop via collaborative, shared faculty discussion, engaged attention, research, organic (and slow) development. They can also powerfully influence broader institutional policy. Vertovec's work on superdiversity points to the importance of scholars helping to redirect imbalances of power in the various worldwide contexts of migration and change; WPAs can contribute locally to reconfiguring an institution's assumptions and implicit or explicit policies. There is some possibility—and this is important for all WPAs to consider— that a certain level of comfort with an activist stance will be necessary. WPAs must look inward to their own assumptions about language and English in relation to writing writ large because if the starting point remains English rather than writing, we're missing the broader key to writing in the world. WPAs must also look outward, across disciplines and contexts.

I explore just a few ideas and paths, first for some general questions about writing instruction and second for a set of suggestions specific to enacting attention to language and English.

Drawing from the World

Generally, the attention to writing programs as situated in the mobile, global, superdiverse world in which we currently work brings multiple benefits: new ideas, new understandings, new practices. There are ways of thinking about writing research and teaching we gain by reflecting on international approaches and the disciplinary approaches sometimes attached to them. Most notably, the focus on upper-level writing and graduate-student writing, the wholehearted embrace of writing in the disciplines, and the research traditions that inform the work at hand can help us question and articulate our priorities and grow our potential sources of collaboration.

Reinventing ourselves via what we read is certainly a strong start: reading sociology, reading education, reading beyond whichever background we might be bringing to our work, and reading economics, international education, and writing research from other contexts and in other languages (go ahead, try Google Translate for that German writing center piece or the Brazilian WAC article . . . it won't be perfect, but it will be useful). The French scholarship, for example, on student writing and "polyphony"—the use, integration, and investment in sources—offers thorough analysis of the ways students dialogue with sources, what they understand, where they are struggling.

Attending to what we can learn from the predominant path outside the United States away from a generic first-year writing experience as separate from the work of other disciplines is key. The recent writing-knowledge "transfer" discussions in US contexts have suggested there is a lot to question in our assumptions about first-year courses that set out to foster "transferrable"-transformable writing research. Models such as learning developers in Australia seem to provide new ways to think about our cross-disciplinary partnerships (with perhaps all the advantages and drawbacks we see in current models of university learning designers who tend to work with educational technology and course design).

Language Practices, English Practices . . .

There is no doubt that the heart of WPA work with faculty is to influence a shift in attention to flexibility, dexterity, nimbleness, and mobility in the kinds and uses of writing knowledge we help students develop. These various terms that suggest mobility have been threading in parallel across many conversations over the past couple of decades and actually inform both linguistic questions and writing-knowledge transfer questions. Guerra (2016, 228), for example, argues for helping students develop a "rhetorical sensibility," a versatility, building from Lorimer Leonard's 2014 call for attention to the need for writers to be "rhetorically attuned."

WPAs might take up specific practices to best develop new student learning outcomes and to prepare writing faculty for work with increasingly heterogeneous classrooms in ways that support teaching all composers the lingual aspects of meaning making and communication (*lingual* here not as restricted to the technical components of language we often associate with linguistics but to its construction and use, always situated). A WPA might start, as Tardy (2011) did, surveying faculty and students about their uses and perceptions of translanguaging. Tardy's study highlights, among other things, students' in-class and out-of-class language practices and faculty attitudes and behaviors in relation to such practices; she notes gaps between student and faculty understandings and choices, as well as faculty recognition of the value of students' linguistic resources but their lack of knowledge about good support practices.

Considering such survey results in relation to research, or querying students and faculty to describe the actual makeup of a student body (cf. Noonan and Gallagher 2014), offers key insights for reconsidering what students know, do, and need. Change should inform specific practices and should foster program-wide work on strategies that build from existing practice. Tardy (2011) suggests, for example, if faculty are already teaching rhetorical analysis, why not try analyzing text in any language? Faculty can actively discuss language diversity and encourage language diversity during writing (654). Even something like taking an active role in assessing with students how the *MLA Handbook* instantiates monolinguist assumptions and discourages experimentation with languages in writing (Swatek 2016) could be both generative and stimulating. WPAs and faculty should also engage in "active language management" via course goals, policy, and handbooks or materials (654). Perhaps most important, they should work within existing institutional values, understanding how the values already express something compatible with productive language expectations or policies (650).

Another key resource for WPAs is the scholarship in writing instruction for modern language learners. That work allows us to study the language aspects of how composers make meaning and communicate. Any method that might highlight linguistic resources for making meaning and communicating (for writers to consider as they design and produce) and encourage students to draw on knowledge from other contexts, languages, language courses, and registers is going to produce new angles on writing and open up new ways to (re)consider language, English, and writing. If we take Pennycook's 2008 definition of code mixing to heart—the action of "sampling of sounds, genres, languages, and cultures" (304) (sampling in the technology-driven twenty-first-century sense of working with, pulling from, remixing, echoing, crafting, (re)creating . . .)—we can work with students' already-occurring translanguaging. Even something as simple as working on paraphrase or close reading—frequent first-year-writing activities—can be transformed via framing them as forms of translations.

CONCLUSION

In the new ecology I explore here, students are mobile, and their writing competence must thus be flexible and dexterous. Today's writing program administrator must understand that mobility and its implications. We have a responsibility to be knowledgeable about writing instruction and research globally so we can resee our work as networked into that larger context. We must in particular understand how our students will be expected to make meaning through writing in a global context, what full discursive and linguistic competence for that work looks like, and how our faculty can rethink writing curricula in response to these new configurations. That is "what's to know."

Notes

1. I am indebted to Bruce Horner for drawing my attention to this field.
2. This distinction doesn't actually hold water in all cases, as some scholars studying multi- or plurilingualism argue (May 2014; Zarate, Levy, and Kramsch 2008; Molina 2011). The way the terms *multi-* or *plurilingualism* are used might in fact matter more, as in Zarate, Levy, and Kramsch's (2008) "précis du plurilinguisme." One key difference, however, is in the critical-political stance of a translingual model as compared to the more often linguistic or broadly educational nature of explorations of multilingualism or plurilingualism.

References

Aparici, Melina. 2015. "Cognitive Effects of Multilingualism" Paper presented at the COST network annual meeting, Barcelona, Spain.

Ballard, Brigid. 1984. "Improving Student Writing: An Integrated Approach to Cultural Adjustment." In *Common Ground: Shared Interests in ESP and Communication Studies*, edited by Ray C. Williams, John Swales, and Alfred John Kirkman, 43–54. Oxford: Pergamon.

Basch, Linda, Nina Glick Schiller, and Cristina Szanton Blanc. 1994. *Nations Unbound: Transnational Projects, Postcolonial Predicaments and Deterritorialized Nation-States.* Amsterdam: Gordon and Breach.

Bawarshi, Anis. 2016. "Beyond the Genre Fixation: A Translingual Perspective on Genre." *College English* 78 (3): 243–49.

Bazerman, Charles, Nataliz Avila, Ana Valeria Bork, Francinia Cristofia Poliseli-Correa, Vera Lucia Cristovao, Monica Ladino, and Elizabeth Narvaez. Forthcoming. "Intellectual Orientations of Studies of Higher Education Writing in Latin America." In *Recherches en ecriture: Regards pluriels /Writing Research from Multiple Perspectives*, edited by Charles Bazerman and Sylvie Plane. Fort Collins, Co: WAC Clearinghouse.

Beasley, Vic. 1988. "Developing Academic Literacy: The Flinders Experience." In *Literacy by Degrees*, edited by Gordon Taylor, Brigid Ballard, Vic Beasley, Hanna K. Bock, John Clanchy, and Peggy Nightingale, 42–52. Buckingham: SRHE & Open University Press.

Beaudet, Céline, and Véronique Rey. 2012. "De l'ecrit professionnel à l'ecrit universitaire." *Scripta* 16 (30): 169–93.

Brereton, John. 2011. "CUNY and the Birth of Modern Composition." Public lecture given at the Mina Shaughnessy Lecture Series, New York, April 1.

Brooks, Kevin Alfred. 1997. *Writing Instruction in Western Canadian Universities: A History of Nation-Building and Professionalism.* PhD diss., Iowa State University.

Canagarajah, A. Suresh. 2013. *Translingual Practice: Global Englishes and Cosmopolitan Relations.* London: Routledge.

Chanock, Kate. 2012. "Academic Writing Instruction in Australian Tertiary Education." In *International Advances in Writing Research: Cultures, Places, Measures*, edited by Charles Bazerman, Chris Dean, Jessica Early, Karen Lunsford, Suzie Null, Paul Rogers, and Amanda Stansell, 7–21. Anderson, SC: Parlor.

Clerehan, Rosemary. 2003. "Transition to Tertiary Education in the Arts and Humanities: Some Academic Initiatives from Australia." *Arts and Humanities in Higher Education* 2 (1): 72–89. https://doi.org/10.1177/1474022203002001007.

Crowley, Sharon. 1998. *Composition in the University*. Pittsburgh, PA: University of Pittsburgh Press. https://doi.org/10.2307/j.ctt5hjpc7.

Cushman, Ellen. 2016. "Translingual and Decolonial Approaches to Meaning Making." *College English* 78 (3): 234–42.

Donahue, Christiane. 2008. *Ecrire à l'université: Analyse comparée, France-Etats Unis*. Villeneuve-d'Ascq, France: Presses Universitaires du Septentrion.

Donahue, Christiane. 2009. "Internationalization and Composition Studies: Reorienting the Discourse." *College Composition and Communication* 61 (2): 212–43.

Donahue, Christiane. Forthcoming. *Writing, English, and a Translingual Model for Composition*.

Ferris, Dana. 2014. "Review: 'English Only' and Multilingualism in Composition Studies: Policy, Philosophy, and Practice." *College English* 77 (1): 73–83.

Gonzalez, Tania. 2013. "Transnationalism." Entry submitted to the CoHab Summer School website, May 17.

Guerra, Juan C. 2012. "From Code-Segregation to Code-Switching to Code-Meshing: Finding Deliverance from Deficit Thinking through Language Awareness and Performance." In *61st Yearbook of the Literacy Research Association*, edited by Pamela J. Dunston, Linda B. Gambrell, Kathy Headley, Susan King Fullerton, and Pamela M. Stecker, 29–39. Oak Creek, WI: Literacy Research Association.

Guerra, Juan C. 2016. "Cultivating a Rhetorical Sensibility in the Translingual Writing Classroom." *College English* 78 (3): 234–42.

Hall, Joan Kelly, An Cheng, and Matthew Carlson. 2006. "Reconceptualizing Multicompetence as a Theory of Language Knowledge." *Applied Linguistics* 27 (2): 220–40. https://doi.org/10.1093/applin/aml013.

Horner, Bruce, Zhan Lu Min, Jacqueline Jones Royster, and John Trimbur. 2011. "Language Difference in Writing: A Translingual Approach." *College English* 73 (3): 303–21.

Kruse, Otto. 2006. "The Origins of Writing in the Disciplines: Traditions of Seminar Writing and the Humboldtian Ideal of the Research University." *Written Communication* 23 (3): 331–52. https://doi.org/10.1177/0741088306289259.

Lorimer Leonard, Rebecca. 2014. "Multilingual Writing as Rhetorical Attunement." *College English* 76 (3): 227–47.

Lorimer Leonard, Rebecca, and Rebecca Nowacek. 2016. "Transfer and Translingualism." *College English* 78 (3): 258–64.

Lu, Min Zhan, and Bruce Horner. 2016. "Introduction: Translingual Work." *College English* 78 (3): 207–18.

Maher, Jan Maree, and Jennifer Mitchell. 2010. "'I'm Not Sure What to Do!' Learning Experiences in the Humanities and Social Sciences." *Issues in Educational Research* 20 (2): 137–48.

Martins, David, ed. 2015. *Transnational Writing Program Administration*. Logan: Utah State University Press. https://doi.org/10.7330/9780874219623.

Matsuda, Paul Kei. 2006. "The Myth of Linguistic Homogeneity in U.S. College Composition." *College English* 68 (6): 637–51. https://doi.org/10.2307/25472180.

May, Stephen, ed. 2014. *The Multilingual Turn: Implications for SLA, TESOL, and Bilingual Education*. New York: Routledge.

McCarthy, Lucille Parkinson. 1987. "A Stranger in Strange Lands: A College Student Writing Across the Curriculum." *Research in the Teaching of English* 21 (3): 233–65.

Molina, Claire. 2011. "Curricular Insights into Translingualism as a Communicative Competence." *Journal of Language Teaching and Research* 2 (6): 1244–51. https://doi.org/10.4304/jltr.2.6.1244-1251.

New London Group. 1996. "A Pedagogy of Multiliteracies: Designing Social Futures." *Harvard Educational Review* 66 (1): 60–93. https://doi.org/10.17763/haer.66.1.17 370n67v22j160u.

Ninnes, Peter, and Meeri Hellsten. 2005. *Internationalizing Higher Education.* Amsterdam: Springer. https://doi.org/10.1007/1-4020-3784-8.

Noonan, Matt, and Chris Gallagher. 2014. "Approaching Translingualism in a 'Global' University." Paper presented at the annual Conference on College Composition and Communication, Tampa, FL.

Pennycook, Alastair. 2008. "Translingual English." *Australian Review of Applied Linguistics* 31 (3): 301–8. https://doi.org/10.2104/aral0830.

Pollet, Marie-Christine. 2012. "From Remediation to the Development of Writing Competencies in Disciplinary Contexts: Thirty Years of Practice and Questions." In *Writing Programs Worldwide,* edited by Chris Thaiss, Gerd Brauer, Paula Carlino, Lisa Ganobscik-Williams, and Aparna Sinha, 93–103. Anderson, SC: Parlor.

Reiff, Mary Jo, Anis Bawarshi, Michelle Baliff, and Christian Weisser. 2015. *Writing Program Ecologies.* Anderson, SC: Parlor.

Russell, David. 1995. "Activity Theory and Its Implications for Writing Instruction." In *Reconceiving Writing, Rethinking Writing Instruction,* edited by Joseph Petraglia, 51–78. Hillsdale, NJ: Lawrence Erlbaum.

Selfe, Cynthia. 2009. "The Movement of the Air, the Breath of Meaning: Aurality and Multimodal Composing." *College Composition and Communication* 60 (4): 616–63.

Skillen, Jan. 2006. "Teaching Academic Writing from the 'Centre' in Australian Universities." In *Teaching Academic Writing in UK Higher Education,* edited by L. Ganobscik-Williams, 140–53. London: Palgrave-Macmillan. https://doi.org/10.1007/978-0-230-20858-2_10.

Skillen, Jan, Margaret Merten, Neil Trivett, and Alisa Percy. 1998. "The IDEALL Approach to Learning Development: A Model for Fostering Improved Literacy and Learning Outcomes for Students." Paper presented at the AARE conference, University of Adelaide.

Smit, David. 2004. *The End of Composition Studies.* Carbondale: Southern Illinois University Press.

Sternglass, Marilyn. 1997. *Time to Know Them: A Longitudinal Study of Writing and Learning at the College Level.* Mahwah, NJ: Lawrence Erlbaum.

Swatek, Aleksandra. 2016. "Foreign Language Text in Academic Writing." Paper presented at the EWCA Conference, Lodz, Poland.

Tardy, Chris. 2011. "Enacting and Transforming Local Language Policies." *College Composition and Communication* 62 (4): 624–61.

Trimbur, John. 2011. "CUNY and the Birth of Modern Composition." Public lecture given at the Mina Shaughnessy Lecture Series, New York, April 1.

Trimbur, John. 2016. "Translingualism and Close Reading." *College English* 78 (3): 219–27.

Vardi, Iris. 2000. "What Lecturers Want: An Investigation of Lecturers' Expectations in First-year Essay Writing Tasks." Paper presented at the First-Year Experience Conference, Brisbane, Australia.

Vardi, Iris. 2009. "Writing Experiences in Multidisciplinary First Years: A Basis for Confusion or Development?" In *Refereed Proceedings of the Communication Skills in University Education,* edited by Colin Beasley. Perth: Murdoch University.

Verstraete, Ginette, and Tim Cresswell. 2002. *Mobilizing Place, Placing Mobility: The Politics of Representation in a Globalized World,* vol. 9. Amsterdam: Rodopi.

Vertovec, Steven. 2007. "Super-Diversity and Its Implications." *Ethnic and Racial Studies* 30 (6): 1024–54. https://doi.org/10.1080/01419870701599465.

Zarate, Geneviève, Danielle Levy, and Claire Kramsch. 2008. "Introduction." In *Précis du plurilinguisme et du pluriculturalisme,* edited by Claire Kramsch, Danielle Levy, and Geneviève Zarate, 15–26. Paris: Contemporary Publishing International.

2

WRITING PROGRAMS AND A NEW ETHOS FOR GLOBALIZATION

Margaret K. Willard-Traub

In this chapter, I use a feminist rhetorical lens to consider the need for explicit and systematic reflexivity built into institution-wide, programmatic, and classroom-based initiatives geared toward recruiting and retaining second language, international students. I draw on my experiences as WPA and writing center director at the same time my campus was ramping up its recruitment of second language (undergraduate, provisionally accepted) students, particularly from China and Oman, while also developing a new English-language proficiency program (ELPP).

I examine simultaneously the ethos of these campus-wide initiatives and that of the writing program's development of cross-cultural and transnational sections of writing courses. These special sections were intended initially to address the needs of domestic, already matriculated L2 and Generation 1.5 students in the linguistically diverse Detroit area: even prior to the push to increase international recruiting, more than 40 percent of students using the university writing center identified a language other than English as their home language. As we began to offer cross-cultural writing sections of various general education courses, the writing program at the same time began to work with the Office of International Affairs to develop "bridge" sections of basic and first-year writing courses that would be available to international students moving from the ELPP into academic majors. Using Jacqueline Jones Royster and Gesa Kirsch's notion of "strategic contemplation," I consider the ways in which reflecting on the experience of students in cross-cultural writing sections on campus can help create an ethos around internationalization not only for the writing program but for the larger institution as well.

CROSS-CULTURAL WRITING ON CAMPUS

As director of the writing program and writing center from 2006 to 2012, and in collaboration with six other full-time faculty (a mix of

DOI: 10.7330/9781607326762.c002

tenure-stream and base-budgeted lecturers), I had stewardship over a curriculum that includes eight different courses taught by about twenty adjunct lecturers and supported by twelve to fifteen writing center undergraduate consultants. Generally, one lecturer and one or two of the peer consultants in this group at any one time are bilingual. By contrast, culturally and linguistically diverse even in the absence of growing international recruiting, UM–Dearborn's undergraduate student population includes English-language learners and Generation 1.5 students from families with roots in countries of the Levant and Middle East (Lebanon, Afghanistan, Iraq, Syria, and Palestine) as well as Eastern Europe and Africa. Most domestic students are drawn from the city of Dearborn and suburban areas around Detroit, though in recent years and as part of its metropolitan mission and strategic plan to increase the current enrollment of nine thousand by about 30 percent, the university has aimed also to enroll more students from the city of Detroit.

As director of the writing program, in 2009 I instituted several themes around which particular sections of our introductory and other writing courses might be organized: multimedia writing, community-based writing, and cross-cultural writing. These themes grew first and foremost out of the explicit teaching interests of our faculty. Second, and subsequent to the development between 2007 and 2009 of new learning outcomes for most of our courses, the themes also reflected how several faculty were practically approaching these learning outcomes in their courses.

The third and most important impetus for creating cross-cultural writing (CCW) sections, however, was to connect the curriculum with the rich linguistic and cultural diversity of domestic students already on campus, leveraging that diversity in the learning of writing and rhetoric. Since moving to UM–Dearborn in 2006, I had had several interactions with tenure-stream faculty in disciplines across campus, and even with a few long-time lecturers within the writing program, whose sense of students' complex linguistic backgrounds was one of deficit. These faculty clearly saw language diversity and even multilinguality as hurdles needing to be cleared before students could move on to the intellectual work of the courses they were in.

Through teaching many of these students myself, however, I knew them in fact to be operating with a surplus of linguistic, cultural, and life knowledge that put them at an advantage in writing courses that focused on rhetoric and inquiry. Early on at the university, as I made my way through teaching most of the core curriculum, I taught an intermediate expository writing course required of transfer students (about 60 percent of our campus's students transfer from another institution) who do poorly on the writing placement exam. This course was also my first foray into transnational teaching: students in the course worked collaboratively with peers in France on a business-memo assignment as part of the course's focus on rhetoric, genre, and culture, including academic/disciplinary, professional, and national culture.

L2 students in the class (speakers of Arabic and French mainly), most of whom were also nontraditional students and mothers of young children—among other nontraditional students and traditionally college-aged students who were monolingual—struggled with both academic English and perceptions of themselves as less capable students because of their English-language ability. One of my students that semester (whom I'll call Huda) was, for example, taking the course after failing a qualifying exam in her education program because of her English skills. As part of a reflective portfolio centered on literacy she put together at the end of the course, Huda wrote of the time she spent as a girl with her family in a Saudi refugee camp after fleeing Iraq, incorporating excerpts of her poetry (written in Arabic) from those years along with a reflection on how her experiences might inform her work as a teacher.

At first resisting the idea that she should incorporate the Arabic poem she had written as a teen, so disciplined had she become in attending to expectations for standard, academic writing in English, Huda was one of several students that semester who exhibited a surplus of potential (especially when compared to her college-aged peers) for reflecting critically on how her lived experience related to the subject material. Thus, from early on at my new campus, working with students like Huda offered me opportunities—and the impetus—to consider curriculum revision that might address the needs of a linguistically diverse student population.

Yet contrast such lived, classroom experiences—for both students like Huda and instructors/administrators like myself—with the realities of learning, teaching, and administering writing (and other programs) in increasingly corporatized university contexts, including my own: growing numbers of administrators who have few opportunities to teach; oversight committees, policies, and infrastructure required to balance attention to budgetary stresses, program enrollments, and the expectations of external accreditation agencies with attention to students' backgrounds and experiences; what at times can appear to be the privileging of learning outcomes over the experience of learners; the consequential commodification of teachers, learners, and knowledge itself.

In increasingly "managed" universities, the systematic development of writing program curriculum that speaks to students' specific backgrounds and lived experiences can help writing programs build and then maintain an ethos for internationalization or globalization independent from—but not in denial about—neoliberal and economic agendas. Furthermore, such an ethos might take the lead in helping shape an ethos for the university writ large. At my institution, for example, where a metropolitan, regionally focused mission has been in place for more than a decade on a campus that already is significantly culturally and linguistically diverse, reflecting on and building curricula that bridge the lives and needs of domestic, L2, and Generation 1.5 students with the lives and needs of a growing international population serves not only to integrate international students more fully into the university but provides space to create a new and more nuanced ethos for the learning of all students.

Originating in a cross-campus, general education writing program, this new ethos begins with a valuing of language and literacy broadly, along with writing and rhetoric, as *projects of inquiry*—not as boluses of knowledge. When I took over as director of the writing program in 2006 (and I continue to some degree still today), there existed a campus culture in which writing and the teaching and learning of writing were (are) seen by many as basic skills apart from the intellectual work of disciplines or students' critical engagement with ideas. The writing program's main bureaucratic functions—placement assessment, staffing sections of required writing courses (entitled Composition) primarily with adjunct faculty, and running the writing center—tended to add to this view about its work being one of developing skills perceived as easily commodifiable.

One first, small step in articulating a new ethos in my program was creating new course titles designated *Writing & Rhetoric*. A second step was developing learning outcomes for our courses and their equivalents that emphasized the learning of writing, rhetoric, and academic research as projects of *intellectual inquiry*.

A third step was the articulation of a more specific identity for writing courses that dovetailed with broader, institutional initiatives. Hence, our theme of community-based writing picked up on the success (and higher administration's support) of a campus-wide, faculty-driven Civic Engagement Project that had included substantial participation from writing program faculty (both full and part time). These community-based writing sections moved civic engagement and service-learning opportunities into first-year writing courses. Similarly, multimedia writing sections both supported several of our new learning outcomes and dovetailed with campus efforts to build programming in areas such as screen studies and digital media.

Our development of cross-cultural writing (CCW) sections, however, was positioned to lead—rather than follow—wider campus curricular initiatives. Though the Office of International Affairs had grown over a number of years, an ELPP was only starting to be conceptualized at the time we instituted CCW sections. (The international students already on campus were mainly at the graduate level in programs in engineering.) CCW sections of various courses—enrolling undergraduate, monolingual, and domestic L2 and Generation 1.5 students who chose these sections rather than being placed into them (as Matsuda and Silva 1999 alternately have described)—highlighted writing, rhetoric, and academic literacy as both objects of inquiry and intellectual pursuits and also spoke to the extant (though seemingly undervalued) "domestic" internationalism already on campus.

In the years since 2009, CCW sections of introductory writing, intermediate exposition, advanced expository writing, and a 300-level course for undergraduate writing center consultants have been taught by a handful of full-time (myself included) and part-time faculty. The sections tagged CCW have involved students in examining literacy and rhetoric as cultural enterprises and have involved students in collaborations with partners in France, Lebanon, and South Africa.

Bruce Horner suggests that WPAs "articulate the value of the courses in their programs in terms that resist tendencies toward the commodification of writing and of the learning and teaching of writing" while at the same time they respond "to the effects of globalization" (Horner 2012, 71). CCW sections, including those that involve transnational collaborations, focus on the links among language, writing, and culture, revealing the ways in which the conventions of Western academic discourse grow out of Western culture and contextualizing those conventions (such as the requirement that a thesis statement appear in the introductory section of an essay or the prohibition against the first-person-singular pronoun *I*) among multiple, other approaches to both academic and nonacademic writing. In challenging received US academic cultural assumptions by not only studying but also practicing writing that embodies difference, CCW sections in effect "negotiate conflicts between specific language users' and global market fundamentalists' definitions of writing [i.e., defined as Western academic discourse and mediated by Standard American English] and its value, both thematically and practically, in the writing produced" (Horner 2012, 71–72).

In addition to its heteroglossic nature, my cross-cultural/transnational classroom, for example, where students are sometimes tasked with interviewing overseas partners via Skype and Facebook in order to compose literacy profiles of those partners, provides a kind of *threshold potential* for student learning because of the overseas, real-world audience it provides for students' work. (In these literacy profiles, students are free to conceive of literacy as the reading, writing, and/or language practices of their overseas partners, or they might conceive of literacy as an even more complex mix of experiences, practices, and beliefs associated with personal experience.) More specifically, such collaborations provide students with an "external gaze" for their work, leading to deep self-reflexivity: "One needs always the eye of the other to recognize (and name) oneself . . . the external gaze is a compensatory way of returning a failed inward gaze" (Phelan 1993, 15).

Especially when such an external gaze or different perspective is incorporated into the writing, students are prompted to engage profoundly with their own situatedness, motivations, and biases—what Pierre Bourdieu has termed "habitus": "Habitus is a *structuring mechanism* that operates from within agents, though it is neither strictly individual nor in itself fully determinative of conduct" (Bourdieu and Wacquant 1992, 18). When students attend to the dispositions and beliefs of their transnational partners in their writing, they are being made aware of and sketching the contours of *their own strategies* for "'cop[ing] with unforeseen and ever-changing situations'" (Bourdieu and Wacquant 1992, 18)—in this case, the unforeseen and dynamic relationships with their partners. These are strategies that are historically constituted and "systemic, yet ad hoc because they are 'triggered' by the encounter with a particular field—in this case the field of the transnational classroom, which itself becomes a *"space of play"*" (Bourdieu and Wacquant 1992, 19; emphasis in original) and agency for students.

As in community-based or service-learning writing courses, but here with additional emphases on linguistic and national difference and boundary crossing, the awareness and self-reflexivity resulting from such transnational collaborations also can help students confront what Bourdieu has identified as the scholarly bias "more profound and more distorting than those rooted in the social origins or location of the analyst in the academic field"—that is, the "*intellectualist bias* which entices [the writer] to construe the world as *spectacle*, as a set of significations to be interpreted rather than as concrete problems to be solved practically" (Bourdieu and Wacquant 1992, 39). Prompted by this external gaze, students are no longer spectators but are active participants in constructing the terms of their own learning as they come into intimate contact with overseas peers and as they inscribe those peers' perspectives into their own analyses.

Further, when students see the focus of their writing as a concrete problem or involvement to be explored practically rather than as a spectacle to be observed and interpreted from a distance, the way in which as writers they are always a part of a particular relationship with their audience(s) also is emphasized. Students in a transnational classroom (not always, but often) recognize their relationship with their audience in part because they see that audience as fully distinct from themselves: at the same time they share with their partner the "space of play" of the classroom, they see that partner as also inhabiting simultaneously one or more distinct fields—for example, a very specific academic, national and/or cultural-linguistic field they have yet (if ever) to enter. Cross-cultural and transnational writing courses, in other words, rely significantly on students reflecting on their learning and collaborations with distinct others.

Finally, the cross-cultural classroom provides a threshold potential for student learning because such collaborations with overseas peers are almost always as much about struggle as they are about dialogue. From the logistical considerations of using digital media across several time zones, to the practical obstacles that come from the need to negotiate language differences, to the kinds of misunderstandings and tensions emerging from differing sociopolitical and historical backgrounds, transnational collaborations are potentially filled with setbacks and *critical incidents*. As such, the transnational classroom strongly invokes the Bakhtinian notion of dialogue as struggle, with its attendant potential for learning and ideological development to occur.

STRATEGIC CONTEMPLATION AND DISRUPTING THE ETHOS OF GLOBALIZATION

Yet disrupting neoliberal approaches to curriculum development and program administration, in particular in the context of economically stressed institutions such as mine, is not simple. Disrupting the neoliberal university through the "brokering" (Horner's term) of writing and its learning and teaching requires deep reflection that takes into account both local and global contexts, a kind of reflection that can be achieved through what Jacqueline Jones Royster and Gesa A. Kirsch have called "strategic contemplation" (Royster and Kirsch 2012, 21). Such an orientation, or "term of engagement" (25), in the context of our writing program has involved not only a valuing of writing and rhetoric as projects of inquiry but, just as important, a focus on the material experiences of students *already* on campus.

In their book *Feminist Rhetorical Practices* (2012), Royster and Kirsch advocate for feminist rhetorical research that "disrupt(s) our assumptions regularly through reflective and reflexive questions" (21). More specifically, they propose to "reclaim the genre of meditation in current scholarly practice in order to claim *strategic contemplation* deliberately as taking the time, space, and resources to think about, through, and around our work as an important meditative dimension of scholarly productivity" and point out that strategic contemplation "becomes especially useful when traditional, more publicly rendered sources of information are in short supply" (21), as is often the case with the documentation of women's experiences.

I propose strategic contemplation as an appropriate and useful orientation for administering writing programs in the context of internationalization and fast capitalism, especially given the paucity of sources of information about the consequences of global capitalism on higher education and especially on the classroom experiences of students. Such an orientation allows "new vistas to come into view," creating a space that allows for reflection rather than an immediate need to "analyze, classify, and establish hierarchies" (Royster and Kirsch 2012, 22). Royster and Kirsch delineate two important aspects of such an orientation. First, strategic contemplation involves "engaging in a dialogue, in an exchange, with the women who are our rhetorical subjects, even if only imaginatively, to understand their words, their visions, their priorities whether and perhaps especially when they differ from our own" (21)—including listening to the silences of those others. In the administration of writing (and other) programs, such dialogue and exchange must be focused on the lived experiences of students already on campus. Programs must actively pursue such dialogue, optimally hardwired into courses such as CCW sections, as a means toward critical reflection that can guide ongoing curriculum development involving even wider, more diverse groups of students—such as international students.

In my context, CCW sections provide a foundation upon which enrollment growth among international students might be built pragmatically, and ethically. Megan Siczek and Shawna Shapiro argue that "in order to be longstanding and transformative, internationalization must be an integrative process," not tacked on to curricula haphazardly or occurring in isolated programs on campus (such as the ELPP). CCW sections provide a space for students already on campus to reflect on how cultural and linguistic differences matter in not just learning and using writing but also in the relationships they build with peers. Such integration of cross-cultural and transnational concerns into an extant curriculum also ensures that "internationalization (is) not only . . . outward-looking, but also inward-looking" (Siczek and Shapiro 2014, 330), including considering the ways in which traditionally marginalized groups of second language writers can contribute to and help shape the project of internationalization. CCW sections, including those that emphasize transnational collaborations, in other words, help instructors avoid the tendency to "oversimplify the needs and abilities of the populations we imagine ourselves to be working with" (Siczek and Shapiro 2014, 424).

A consideration of students' reflections on the processes and products of transnational collaborations, for example, offers insights about a larger institutional ethos for such projects—an ethos centered not simply on preparing students for living and working in globalized economies but rather (or also) centered on students' ongoing development as language users and as critical thinkers about language use within contexts both local and global simultaneously. Beyond this, students' reflections suggest reasons instructors, programs, and universities might themselves seek collaborations and partnerships based not only on similarity but also on significant difference, for it is partnerships of difference, especially, that help drive change over time.

In addition to the important aspect of dialogue with current L2 students, "strategic contemplation" in the context of administering a writing program within an internationalizing institution, requires "pay(ing) attention to how lived experiences shape our (own) perspectives" (Royster and Kirsch 2012, 22) as administrators and instructors. Royster and Kirsch call researchers' own lived, embodied experience "a powerful yet often-neglected source of insight, inspiration, and passion" (22): strategic contemplation makes "time and space for contemplation, reflection, and meditation . . . and makes room for the researcher [or administrator or instructor] to acknowledge her or his own *embodied* experiences while engaging in inquiries that permit (her or him) to gain perspective from both close and distant views of a particular rhetorical situation or event" (89; my emphasis). In the context of internationalizing efforts such as the ELPP, which are driven chiefly by economic and enrollment motives, program administration and curriculum development that build an adequate foundation for integrating—not just tacking on—these efforts must consider the material, embodied experiences of current instructors as well as students. In my writing program, 85 percent of classes are taught by adjunct faculty primarily with degrees in areas other than composition and rhetoric. Only one of these teachers has formal training in second language writing, and no more than a couple are bilingual. The institutional status of the vast majority of writing program instructors alone impacts how CCW sections are perceived on campus and so impacts their potential for helping shape the ethos of other campus initiatives.

RISE OF THE ELPP

The discourse on my campus surrounding international programming, transnational partnerships, and cross-cultural pedagogies across a range of levels of institutional initiatives suggests a paradox often duplicated on other campuses: as internationalism may be proffered as a way of increasing cultural diversity or even jettisoning Western cultural and epistemological privilege, its raison d'être simultaneously remains the propping up of revenue streams and successful competition in the worldwide, academic marketplace through, for example, the leveraging of English-language (and US economic) dominance to prospective students both at home and abroad (see also Tardy 2015).

On my campus, the creation of the ELPP (circa 2012) and expansion of its institutional home in the Office of International Affairs (OIA) was a consequence of the push to increase university enrollments and attendant revenues. There are currently about fifty international students at my university taking classes in the ELPP, among about seven hundred international students in all (most of them on the graduate level). The program's recent accreditation bid to the CEA (Commission on English Language Program Accreditation) was geared specifically to increase those numbers: such status would make the ELPP eligible to apply with the federal government to issue ESL I-20 visas and so increase significantly enrollments by attracting students not yet provisionally admitted.

The ELPP cross-campus advisory committee, of which I am the College of Arts, Sciences & Letters representative, was established (according to a recent self-study report) to "revise and review on a regular basis the ELPP mission statement and the program's basic policies and procedures." The report continues: "The reason this committee . . . was created was to ensure that various University stakeholders could voice their opinions regarding the role that the ELPP plays on campus and to make sure that inter-departmental interactions run smoothly" (English Language Proficiency Program 2016). This advisory group includes faculty representatives from each of the academic units, along with representatives from enrollment management and student affairs.

Feedback I have received from faculty beyond the ELPP, however, makes it clear that most of those on the academic side of the house are not particularly aware of the new program or its goals. Those who are supportive see the ELPP positively not necessarily because of its potential for increasing university enrollments but because of its potential for culturally and/or linguistically diversifying the campus still further. (Many faculty members in humanities disciplines, for example, responded enthusiastically to a recent e-mail announcement that the ELPP was given a five-year accreditation from the CEA.) Nonetheless, there are few opportunities for faculty generally to engage in dialogue or exchange with the ELPP coordinator, ELPP instructors, or students.

The OIA's website offers pragmatic information for international students related to health insurance, housing, visas, and the like. Unremarkable in many ways, the site is surprisingly scant in its articulation of a mission and largely silent on how its work relates to the rest of the university or could contribute to the learning experiences of other students. (According to Royster and Kirsch, strategic contemplation pays attention to such silences.) The one sentence statement reads, "The mission of the Office of International Affairs (OIA) is to enrich the University of Michigan-Dearborn community through inclusive learning experiences that promote acculturation" (University of Michigan–Dearborn 2016b).

It is a metaphor of "fit" at work here: that is, learning experiences are deemed "inclusive" for international students if they are also ones that promote these students' *acculturation* to the dominant context—rather than articulating any sense that the dominant context will also need to adjust itself by virtue of having these students on campus, or that a mutual exchange is what is hoped for. In other words, there is little sense in this mission that international students who are second language writers would be called upon as participants in an exchange that might help shape the broader project of internationalization on campus. Instead, international students are objects of inclusion into a dominant culture—to be consumed by that culture.

The OIA's website does offer information to already matriculated students interested in studying abroad: "**Change your life with Study Abroad!** Become globally literate by experiencing an in-depth study of another country and culture, while at the same time, getting credit towards your degree. Study abroad assists students in the development of the academic, intercultural, professional, and personal skills and attitudes that today's employers are looking for" (University of Michigan–Dearborn 2016c). Here, for an audience of presumably domestic (and mostly monolingual) students, the website portrays becoming "globally literate" as the acquiring of certain intercultural "skills and attitudes"—commodities that should be of interest to students because of their desirability for prospective employers.

In contrast, the ELPP page gestures toward the significance attached by the university to the diversity that already exists on campus, noting that the "campus celebrates individual and cultural differences in a highly diverse campus community," which itself is situated in Dearborn, "a uniquely international city that welcomes and supports all people" (University of Michigan–Dearborn 2016a). But the ELPP page also fails to address an ethos for its courses geared toward international students other than suggesting these courses will increase students' success in a global marketplace. Neither does the page articulate a sense that prospective students' presence would entail the campus (or its broader curriculum) to change and grow. The program's mission is simply to "provide quality English language education and an orientation to the academic culture of the United States for non-native speakers of Standard American English" (University of Michigan–Dearborn 2016a).

CONCLUSION: THE THRESHOLD POTENTIAL OF CROSS-CULTURAL CURRICULUM

Internationalization is implicated in universities' participation in fast capitalism, privileging as it often does acculturation to the dominant, academic culture. At the same time, at least for some audiences, internationalization is assumed to address concerns for diversity and inclusion. The teaching and learning of writing in US contexts have become "commodities for exchange in the current marketplace of globalizing capital" (Horner 2012, 58), in particular because of writing's central role in university curricula and the central role of written communication in assessing students' readiness for college coursework. As an intellectual and also material crossroads of the ELPP—where many international students begin their university experiences—and the rest of the curriculum, the university's writing program is uniquely positioned to help at least slow down the commodification of students and their experiences through modeling *reflective practice* in teaching and curriculum development. Equally important are the writing program's efforts to support the role of reflection in students' individual learning and writing in courses that encourage their awareness of a larger, global context. The development of curriculum, as exemplified in my writing program of cross-cultural writing sections of core writing courses and other bridge sections of required courses, can create the necessary space for strategic contemplation about patterns of experience in the administrative contexts related to internationalism and the student learning contexts of various classrooms.

Because cross-cultural and transnational writing is situated at the crossroads of multiple disciplines and communities of teaching and research—rhetoric and composition, rhetorical genre analysis, theories of writing and identity, intercultural rhetoric, second language writing, and English for academic/specific purposes—an understanding of how students develop an awareness of a transnational or transcultural, rhetorical space, and in turn what these reflections might contribute to internationalizing the curriculum, cannot be gauged simply at the end of a semester-long exchange. There is a great need to consider more fully and over a greater range of contexts the notion of cross-cultural/transnational space, its threshold potential, and the ways in which learning and transfer of that learning take place.

For example, in many of the collaborative, transnational exchanges my students have participated in with peers overseas, their written reflections suggest a struggle not only with logistical, cultural, and linguistic differences but also, significantly, with the pressures of globalization. In past semesters as they've interviewed and written literacy profiles of each other, my students and their Lebanese partners (who were studying at an elite, private university) have engaged in a kind of discourse that might be said to typify globalization: Lebanese students assuming a cultural impoverishment on the part of US partners whose views of the world they believed would be structured primarily by Western media and pop culture; my students assuming a civic impoverishment on the part of their Lebanese partners who they believed would have experienced less freedom of choice in their lives. At the same time, US students recognized their Lebanese partners as surprisingly rich in knowledge of multiple languages, especially English (a recognition that seemed to bring with it newfound appreciation for the linguistic wealth of their domestic, L2 peers), in addition to rich in opportunities for travel and private education. And many Lebanese students were amazed at the degree to which my students had developed independent lives, working at jobs to pay for their educations and sometimes living apart from their families. While students at both institutions very often also described in their texts burgeoning relationships with their overseas partners—the kinds of friendships and connections that embody what it means "to approach another person as a soul, rather than as a mere useful instrument or an obstacle to one's own plans" (Nussbaum 2010, 5–6)—they seemed also to be working out some kind of balance sheet related to goods associated with the global marketplace and others' and their own position relative to those goods.

Individual instructors, programs (including first-year writing and general education programs), and institutions engaged in transnational and international initiatives must critically reflect on how their efforts could work to exploit such preoccupation with the global marketplace—especially when such initiatives are framed with the suggestion that they lead to the transfer of knowledge or abilities that make students more "competitive." All kinds of pedagogies and programming are at risk of becoming complicit with neoliberal practices characterizing universities' own movement into a fiercely competitive, globalized marketplace: the effects of globalization and market-driven considerations, having affected for decades our students' experiences outside the classroom, increasingly now also affect their varied experiences inside the classroom. This risk is perhaps especially acute within a higher education context where a liberal arts curriculum—traditionally a companion piece to professional training and integral for an understanding of education for such humanistic purposes as democratic citizenship—is increasingly threatened and publicly perceived as lacking adequate return on investment for economically stressed students and their families.

Developing an ethos around globalization and internationalization in writing program administration, curriculum development, and classroom pedagogy is essential. In my classrooms over the last several years, it is the rare student who reports not having been affected by the economic downturn, Detroit's bankruptcy, and/or the city and the state's drastically shrinking population. Lebanese students' day-to-day lives—though generally involving more time to devote to school work and civic organizations, for example—differ significantly from their older and working-their-way-through-college peers in the United States, and from students in France for that matter, many of whom come from immigrant families of more modest means. Yet all three cohorts, in writing and reflecting on their experiences with literacy, education, and identity in the context of cross-cultural writing sections, express surprisingly (or not so surprisingly) similar career and success-related anxiety.

These students, themselves so different in so many ways, are arguably linked not only by communications technologies that make their collaborations possible but also by the yoke of the marketplace. Given this, it would be easy for an institution aiming to increase enrollments by building an ELPP, for example—as it competes for students, rankings, and prestige—to prey on students' fears and anxieties, proffering cross-cultural learning (or related experiences such as study abroad and international internships) as absolute requirements for knowledge transfer to globalized workplaces or for long-term success. An orientation of strategic contemplation—trained on the embodied experiences and reflections of L2 learners already on campus and of their instructors—offers an opportunity for considering the ways in which initiatives at the programmatic and institutional levels such as the ELPP might ethically develop: What does each program/institution have at stake in any given project? What are the implications for the lived experiences of students? How do various initiatives encourage (or not) "the faculties of thought and imagination that make [students and their teachers] human and make [their] relationships rich human relationships, rather than relationships of mere use and manipulation" (Nussbaum 2010, 6)? In what ways (if any) do students have opportunities to examine their university's stake—and to help shape it? Are students even encouraged to understand their involvement in such questions as part their education in the first place?

In the absence of such an orientation, and as the university-as-corporation becomes ever more fully realized, however, we inevitably approach another kind of threshold potential. This is the point beyond which even innovations such as cross-cultural courses and transnational teaching might accelerate a corporatized ethos, reaffirming discourses characteristic of fast capitalism with its attendant cultural and linguistic hegemonies instead of sparking intellectual, ideological, and material change more resonant with the best traditions of the liberal arts that emphasize the study of human experience and the building of rich human relationships.

References

Bourdieu, Pierre, and Loï J. D. Wacquant. 1992. *An Invitation to Reflexive Sociology.* Chicago, IL: University of Chicago Press.

Horner, Bruce. 2012. "The WPA as Broker: Globalization and the Composition Program." In *Teaching Writing in Globalization: Remapping Disciplinary Work,* edited by Darin Payne and Daphne Desser, 57–78. Lanham, MD: Lexington.

Matsuda, Paul Kei, and Tony Silva. 1999. "Cross-Cultural Composition: Mediated Integration of US and International Students." *Composition Studies* 27 (1): 15–30.

Nussbaum, Martha. 2010. *Not for Profit: Why Democracy Needs the Humanities.* Princeton, NJ: Princeton University Press.

Phelan, Peggy. 1993. *Unmarked: The Politics of Performance.* London: Routledge. https://doi.org/10.4324/9780203359433.

Royster, Jacqueline Jones, and Gesa A. Kirsch. 2012. *Feminist Rhetorical Practices: New Horizons for Rhetoric, Composition, and Literacy Studies.* Carbondale: Southern Illinois University Press.

Siczek, Megan, and Shawna Shapiro. 2014. "Developing Writing-Intensive Courses for a Globalized Curriculum through WAC-TESOL Collaborations." In *WAC and Second-Language Writers: Research Towards Linguistically and Culturally Inclusive Programs and Practices,* edited by Terry Myers Zawacki and Michelle Cox. Fort Collins, CO: WAC Clearinghouse and Parlor. https://wac.colostate.edu/books/12/.

Tardy, Christine M. 2015. "Discourses of Internationalization and Diversity in US Universities and Writing Programs." In *Transnational Writing Program Administration,* edited by David S. Martins, 243–62. Logan: Utah State University Press. https://doi .org/10.7330/9780874219623.c010.

University of Michigan–Dearborn. 2016a. "English Language Proficiency Program." https://umdearborn.edu/io_elpp/.

University of Michigan–Dearborn. 2016b. "International Affairs." https://umdearborn .edu/internationaloffice/.

University of Michigan–Dearborn. 2016c. "Travel Abroad." https://umdearborn.edu/io _overseas/.

3

ADMINISTRATIVE STRUCTURES AND SUPPORT FOR INTERNATIONAL L2 WRITERS
A Heuristic for WPAs

Christine M. Tardy and Susan Miller-Cochran

As the number of international students continues to rise at many US colleges and universities, writing programs often find themselves examining, or reexamining, the extent to which their current curriculum, placement practices, and teacher development adequately support this expanding population. Because of the rapidity with which international student enrollments have grown, with some universities seeing undergraduate numbers double over just a few years (e.g., University of Arizona 2014), the situation is frequently framed as a problem that must be solved, perhaps urgently. Proposed solutions are often short-term changes that can be implemented quickly with little financial burden on the program or institution—such as guest speakers or workshops focused on L2 writing or simply adding new responsibilities to existing faculty or administrators to help address gaps and concerns. Such changes can serve a useful temporary role and are often the only immediate options available to writing programs, but they are insufficient for addressing the kinds of systemic changes that come with the responsibilities of supporting a substantial student population with linguistic, cultural, and educational backgrounds that often differ significantly from those of domestic students.

We believe the larger administrative structures of writing programs can and do play critical roles in supporting an international student population and reenvisioning writing programs as international spaces. While some work in writing program administration has provided guidance on offering various types of support for international students in writing programs (e.g., Preto-Bay and Hansen 2006; Shuck 2006), little work has addressed (re)designing administrative structures in writing programs, as the growth in international student populations is so recent. The goal of this chapter is to outline some of the most common

DOI: 10.7330/9781607326762.c003

structures and to examine each through a framework that can help individual programs identify administrative configurations best suited to their own institutional spaces and circumstances. Although we realize there is a need to address these issues at all levels of undergraduate and graduate education, we focus here on first-year writing (FYW) because of its unique and ubiquitous role in supporting international L2 writers at institutions of varying sizes and types.

BACKGROUND ON ADMINISTRATIVE STRUCTURES AND L2 WRITING

We see the increasingly international character of US colleges and universities as a welcome opportunity for writing programs to reexamine the extent to which existing administrative structures align with the needs of students and teachers in the program. This increasing internationalization means expertise in L2 writing is an essential component of writing program administration, however. Second language writing scholarship suggests that such expertise might include familiarity with research on L2 writers' language, writing, and genre development; multilingual composing processes; textbooks; and sociocultural and sociopolitical interactions and relations (see Leki, Cumming, and Silva [2008] and Manchón and Matsuda [forthcoming] for recent syntheses of such scholarship).

While not specifically addressing administrative structures, second language writing specialists have been addressing issues of support for L2 writers for decades, including Tony Silva's (1997) foundational article "On the Ethical Treatment of ESL Writers." A piece perhaps even more relevant in today's context, Silva's article is grounded on the premise that respect for students should be central to programmatic decisions and structures. He writes, "An instructional program that does not respect its students is primed for failure and almost certain to engender resentment" (359). Toward this aim, he offers four guiding principles for such respect, including (1) understanding the diversity in linguistic, rhetorical, cultural, and educational backgrounds of L2 writers, (2) offering suitable placement options to support students' diverse backgrounds, (3) providing appropriate instruction for students, and (4) evaluating L2 students' writing in a fair and equitable way.

These principles are certainly applicable to supporting any student population, but Silva's (1997) discussion very clearly and directly emphasizes the need for programmatic decisions—of curriculum, placement, instructional approaches, and assessment—to be based on a strong understanding of what second language writing is and what second language acquisition entails. Such decisions are administrative in nature, and they necessitate having appropriate people working within effective structures. In this same spirit, the "CCCC Statement on Second Language Writing and Writers" (referred to herein as the "CCCC-SLW Statement") asks for writing program administrators (WPAs) to offer teacher support (e.g., through required graduate coursework in second language writing), to include second language writing and writers in program research, and "to develop instructional and administrative practices that are sensitive to [L2 writers'] linguistic and cultural needs" (Conference on College Composition and Communication 2014).

Unfortunately, several barriers have made it challenging to incorporate L2 writing expertise (or experts) into typical frameworks of writing program administration. Disciplinary divisions—related to historical circumstances (Matsuda 2003, 2006), epistemological and ideological differences (Atkinson and Ramanathan 1995; Silva and Leki 2004), and graduate-program curricula (Kilfoil 2014)—have meant that much L2 writing scholarship is situated more firmly within the fields of applied linguistics and TESOL than in composition studies. Writing programs, on the other hand, tend to be administered by composition scholars and housed in English departments, which only occasionally include TESOL or applied linguistics programs. Institutional structures, then, may separate L2 and L1 writing specialists, further limiting opportunities for collaboration. In an analysis of L2 writing support at an English-speaking university in French-speaking Québec, Guillaume Gentil (2006) similarly found that resources for supporting biliteracy development "were available on campus but not accessible . . . because knowledge was compartmentalized along disciplinary and administrative lines rather than allowed to circulate across departments and disciplines" (161).

This disciplinary and institutional compartmentalization additionally, and perhaps inadvertently, contributes to what Paul Kei Matsuda (2006) has termed a "policy of containment" that delegates students "to remedial or parallel courses that were designed to keep language differences from entering the composition course in the first place" (648). In such a model, linguistically diverse students, and most particularly international students, are deemed to be best supported by L2 experts, who are often not associated directly with writing programs. It may therefore not be a surprise that Christine M. Tardy's (2015) analysis of university writing program websites found that references to internationalization, language, and diversity were minimal, often because language difference and linguistically diverse students are set apart from "mainstream" concerns of writing programs. Programs that lack L2 writing specialists in central administrative roles may also overlook language issues when articulating policies, mission statements, and learning outcomes so that language difference becomes invisible by default rather than by choice (Miller-Cochran 2010; Tardy 2011). Of course, even when L2 writing specialists are part of a writing program's administrative team, their roles may be diminished simply because of the relative size of L1 and L2 student populations. As Ilona Leki (2006) elegantly laments, "At a major non-border state institution like mine, L2 students and their needs count for rather little. Their voices are lost in the roar as we and they more or less follow what is put in place for L1 students" (70).

Clearly, a confluence of issues is involved in the support of international L2 writers in university writing programs, but administrative structures emerge for us as one of the key areas worth examining. WPAs, after all, are the ones at the table when decisions regarding curriculum, placement, instruction, assessment, and hiring are made. WPAs are directly involved in the preparation of mission statements, learning outcomes, and program assessment. And WPAs represent the program, its students, and its needs to faculty across the institution and to upper-level administrators. The visibility of L2 writers within a program can therefore be highlighted or diminished through a program's administrative structure and the distribution of responsibilities and expertise on an administrative team. In our analysis of potential administrative structures of writing programs, we explore how various configurations might enhance a writing program's support of L2 writers and reenvision a program as an international space.

A FRAMEWORK AND TOOL FOR ANALYZING ADMINISTRATIVE STRUCTURES

To develop a framework for assessing the suitability of an administrative structure within one's local context, we turned first to the "CCCC-SLW Statement," which outlines a range of areas central to the support of L2 student writers. While the statement offered initial guidance in developing our analytic framework, we quickly found ourselves turning to other influential scholarship (e.g., Matsuda, Ortmeier-Hooper, and You 2006; Silva 1997) and our own experiences as writing program administrators to identify meaningful categories that could create a general framework or heuristic for assessing appropriate and *feasible* administrative structures. In the end, we identified six categories we explain below and summarize with sample questions in table 3.1.[1]

Table 3.1. A heuristic for examining writing program administrative structures and support for international L2 writers.

Category	Sample Questions
International student population	• How large is the population of undergraduate international students? Is it growing, stable, or decreasing?
	• What nationalities and language groups are represented among the international student population and in what kind of distribution?
	• What percentage of students enter the university directly and what percentage enter through an intensive English program (IEP) or bridge program?
Institution	• What is the size of the institution's total undergraduate population? What percentage of these students are international versus domestic?
	• What is the institutional admission requirement for English-language proficiency?
	• What units of support for international students and for multilingual students exist at the institution? How well coordinated are these units?
Curriculum	• What curricular options are available to international L2 writers in the FYW program?
	• To what extent are FYW program textbooks and required assignments designed for students with international educational and linguistic backgrounds?
	• To what extent do program student-learning outcomes (SLOs) take into account students with international educational and linguistic backgrounds?
Placement	• What placement options are available to international L2 writers?
	• How are placement decisions made? What information are they based on?
	• Does the institution offer developmental L2 (pre-FYW) courses? If so, how are students placed into these courses? How many and what percentage of students are placed into these courses?
	• What expertise and experience in SLW is drawn on in placement practices, including the design of tools, scoring of student writing, final placement decisions, and ongoing assessment and development of placement practices?
Local expertise	• What expertise in L2 writing do faculty and writing program administrators have?
	• Where are L2 writing experts located at the institution?
	• What availability do local L2 writing experts have for providing teacher support? What kind of support?

continued on next page

Table 3.1—*continued*

Category	Sample Questions
Teacher preparation and support	• What qualifications in L2 writing are required for all FYW instructors in the program?
	• What qualifications in L2 writing are required for FYW instructors who teach sections specifically for L2 writers?
	• Is there a sufficient population of instructors with backgrounds and knowledge in teaching L2 writing?
	• What preservice and inservice support is offered for instructors, including those predominantly teaching L2 writers?
	• What kinds of requirements for teacher preparation can be mandated (e.g., participation in credit-bearing graduate courses on L2 writing)?

International student population. Institutions of higher education differ, often radically, in the size and nature of their international student population. Some large research universities, for example, have maintained a sizable population of international students for decades, and that population has continued to grow; for other institutions, such growth is very recent, so fewer support structures are already in place. But while numbers of students are important, it is also necessary to consider the relative proportion of international and domestic students. For instance, seven thousand international students may make up 25 percent of a student population at one school and only 10 percent at another. Furthermore, demographic details of student populations are important in understanding the nature of support. Do students come from a broad range of countries? Has this distribution changed over time? Many universities, for example, have a long history of a large international student population but find that the nature of their support has had to change with shifts in students' countries of origin and language backgrounds. Institutions must also consider students' previous educational experiences, whether in the United States or other countries: Have many students studied in the United States before, either as high-school exchange students or in intensive English programs (IEPs) or bridge programs? How many students have completed high-school education in an English-medium environment outside the United States?

Institution. The factors described above are all contextualized within an institutional context, and, again, institutions vary in numerous ways. Information especially pertinent to consider includes the overall presence and visibility of an institution's international student population, including at the undergraduate level, and the history of that population within the institution. Institutional language policies are also of relevance, including the requirements for English-language proficiency in the school as a whole and perhaps even distinctions made across units within the institution. In addition, the range of support services for international and multilingual students within an institution is important. Are these compartmentalized or do they communicate and collaborate? To what extent does a student's visa status influence the kinds of support they might receive? How closely do various units collaborate with the writing program?

Curriculum. Closely related to administrative structures are the curricular options a program offers for L2 writers in general and international L2 writers in particular. Are there courses designed especially for L2 writers? Are these equivalent to other FYW requirements? If not, do they receive credit? Where are they taught? If a program has a standardized curriculum, to what extent is it appropriate for an international L2 writer? Do program learning outcomes and rubrics take into account students who are new to US educational practices and/or still developing English-language skills? Put another way, are all students treated *equally* or *equitably*, and how are these distinctions represented throughout the curriculum?

Placement. Placement options and practices are closely tied to curriculum but focus on the options for and processes of placing students into a writing program's curriculum. Issues of particular importance include the range of developmental or English for academic purposes (EAP) courses (pre-FYW) offered, the means for placing students into such courses, and the relative percentage of students who might take these courses. Some institutions require in-house placement exams, which might be taken once a student has arrived on campus or may be taken online prior to arrival, and the exams might be administered within any number of units on campus. Other institutions may have no placement procedures because they have no unique curricular options for international students. In some cases, this may be appropriate, while in others it may be outdated and insufficient.

Local expertise. As our earlier discussion notes, expertise emerges as a critical factor in the creation of appropriate administrative structures, but most institutions must balance their vision of an ideal structure with what is logistically feasible in relation to local expertise. Programs should consider the L2 writing expertise present within their program and across the institution. Are experts tenured professors, junior faculty, contingent faculty, staff, and/or graduate students? What kinds of support can they contribute to the writing program in various areas (e.g., curriculum, placement, teacher support)? To what extent will the institution compensate them for such work? We find this category to be especially important to tease apart because of its complexities. Some institutions, for example, may have L2 writing specialists, but those people are already committed to other teaching and administrative duties or lack close ties to the writing program. In other cases, expertise may be readily available but an institution is unable to offer appropriate compensation.

Teacher preparation and support. One final area to be considered is the preparation of teachers and the ongoing support they receive. The issue of teacher preparation for and confidence in supporting international L2 writers has been raised by numerous scholars (e.g., Matsuda, Saenkhum, and Accardi 2013; Tardy 2011), noting many teachers of FYW feel ill-equipped in this area. Nevertheless, institutions vary widely in their population of teachers and students, so this issue must be considered on a local level. Programs should consider the expertise and experience of teachers *throughout* the program as well as teachers who are responsible specifically for L2 writing instruction, if such options exist. Ongoing support is also important, including the availability of and incentives and support for continued professional development. Local program policies and practices for teacher hiring and course assignments are also important factors.

These six categories provide a heuristic framework for analyzing and understanding administrative structures in writing programs. As we began to apply the framework in an analysis of four common structures, we recognized three clear categories emerging from connections that tied together questions of context (student population and institution), curriculum (curriculum and placement), and instruction (local expertise and teacher support). Therefore, we organize our discussion of each administrative structure in the next section around these three combined categories.

ANALYSIS OF COMMON ADMINISTRATIVE STRUCTURES

To illustrate how we envision this framework's being used productively by writing programs, we turn now to applying it to the discussion of four common administrative structures. We identified these structures based on published accounts (e.g., Matsuda, Ortmeier-Hooper, and You 2006), consulting we have done at various institutions, and discussions with colleagues at conferences and through professional listservs. These structures are familiar to us from our own institutional experiences; indeed, between the two of us, we have worked within each of these models as either an instructor or an administrator, or sometimes as both. We have also been directly involved as administrators in various transitions from one model to another, giving us firsthand insight into the institutional factors at play in assessing the effectiveness of a given structure and in redesigning an existing administrative model.

1. No Distinct Administrative Support for L2 Writers

It is not uncommon for writing programs to lack distinct administrative support for international L2 writers. Typically, in such programs, international L2 writers take the same courses as domestic students and there are no administrative positions dedicated to working with L2 writers or their teachers. According to the National Census of Writing (2014), 40 percent of 408 programs surveyed indicated offering no L2 writing courses. In some contexts, this programmatic approach may have many benefits; when international and domestic students take courses together, both populations have opportunities to learn from one another and to widen their perspectives. Some institutions may adopt this administrative structure by choice, diffusing L2 support throughout an administrative team rather than tasking one individual or set of individuals with the work. Other programs may lack distinct administrative support for international L2 writers simply because they do not have the resources to do otherwise.

Student population and institution. The size of a program's international L2 student population may have the greatest impact on whether a program's administrative infrastructure explicitly addresses L2 writers. An institution with a very small international student population, for example, may not be able to offer enough course sections specifically for L2 writers to allow scheduling choices that meet their students' constraints. In lieu of such offerings, institutions might be able to support international L2 students through other campus support services or by hiring teachers who have teaching experience and knowledge in second language writing so all instructors are prepared to support linguistically diverse students.

Curriculum and placement. Courses within FYW programs often rely on assumptions of students' familiarity with certain US educational practices (e.g., extensive use of group work, peer-review practices, process writing) and reading content (e.g., US popular culture, national cultural references), which can pose challenges to international L2 writers. Programs that make an intentional effort to design courses and implement approaches that do *not* assume such familiarity are likely to be more successful at supporting L2 writers within mainstream courses compared with those programs that do not take such factors into account. Some programs may offer cross-cultural sections of composition that purposefully mix domestic and international students in relatively equal numbers, allowing for spaces in which international students are not in a minority (see, for example, Vann and Myers 2001).

Placement is also a very important factor to consider for programs adopting the no-distinct-support model. In some institutions, for example, international students may be required to complete a range of courses in EAP prior to enrolling in FYW, sometimes up to one year of coursework, typically determined through in-house placement testing (see Developmental-EAP-Courses model below). If such requirements are in place, it may be that the majority of students in the FYW courses have already received sufficient language support and are largely familiar with US academic practices by the time they enroll in FYW.

Local expertise and teacher support. If an institution does not offer distinct support for L2 writers, local expertise and teacher support become essential. In our experience, the presence of L2 writing specialists in program conversations (including teacher workshops, policy meetings, and curriculum development) can be pivotal in raising awareness of such issues across a program and in implementing practices that support these students. In some cases, such expertise may come from faculty who do not hold an administrative or teaching role in the writing program but who could be affiliated with the program in a less formal manner, serving as a consultant, regular workshop presenter, or ex officio committee member.

Ongoing teacher support is also essential if a program lacks a dedicated pool of L2 writing instructors. L2 writing issues should be integrated throughout pre- and inservice teacher support in this case. For example, workshops on feedback should include L2 student texts, sample student papers should include those by L2 writers, and discussions of rubrics and outcomes should take into account students writing in an additional language.

We want to acknowledge that the no-distinct-support administrative model is rarely ideal but sometimes is the only option available to programs. Application of our heuristic to this model helps illuminate not only some limitations of the model but also ways other resources might be leveraged to help bolster the effectiveness of this model within a given institutional context.

2. L2 Writing Program within a First-Year Writing Program

A second common model incorporates administration of L2 writing as a kind of subprogram within a larger FYW program. There are numerous variations, ranging from the simple incorporation of L2 writing sections administered by a coordinator or the WP director to something more fully developed with an L2 writing director and perhaps even assistant director. In the latter model, we would be more likely to find L2 writing specialists involved in placement, teacher support, and curriculum development.

Student population and institution. Size again is a crucial factor in the decision to develop administrative structures specifically devoted to L2 international student writers. Many institutions may move from the no-distinct-support model to the development of L2 writing administrative structures as the student population becomes larger and, thus, more visible throughout the program. Indeed, it may be difficult to argue for an L2 WPA until the numbers of international students and L2 writing sections increase to a kind of tipping point, at which time the need for development of appropriate placement, curricula, and teacher support becomes indisputable. Institutions with lower English-language-proficiency admission requirements may especially benefit from this model because of the need to support students developing language skills within, or in addition to, FYW courses.

Curriculum and placement. In general, more curricular options for international L2 writers might suggest more need for distinct L2 writing administrative structures. When students have options for "mainstream" writing courses, L2 writing courses, and possibly developmental writing or cross-cultural composition sections, most institutions would find it valuable to have an administrator devoted to coordinating these options, being involved in placement decisions, and assessing the appropriateness of course content and program learning outcomes for linguistically diverse students.

In our experience, we have found placement of L2 writers to be particularly challenging. Traditional placement tools for L1 writers generally do not take into account language development, so they are insufficient for L2 writers. Similarly, traditional language-placement tools tend to be quite distinct from the writing-focused content and learning outcomes of FYW programs. Without some administrative role dedicated to L2 writing, we suspect placement of L2 writers is less likely to take into account both writing competencies, as linked to the FYW curriculum, and English-language development.

Local expertise and teacher support. Incorporating an administrative model that explicitly includes L2 writing requires expertise at several levels. First, there must be a sufficient population of instructors who are experienced and qualified in teaching L2 writing. Writing programs with limited access to such teachers will need to incorporate more robust inservice teacher support. This approach requires L2 writing experts to play administrative and/or professional-development roles, offering regular workshops, reading groups, classroom observations, and other activities for teacher development.

There are also institutional constraints. Some writing programs may have local L2 writing experts who could serve some administrative role, but those individuals are already fulfilling other duties. Writing programs, then, might identify the most pressing needs for administrative duties and teacher support, examine the available expertise at all levels of faculty and administration, and then develop structures that draw on existing resources while also pursuing the hiring of additional experts to fill needed gaps.

3. L2 Writing Program outside a First-Year Writing Program

Often due to historical and/or institutional circumstances, some colleges and universities compartmentalize L2 writing instruction for first-year students, assigning administrative and instructional oversight of L2 writing courses to a unit outside the writing program. The National Census of Writing (2014) reports that only 17 percent of 241 programs surveyed house L2 writing courses within the writing program or department. Instead, such courses (and programs) might be found in a department of languages, applied linguistics, or linguistics, or in a university-wide ESL center or intensive English program. In this model, international L2 writers might be automatically streamed into L2 writing courses, or they might be assigned to L2 courses according to standardized language-proficiency scores or in-house placement testing.

Student population and institution. The size and nature of an institution's international student population may not have a great impact on the decision to create a distinct administrative home for L2 writing courses. Data from the National Census of Writing (2014) demonstrate that this structure exists at large universities but also at smaller colleges. This outside-L2-writing-program model may be suited to institutions in which a large number of international students are still developing language-proficiency skills and the university writing program is unable to support students but a separate unit is. This model also seems most effective when there is strong collaboration, coordination, and communication among the units delivering writing instruction.

Curriculum and placement. Theoretically, this model may provide more opportunity for L2 writing courses to develop placement, learning outcomes, and curricular options well suited to the characteristics of international EAL students simply because of the autonomous administrative oversight. Nevertheless, the extent to which such options might be appropriately developed and managed depends largely on the expertise available in the L2 writing administrative unit as well as the communication between that unit and the writing program. One danger of this model is that the programs might evolve in ways so distinct that they might not adequately fulfill the same university requirement. Dwight Atkinson and Vai Ramanathan's (Atkinson and Ramanathan 1995) ethnography of a university's IEP and writing program, for example, demonstrates the potential for programs to become very different cultural spaces in terms of how they conceptualize and teach writing.

Local expertise and teacher support. At many institutions, historical, political, and personal circumstances are often as important, or more important, than intellectual arguments in determining who has institutional authority of writing support for international L2 writers. This model may be most likely found in contexts in which a writing program lacks an administrative team or faculty with L2 writing expertise *and* in which another unit can claim this expertise to upper-level administration. The presence of available graduate-student instructors is relevant here as well. When graduate programs in TESOL or applied linguistics are in home departments separate from the writing program, it may make the outside-L2-writing-program the most viable and appropriate at an institution, particularly if those programs also include faculty with expertise in L2 writing.

4. Developmental (Pre-FYW) EAP Courses

This fourth model can co-occur with any of the above models, but we mention it here because it may be influential in the first-year L2 writing administrative options available to institutions. At some institutions, once admitted, all students enroll in FYW courses; at other institutions, some students may be placed into developmental courses prior to enrolling in FYW. These developmental courses for matriculated L2 students are found under many different labels, but one common label for them is "English for academic purposes (EAP) courses," so we have adopted that term here. Placement into pre-FYW EAP courses is often based on standardized language-proficiency test scores and/or institutional placement exams.

Student population and institution. Currently, the rush to recruit international students has been accompanied at some institutions by a reduction in language-proficiency requirements. In these cases especially, writing programs may find that the one or two semesters of FYW are insufficient for supporting students, and the availability of EAP courses may be a valuable resource for developing academic language and literacy skills. Whether these courses should be administratively managed by the writing program or another unit depends on the numbers of students and teachers involved and the ability of the writing program to incorporate an EAP program into its larger structure. At institutions where large percentages of students complete one or more EAP courses prior to FYW, there is a strong need for communication between the EAP and FYW administrators and teachers, but it may not be logistically feasible for the EAP courses to be administered by the writing program.

Curriculum and placement. Considering the ideal administrative relationship between EAP and FYW courses also involves examining the curricular options available to international L2 writers in both programs. Are the two programs striving to be clearly articulated so the EAP courses prepare students for success in the FYW courses (in areas like writing tasks/genres and learning outcomes) while the FYW courses take into account the content and strategies of the EAP courses? What placement tools are used to determine where international L2 writers will begin? Even when clear articulation to the writing program is desirable (or may exist), EAP courses are often distinct because of their relatively greater focus on integrated academic language and literacy skills (particularly reading). The extent of administrative connection between EAP programs and the writing program therefore becomes further complicated.

Local expertise and teacher support. As in the other models, the presence and location of L2 writing experts is likely to be one of the most important factors regarding the administrative relationship between EAP and FYW programs. Programs must consider issues of workload for L2 writing administrators as well. Depending on the size of the EAP program and any L2 writing program at the first-year level, it may not be feasible for a single individual to administer both.

And once again, the pool of qualified teachers will impact the administrative options as well. Institutions that enjoy access to a large number of teachers qualified to teach L2 FYW and EAP courses may be able to maintain closely linked programs so teachers can move across the curriculum, itself a benefit as it gives instructors a wide-angle view of writing instruction. At other institutions, though, there may be separate pools of instructors for EAP and FYW courses, perhaps based on institutional funding streams and instructional expertise. When instructor pools are distinct, it may be challenging to create shared administrative oversight between the EAP and FYW programs. For example, at institutions with clear credentialing criteria for teaching in different areas, the credentials for EAP and FYW might be quite different. And if instructor pools are separate, funding for instructional support and professional development might be separate as well. These sorts of divisions can lead to silos of disciplinary domains that can be challenging to bridge, especially from an administrative perspective.

CONCLUSION

Our analysis of four common administrative structures for supporting international L2 writers demonstrates that there is a wide range of factors to consider when evaluating the suitability of any particular administrative structure for any given institution as well as its effectiveness for supporting international students. As WPAs ourselves, we have come to see the notion of any one ideal structure to be of less practical value than a framework for understanding the opportunities that may be possible locally. It is our hope that the framework we offer in this chapter may serve as a heuristic for others involved in assessing existing administrative structures and perhaps building new ones that serve the needs of a growing international population. We understand some of these structures might demand fairly substantive shifts in human and material resources. They should, therefore, be seen as long-term investments in student and faculty support, and care should be taken in decisions of hiring and (re)distribution of responsibilities.

Our emphasis here has been primarily on supporting an international student population from a linguistic perspective, though we have also considered issues of educational and cultural backgrounds. We feel this dimension is critical to supporting L2 writers, but we also acknowledge that the administrative structures we have outlined can inadvertently construct a linguistic binary of L1 versus L2 writers when students' linguistic backgrounds in fact represent a much richer and more nuanced spectrum. It is important, we believe, for writing programs to imagine administrative and curricular structures that fully recognize the broad range of linguistic backgrounds international students bring. One example includes the large population of students from India, where English is often used as a dominant language. India was the second-largest place of origin for international students in the United States in 2015 and one of the fastest-growing groups overall (Institute of International Education 2015). Currently, these students are primarily studying at the graduate level, but the number of Indian undergraduates increased by 30 percent between the 2013–14 and 2014–15 academic years. WPAs might begin asking how well prepared their writing programs are to support students like these, who are users of world Englishes.

Because language support is often most urgent for students and most visible to teachers, we feel our focus on language within administrative models remains important in most institutions. However, truly internationalizing a writing program involves reexamining and reimagining multiple assumptions about writing in an academic context, where students and professors are globally mobile, linguistically diverse, and concerned with local and global issues. We are hopeful that in the future we might be in a position at our own institution to imagine what it would mean administratively to truly internationalize our programs for all students, whether they grew up a mile from campus or on the other side of the globe.

Note

1. There are, of course, many other related and relevant categories and issues that we have omitted here due to space constraints but that we also encourage programs to consider, including student assessment, visibility on campus, and institutional discourses and attitudes regarding internationalization and diversity.

References

Atkinson, Dwight, and Vai Ramanathan. 1995. "Cultures of Writing: An Ethnographic Comparison of L1 and L2 University Writing/Language Programs." *TESOL Quarterly* 29 (3): 539–68. https://doi.org/10.2307/3588074.

Conference on College Composition and Communication. 2014. "CCCC Statement on Second Language Writing and Writers." http://www.ncte.org/cccc/resources/positions/secondlangwriting.

Gentil, Guillaume. 2006. "EAP and Technical Writing without Borders: The Impact of Departmentalization on the Teaching and Learning of Academic Writing in a First and Second Language." In *The Politics of Second Language Writing*, edited by Paul Kei Matsuda, Christina Ortmeier-Hooper, and Xiaoye You, 147–67. West Lafayette, IN: Parlor.

Institute of International Education. 2015. *Open Doors*. https://www.iie.org/Research-and-Publications/Open-Doors/Data/International students/By-Academic-Level-and-Place-of-Origin/2014-15.

Kilfoil, Carrie Byars. 2014. "The Language Politics of Doctoral Students in Rhetoric and Composition: Toward a Translingual Revision of Graduate Education in the Field." PhD diss., University of Louisville.

Leki, Ilona. 2006. "The Legacy of First-Year Composition." In *The Politics of Second Language Writing*, edited by Paul Kei Matsuda, Christina Ortmeier-Hooper, and Xiaoye You, 59–74. West Lafayette, IN: Parlor.

Leki, Ilona, Alister Cumming, and Tony Silva. 2008. *A Synthesis of Research in Second Language Writing in English.* New York: Routledge.

Manchón, Rosa M., and Paul Kei Matsuda. Forthcoming. *Handbook of Second and Foreign Language Writing.* Berlin: De Gruyter. https://doi.org/10.1515/9781614511335.

Matsuda, Paul Kei. 2003. "Second Language Writing in the Twentieth Century: A Situated Historical Perspective." In *Exploring the Dynamics of Second Language Writing,* edited by Barbara Kroll, 15–34. Cambridge: Cambridge University Press. https://doi.org/10.1017/CBO9781139524810.004.

Matsuda, Paul Kei. 2006. "The Myth of Linguistic Homogeneity in U.S. College Composition." *College English* 68 (6): 637–51. https://doi.org/10.2307/25472180.

Matsuda, Paul Kei, Christina Ortmeier-Hooper, and Xiaoye You, eds. 2006. *The Politics of Second Language Writing: In Search of the Promised Land.* West Lafayette, IN: Parlor.

Matsuda, Paul Kei, Tanita Saenkhum, and Steven Accardi. 2013. "Writing Teachers' Perceptions of the Presence and Needs of Second Language Writers: An Institutional Case Study." *Journal of Second Language Writing* 22 (1): 68–86. https://doi.org/10.1016/j.jslw.2012.10.001.

Miller-Cochran, Susan. 2010. "Language Diversity and the Responsibility of the WPA." In *Cross-Language Relations in Composition,* edited by Bruce Horner, Min-Zhan Lu, and Paul Kei Matsuda, 212–20. Carbondale: Southern Illinois University Press.

National Census of Writing. 2014. *Four-Year Institution Survey.* http://writingcensus.swarthmore.edu/survey/4.

Preto-Bay, Ana Maria, and Kristine Hansen. 2006. "Preparing for the Tipping Point: Designing Writing Programs to Meet the Needs of the Changing Population." *WPA: Writing Program Administration* 30 (1–2): 37–57.

Shuck, Gail. 2006. "Combating Monolingualism: A Novice Administrator's Challenge." *WPA: Writing Program Administration* 30 (1–2): 59–82.

Silva, Tony. 1997. "On the Ethical Treatment of ESL Writers." *TESOL Quarterly* 31 (2): 359–63. https://doi.org/10.2307/3588052.

Silva, Tony, and Ilona Leki. 2004. "Family Matters: The Influence of Applied Linguistics and Composition Studies on Second Language Writing Studies—Past, Present, and Future." *Modern Language Journal* 88 (1): 1–13. https://doi.org/10.1111/j.0026-7902.2004.00215.x.

Tardy, Christine M. 2011. "Enacting and Transforming Local Language Policies." *College Composition and Communication* 62 (4): 634–61.

Tardy, Christine M. 2015. "Discourses of Internationalization and Diversity in US Universities and Writing Programs." In *Transnational Writing Program Administration,* edited by David S. Martins, 243–62. Boulder: University Press of Colorado. https://doi.org/10.7330/9780874219623.c010.

University of Arizona. 2014. "2014–15 Fact Book—International Students." http://factbook.arizona.edu/2014-15/students/international.

Vann, Roberta J., and Cynthia Myers. 2001. "Capitalizing on Contacts, Collaboration, and Disciplinary Communities: Academic ESL Options in a Large Research University." In *Academic Writing Programs,* edited by Ilona Leki, 73–84. Alexandria, VA: Teachers of English to Speakers of Other Language.

PART II

Program Development

4

CONFRONTING SUPERDIVERSITY IN US WRITING PROGRAMS

Jonathan Benda, Michael Dedek, Chris Gallagher,
Kristi Girdharry, Neal Lerner, and Matt Noonan

Over the past ten years, Northeastern University, like many US colleges and universities, has branded itself as a global institution, placing enormous emphasis on the recruitment of international students and the engagement of students in international experiences such as semesters abroad and global co-ops. For the university's writing program, in which the coauthors work, the most palpable change has been the sharp rise in the number of international students in our classrooms: a reported a 445 percent increase between 2006 and 2016 (https://www.northeastern .edu/accomplishments/). The over twenty-five hundred international students at Northeastern comprise 19.1 percent of the undergraduate-student enrollment (Powell 2016). This shift in demographics has proven both salutary and challenging. The increased diversity has made all our classrooms, not only those designated for multilingual writers, sites of rich, meaningful global encounters. At the same time, as teachers and administrators, we have struggled to keep pace with these changes— to learn about and from our students so we can teach them well.

As we began interacting with our students through these dynamic shifts, we quickly recognized that the designation *international* is insufficiently robust as an analytical category. First of all, we realized the category is difficult to define. Are students international by virtue of their visa status? by country of origin? by citizenship status? by history of schooling? by racial, cultural, linguistic, religious, or tribal-group membership? Moreover, among our students, nationality and language often do not neatly align: many of our international students are fluent (and sometimes L1) English speakers, just as many of our US students are multilingual—and sometimes L2 (or L3) speakers. Even within national and language or cultural groups, we see huge ranges in academic preparation, language and literacy experiences, and cultural and personal perspectives.

DOI: 10.7330/9781607326762.c004

We have also come to see the dangers of casual reliance on nation-based identity. We suspect we are not alone in observing at our university sweeping characterizations (and, inevitably, caricatures) of students by nationality—"these Chinese students don't know English," for instance.

With apologies to our editors, then, the coauthors of this chapter resist the concept of internationalization. When we think and talk about our students, or our campuses or programs, as international(ized), we say very little about them—and we may court dangerous generalizations and stereotypes. Our students increasingly exemplify what Steven Vertovec (2007) has called "super-diversity," characterized by an explosion of identity categories brought about by increased mobility in a globalizing world. Confronting superdiversity, we contend, will require us to move beyond broad descriptors like *international* in order to become better attuned to the diverse language, literacy, and cultural experiences, expectations, and practices of all our students in this era of globalization.

This chapter describes one writing program's attempts to address the growing superdiversity of its students. We feature three initiatives designed to help us learn about our students in order to better teach them across key areas of any writing program's enterprise: assessment (our guided self-placement process), research (our Multilingual Writers Research Project), and curriculum (our experimental Intercultural Writing and World Englishes course). Each of these initiatives was prompted by a recognition of a deficiency not in our students but in our understanding of our dynamic student body. Each has allowed us to deepen and complicate our understandings of who our students are and how best to serve them. And each, critically, is a work in progress: an imperfect and evolving effort to develop new ways to think about, talk about, and teach our superdiverse students.

THE NORTHEASTERN UNIVERSITY WRITING PROGRAM ENCOUNTERS THE WORLD

The Northeastern Writing Program offers approximately 350 sections of required first-year and advanced writing courses per year. The first-year courses include First-Year Writing, Introductory First-Year Writing, and First-Year Writing for Multilingual Writers. The advanced writing courses are offered in different disciplines or collections of disciplines including law, education, science, humanities, social science, and the technical professions, and there is also an interdisciplinary version. The writing program also houses a busy writing center and an undergraduate journal. It is staffed by a mix of tenure-stream faculty, full-time teaching professors, part-time lecturers, and PhD students.

As we noted at the start of this chapter, over the past several years, we have seen a rapid and significant increase in the number of international students at Northeastern, accompanied by what we perceived to be problematic responses on campus to this demographic shift. While many on campus, including most students, have embraced the university's growing cultural and linguistic diversity, as well as its global profile, some have chafed. We have heard persistent complaints about "these international students" and "their English." Some students have attempted to avoid collaborating on group projects with international students.

To be sure, we in the writing program have encountered students with limited English-language ability in our classrooms and in the writing center. However, they are a small percentage of the overall international-student population, which runs roughly the same gamut as our domestic students: from those who struggle daily to comprehend and keep up with their work to the very best students at the university. Even more to the point, *all* these students bring cultural and linguistic assets that, far from undermining the educational experience of others (presumably our white, domestic students), enrich and enliven that experience. For us—the authors of this chapter—the problem lies not in our students but in an institution that has not yet learned how to teach them.

Within the Northeastern Writing Program, then, we see the need to revisit our own practices and build our own capacity to serve our changing student population. We have taken several steps to help us better serve multilingual writers, including

- a series of both mandatory and optional workshops facilitated by leading ESL and translingualism scholars, including Christina Ortmeier-Hooper, Paul Kei Matsuda, Bruce Horner and Min-Zhan Lu, Juan Guerra, and Asao Inoue and Mya Poe;
- a multilingual writers inquiry group, facilitated by full-time lecturer Matt Noonan, who wrote his dissertation on teacher inquiry and assessment of ESL writers;
- the hiring of two faculty members, Jonathan Benda and Mya Poe, with expertise in teaching and assessing diverse writers;
- training of writing center tutors on working with multilingual writers;
- participation in national conversations on translingualism, including a featured session at CCCC (2014) and a chapter in Bruce Horner and Laura Tetrault's collection *Crossing Divides: Exploring Translingual Writing Pedagogies and Programs*.

At the same time, we have designed larger, ongoing initiatives to help us learn about and better serve our dynamic student body. In the following sections, we highlight three such initiatives spanning assessment (specifically placement), research, and curriculum.

GUIDED SELF-PLACEMENT

In 2009, when the number of international students at Northeastern was beginning to grow, the writing program used a placement process that relied entirely on an in-class essay. The essays, written in response to a prompt in the then-required textbook, were evaluated by instructors and program administrators, and students who were deemed unready for the rigors of the standard first-year course were placed either into a "basic" version of the course or into a section designated for speakers of other languages (SOL). Beyond the obvious problems with such an assessment—using a single, on-demand exam to make a high-stakes decision; putting instructors in the role of examiners on the first day of class; stigmatizing students by requiring them to switch classes; and so forth—we recognized our rapidly diversifying student body would be increasingly ill served by the placement process. Multilingual writers were more likely to face challenges during a timed, impromptu exam, and their essays were more likely to be flagged for minor grammatical and usage issues. What this placement exam could tell us about our students—how well they could perform in a remarkably inauthentic and limiting testing environment on the first day of classes—was insufficient to determine how best to serve their needs as learners and writers.

After surveying various placement models, we designed what we call a *guided self-placement process* (GSP) and implemented it in 2010 (see http://www.northeastern.edu/writing/first-year-writing/course-place ment/). The GSP is a version of what Daniel Royer and Roger Gilles call "directed self-placement" (Royer and Gilles 1998, 2003). During the summer, before arriving on campus and meeting with their advisors, students first review our first-year course offerings and conduct a self-assessment using guidelines we provide. After consulting with their advisors during freshman orientation on campus, they choose one of the three courses (including what we now call First-Year Writing for Multilingual Writers). They then write a short essay describing their prior experiences with writing and reading, as well as their current level of confidence and competence, and they submit these essays to their instructor on the first day of their writing class. During the first week of classes, instructors read the essays and consult with students and with program administrators about possible recommendations for changes in course selection. Students and their advisors ultimately determine whether to accept recommendations.

The GSP has several aims:

- to help students learn about our courses before taking them;
- to use multiple data sources for placement;
- to empower students in the course-selection process by trusting them as informants about their own learning experiences and needs;
- to involve program administrators and instructors as consultants to students rather than sole judges and juries; and
- to provide instructors and administrators with a wealth of information about students' literacy experiences and self-perceptions at the beginning of the class.

The last two goals were critical in the context of our shifting student demographics: we envisioned GSP as a tool for learning about and from students how we could best teach them.

The results of the GSP have been mixed. Certainly it is an improvement over the previous placement method. We now begin the semester by learning a great deal about students, including and especially their perceptions of themselves as writers and learners. Instead of asking only, can this student produce the kind of prose we are looking for in the standard first-year writing course?, we are asking, how can we use what we learn about this student to make a recommendation about the best possible curricular fit? Many instructors use the placement essay as part of the first project of the course, thus building students' literacy histories into their learning. Each semester, instructors and administrators have searching conversations with each other and with students about how best to serve our writers. Finally, the process has affirmed our disinclination to simply place international students in segregated courses; the majority of international and multilingual writers take the standard version of the first-year writing course.

At the same time, the GSP is not perfect and in some ways has reified the problems it was intended to address. Some instructors—though fewer and fewer—still flag student essays for surface-level correctness and place undue emphasis on the essay itself rather than taking a more holistic approach to assessment, including conversation with students. Some students do not fully understand their curricular options and what it would mean to avail themselves of one rather than another. It may be that multilingual writers are especially susceptible to this difficulty; DSP has been criticized along these lines (Bedore and Rossen-Knill

2004; DasBender 2012; Lewiecki-Wilson, Sommers, and Tassoni 2000; Saenkhum 2016). Students are sometimes placed and decide to stay in courses for reasons other than where they are most likely to succeed— their schedules, for instance. Perhaps most distressingly, some advisors automatically place international students in the course for multilingual writers, and those students feel they belong in those sections, whether or not that is the case. This undermines the entire purpose of the GSP.

The GSP remains a work in progress. We have formed a working group to explore ways to better inform students and their advisors—and sometimes ourselves!—about its purpose and about the curricular choices available. We are also trying to build a better understanding of how multilingual students in particular fare under the GSP. We know the number of international students placed into the course for multilingual writers has decreased sharply over the past several years, with no corresponding drop in students' grades. This could be because more students are initially placed into multilingual sections, because our instructors' capacity to teach diverse groups of learners has grown, because our population of international and multilingual writers has grown stronger—or, most likely, some combination of these. In any case, what we need now are more sophisticated ways to understand not just who our diverse writers are as they enter our courses but also how they experience the GSP and the courses themselves.

THE MULTILINGUAL WRITERS RESEARCH PROJECT

While the GSP process has told us a great deal about who our multilingual writers are at Northeastern, we still feel hampered in our efforts to make curricular decisions given a growing and changing multilingual population, a group of students we still know in only limited ways. To address this need, we formed a writing program subcommittee consisting of instructors at all ranks: PhD students, full-time lecturers, and tenure-stream faculty. We wanted to answer a seemingly simple question: who are our multilingual writers at Northeastern? We chose the term *multilingual* for three reasons: (1) to resist easy generalizations about international students, (2) to capture multilinguality among our domestic students, and (3) to emphasize what these students *could* do—work with multiple languages—rather than what they could not do. The Multilingual Writers Research Project (MLWRP), then, grew out of dissonance between the ways in which we were experiencing our multilingual writers and the ways in which some in our institution were describing "those international students."

To begin to answer our central question—who are our multilingual students at Northeastern?—we applied for and received funding through an assessment initiative from our university's teaching and learning center and then obtained IRB approval[1] starting in 2013 to conduct a large quantitative survey, administered annually, with follow-up qualitative interviews. The purpose of the survey and follow-up interviews was to better understand multilingual students' expectations, experiences, and aspirations for writing in English at Northeastern and beyond.

To draft our survey, we first looked to similar studies on multilingual students and writing (see especially Ferris and Thaiss 2011; Jarratt, Losh, and Puente 2006). We divided our survey into four parts: demographics, expectations of writing at NU, experiences of writing at NU, and expectations of using English in the future. Once we collaboratively designed the survey questions, we piloted the instrument with a first-year writing class designated for multilingual writers and taught by one of the coauthors. With feedback from those students, we revised questions to ensure consistent response.

An invitation to complete the online survey was sent to all students who had completed our required Advanced Writing in the Disciplines course (this course can be taken after students complete sixty-four academic credits, which puts most students in their junior and senior years), and all students were offered the chance to win a $50 Amazon gift card for their participation. Students who did not identify a language other than English as important to them personally or culturally were excluded from the survey after a couple of preliminary questions (though they still qualified for the gift-card lottery).

Sample Survey Questions[2]

Demographics	Expectations for writing at NU
• Are languages other than English spoken in your family home? If yes, what are these languages?	• When you first came to Northeastern University, what was your confidence in writing in English?
• For your instruction previous to coming to Northeastern, were all of your classes taught in English (not including foreign-language classes)?	• Before coming to Northeastern, how challenging did you expect the writing assignments to be?
• Where did you go to high school?	• Before coming to Northeastern, what kinds of activities did you expect in your writing courses at Northeastern?
• Were you enrolled in any English-language transitional or preparatory programs (e.g., Global Pathways or the US-Sino Pathway Program)?	• Before coming to Northeastern University, what did you expect to learn in your writing courses?

Experiences of Writing at NU	Expectations for English in the Future
• What is your confidence in writing in English now?	• What do you plan to do immediately after graduation?
• How challenging have you found the writing assignments?	• Where do you expect to live and work after graduation?
• In your writing courses at Northeastern, which kinds of activities took place in your classes?	• How often do you expect to use English after graduation at work, at home, and in public?
• Consider the writing courses you took at Northeastern; what do you feel you learned?	• How well do you expect you will need to speak and write in English to achieve your goals after graduation?

After a pilot administration of our survey in 2013, we learned two important things: (1) the diversity of our students—as we report on in this chapter—belied simple categorizations, and (2) we needed to revise several survey questions because they were misinterpreted by large numbers of respondents. We realized that many of our language questions needed to focus on writing specifically.[3] In the 2014 and 2015 administrations of the survey, we used the revised instrument, and the survey data we report on here come from those two administrations. We also show aggregate results from the 2014 and 2015 administrations, as we did not see statistically significant differences between the two data sets. Given space constraints, we primarily address what we learned from those two survey administrations about who our multilingual writers are at Northeastern, findings that further complicate broad notions of the international student.

As shown in table 4.1, in both 2014 and 2015, we received about a 20 percent response rate to our survey invitations, and in both years a bit more than 40 percent of the students who started the survey self-identified as multilingual writers and thus were able to complete the entire survey.

In both survey years, students also consistently reported tremendous language variation. In the 2014 survey, students indicated proficiency in a total of fifty-nine languages other than English; in the 2015 survey, this figure was seventy-six languages. We also saw this variation in terms of how many students reported proficiency in two or more languages other than English, as shown in table 4.2.

Another example of language diversity comes from students' responses to our survey question, "While you have been at Northeastern, what kinds of writing have you done outside of school?" As shown in table 4.3, students reported engaging in a wide range of writing activities, both in English and in other languages. Perhaps it's not a surprise

Table 4.1. MLWRP survey demographics, 2014 and 2015.

	2014	2015
Surveys distributed	8,364	5,985
Students who started survey	1,628 (20%)	1,132 (19%)
Students who identified as multilingual writers	704 (43%)	506 (45%)

to see the frequency with which e-mail, texting, and Facebook were cited by a large majority of respondents, but as writers and writing teachers ourselves, we were very pleased to see the strong presence of bloggers, poets, fiction writers, and diarists, both in English and in languages other than English.

To better understand how students were using their primary language other than English, we asked about their confidence in writing in this language, as well as whether they wrote in L1 with friends and other students. We also asked students to rate their confidence as writers, both upon entry to Northeastern and at the time they were taking the survey (most likely as juniors or seniors) as shown in table 4.4.

When we first discussed the results of our survey after the 2013 pilot administration, results such as those shown in table 4.4 came as a surprise. Our preconceived notions of who our multilingual writers were did not take into consideration that they might not be particularly fluent writing in L1 (though this finding is consistent with Chiang and Schmida's [1999] study of Asian American students at UC Berkeley). Also, we were surprised that fewer than half reported writing in L1 with friends and other students, particularly given the use of texting and international keyboards. Finally, we were surprised by how highly students rated their confidence writing in English upon entry. Overall, we wondered whether overall averages or totals might be masking results for particular subgroups, particularly less able users of English.

To investigate that possibility, we used the results of two demographic questions to create two breakout groups: (1) survey respondents who reported attending high school outside the United States and (2) those who entered Northeastern through a "pathway" program or a year-long, language-intensive preparatory program that recruits international students (see http://www.global-pathways.com/northeastern-boston/). We focused on these groups because, as shown in table 4.5, they were as a whole more likely to have had instruction in a language other than English before coming to Northeastern, and thus we assumed their perceived written proficiency in and use of English might be different than for multilingual writers as a whole.

Table 4.2. Students' language diversity, 2014 and 2015.

Students identifying two languages other than English	46% (550)
Students identifying three languages other than English	13% (159)
Languages cited most often for L1	Spanish = 24% (289)
	Chinese = 16% (192)
	French = 11% (127)

Table 4.3. Percent of all students reporting outside-of-school writing by type, 2014 and 2015.

Type of writing	In English	In other language(s)
E-mail	87%	32%
Text messages	86%	42%
Facebook updates/tweets	83%	29%
Letters/postcards	61%	18%
Comments on blogs, online forums, or other online venues	54%	14%
Keeping a private diary/journal	38%	9%
Computer code/programs	32%	3%
Keeping a blog	31%	6%
Newspaper articles, editorials, or letters to the editor	25%	6%
Fiction (short stories, plays)	24%	4%
Poetry	22%	4%
Magazine articles	20%	5%
Comics, graphic novels, and other forms of graphic texts	16%	5%

Table 4.4. Fluency in L1, confidence as a writer: 2014 and 2015.

Avg. written fluency in L1 (4 = very fluent; 1 = not fluent)	2.4/4
Do you write L1 with friends or other students at Northeastern?	Yes = 39% (469)
	No = 61% (733)
Avg. confidence as a writer in English upon entry (4 = high; 1 = low)	3.5/4
Avg. confidence as a writer in English now (4 = high; 1 = low)	3.5/4

As shown in table 4.6, students who went to high school outside the United States reported a higher written proficiency in L1 and lower confidence as writers upon entry to Northeastern but a confidence equal to

Table 4.5. For your instruction previous to coming to Northeastern, were all of your classes taught in English (not including foreign-language classes)?

	All respondents 2014 and 2015	*HS outside US 2014 and 2015*	*Pathways 2014 and 2015*
Yes	84% (974)[a]	51% (128)[a]	42% (28)[a]
No	16% (188)[b]	49% (123)[b]	58% (38)[b]

[a] Differences between subgroup and all survey respondents are statistically significant at $p < 0.01$.

[b] Differences between subgroup and all survey respondents are statistically significant at $p < 0.01$.

all survey respondents at the point of survey administration. Students who entered via Pathways programs (some, but not all, of whom overlap with those who went to high school outside the United States) also reported higher written proficiency in L1 and even lower confidence as writers in English than did the overall group and those who went to high school outside the United States, both at the point of entry to Northeastern and at the point at which they took the survey. We also note that these students were more likely to cite Chinese as their first language, particularly the Pathways-entry students. Still, that broad finding once again masks individual variation for a country of 1.3 billion inhabitants from a range of school systems and for college-age students with varying degrees of English-language preparation. To further investigate the experiences of these students, after the 2017 survey administration, we plan to conduct individual interviews with students who reported having attending high school in China.

Overall, the findings from the MLWRP remind us to resist broad categorizations of multilingual student writers at Northeastern and make us more aware of the diversity of languages, cultures, experiences, and expectations students bring to bear in our work with them in and out of the classroom. As we noted previously, the MLWRP came out of a programmatic need to understand who our multilingual students are as writers and thus to make informed decisions about teaching and curriculum. We next describe one particular curricular effort.

INTERCULTURAL WRITING AND WORLD ENGLISHES

One curricular response to our growing population of multilingual writers was to pilot a themed first-year writing course that focused, in part, on language and language difference. We titled this piloted version Intercultural Writing and World Englishes (IWWE). The course

Table 4.6. Comparison of breakout groups with all survey respondents, 2014 and 2015.

	All respondents	HS outside United States	Pathways entry[a]
Students who identified as multilingual writers	1,210	21% (251)	5% (65)
Students identifying two languages other than English	46% (550)	66% (166)	48% (31)
Students identifying three languages other than English	13% (159)	29% (73)	12% (8)
Languages cited most often for L1	Spanish = 24% (289)	Chinese = 23% (58)	Chinese = 52% (34)
	Chinese = 16% (192)	Spanish = 20% (50)	Spanish = 8% (5)
	French = 11% (127)	French = 15% (37)	French = 6% (4)
Avg. written fluency in L1 (4 = very fluent; 1 = not fluent)[a]	2.4/4	3.5/4	3.5/4
Do you write L1 with friends or other students at Northeastern?[b]	Yes = 39% (469)	Yes = 74% (185)	Yes = 72% (47)
	No = 61% (313)	No = 26% (66)	No = 28% (28)
Avg. confidence as a writer upon entry (4 = high; 1 = low)	3.5/4	3.1/4	2.8/4
Avg. confidence as a writer now (4 = high; 1 = low)	3.5/4	3.5/4	3/4

[a] 29% (19) of these students reported attending high school in the United States.

[b] Differences are statistically significant at p <0.01.

was initially conceived during the spring 2012 semester by our writing program's Multilingual Writers Committee, comprised of three lecturers, two full time and one part time. These lecturers, including Jonathan and Matt, took responsibility for inventing and piloting IWWE. Chris also assisted in revising the official course description. A major feature of IWWE was that it was designed to enroll what our institution labels "US domestic" and "international" students in equal proportions. The official course description for IWWE stated that, in the course,

- students "will be focusing on the use of English around the world, and the implications of that use for language standards and language learning";
- "intercultural communication will become both the means and the object of study";

- students "will compose . . . writing projects . . . that simultaneously explore and enact language difference";
- and "language difference will be approached as an asset, rather than an impediment, to learning."

Initial discussions about IWWE centered on how we might combine two first-year writing courses: (1) ENGW1102, which was then called College Writing—SOL (Speakers of Other Languages) and (2) ENGW1111, then called College Writing. Our integrated course resembled the model offered by Paul Kei Matsuda and Tony Silva (Matsuda and Silva 1999)—Matsuda had also visited our campus during the fall of 2011—and was motivated in part by conversations about translingualism, which were gaining popularity in disciplinary publications at the time (Horner et al. 2011). The intention was to mix students who had different cultural and linguistic backgrounds in order to offer all students opportunities to learn about, experience, and write with a variety of linguistic resources.

Though IWWE was taught in significantly different ways by each instructor who piloted it, all sections of IWWE included writing assignments and course readings that directed students' attention toward their own experiences with Englishes and other languages and that encouraged students to draw on their English and multilingual repertoires as they composed. In one version of IWWE taught by Jonathan, an assignment titled "English and Me" instructed students, "Introduce yourself to me by describing your previous experiences with the English language. Relate some specific incidents that describe your attitude (or attitudes—maybe you have several different or conflicting feelings) and experiences related to English." This assignment was particularly challenging to students who self-identified as monolingual or as native speakers of English because, as some of them admitted, English was something they took for granted.

Meanwhile, in Matt's version of the course, students were invited to write a "collage" essay that imitated Susan Griffin (2011) and that engaged with A. Suresh Canagarajah (2006) by code meshing, or by directly writing about Canagarajah's ideas, or both. In addition to Canagarajah (2006) and Griffin (2011), course readings included texts from David Bartholomae and Anthony Petrosky (Bartholomae and Petrosky 2011) that demonstrated writers drawing on a range of linguistic resources. Such texts included Gloria Anzaldúa (2011a; 2011b) and John E. Wideman (2011). In some sections of IWWE, students also read excerpts from Rosina Lippi-Green's (1997) *English with an Accent*, which scrutinizes monolingual ideology in the United States.

Students' responses to course readings and writing assignments and our interactions with students in IWWE have helped us develop insight into our students' diverse backgrounds and expectations as learners. Through IWWE we have learned more about the unpredictability of students' backgrounds and expectations. IWWE has helped us become more aware that it is not uncommon for our students—whether international or US domestic—to move daily among multiple languages, to have biographies that traverse national boundaries, and to have educational experiences and aims that are impossible to predict on the basis of nationality or trajectory of migration. An example of our students' multifaceted cultural, social, linguistic, and geographic identities appears in a passage excerpted from a student's project in a section of IWWE taught by Matt.

> I was born in Los Angeles, California, and moved to the Dominican Republic when I was eight years old. My mother is Philippine and my father is Belgian. I have a younger brother, Tristan, who lives at a tennis academy in Florida. Up to elementary school, all of my education had been American, until my parents placed me in a Lycée Français. Paradoxically, at school I learned to speak Spanish because that was all my classmates spoke outside of the classroom. So I am trilingual, which sometimes has me jumping from language to language, looking for the translation of a word that doesn't exist.

Such examples have suggested to us the limited usefulness of creating pedagogical and curricular interventions based on knowledge about students' citizenship or residency status. Our experiences with teaching IWWE—which has opened up a space for students to explore their complex relationships with language, culture, and geography—has contributed to our view of the presence of superdiversity. Our experience with IWWE supports the view that "the predictability of the category of 'migrant' and his/her sociocultural features has disappeared" (Blommaert and Rampton 2011, 1).

This superdiversity is also illustrated in the changes in demographics in IWWE over the two-year period in which it was piloted. Matt has recorded that, in the first round of piloting of the course (fall 2012), three of nineteen writers in his class identified or could be identified as multilingual. By the fall of 2013, thirteen of nineteen writers could be categorized as multilingual. Perhaps even more telling is a list culled from the projects writers worked on in Matt's 2013 course. The prompt, working off of Wideman's (2011) descriptions of Homewood in his essay "Our Time" published in the course text, *Ways of Reading*, invited writers to write about a place and its people. This list includes places the writers lived in for some period of time:

- Mexico City, Caracas (Venezuela), Kenya
- Los Angeles California, Dominican Republic, Florida, Belgium
- New Jersey
- New York
- India
- Valencia (Venezuela)
- Northbridge, Massachusetts
- Plymouth, Massachusetts
- Jeddah, Saudi Arabia, then New Hampshire
- Puerto Rico
- Amesbury, Massachusetts
- Lagos, Africa, then Dubai, United Arab Emirates (with rich Indian background)
- Beijing, China
- Toronto, Canada, then Yemen, then Jeddah, Saudi Arabia
- Mexico City
- West Hartford, Connecticut
- Shenzhen and Hong Kong
- Brookline, Massachusetts, and Russia
- Beirut, Lebanon, then Boston, Massachusetts

As shorthand, though, this list fails to account for the even greater complexity in many of the linguistic lives of our students. The list only hints at the superdiversity of the writers in the class, the layered origins, the richness within the larger categories—a better (more complex) representation is found in the words of the writers themselves.

DIVERSITY AS A STRENGTH FOR NORTHEASTERN'S WRITING PROGRAM

Overall, the assessment, research, and curriculum/teaching we describe in this chapter have shown us what is often asserted in the literature: students' diversity, whether in terms of language, culture, history, race, gender, sexuality, or other factors, offers great strength and opportunity. It is too easy to group students by region or culture or assumed educational background. The challenge is not merely to meet students where they are but to investigate in meaningful ways where they might be and to use that information in creating curriculum and pedagogical interventions.

We are also mindful of the dynamic nature of our students' lives and of writing programs as particular contexts for learning. As Canagarajah (2013) writes, citing Jan Blommaert (2010), "We have to also remember that contexts should not be treated as static. Interactants construct the context that is operative in their talk by invoking different scales of time, space, and social life" (155). Further, Canagarajah (2013) argues that

> context is a relational construct, that is: is a particular context home or alien? Contexts are overlapping, that is: is a particular context local or global, when we know that the global interpenetrates the local? Context is dynamic, that is: how do space, time, and social structure interact in reshaping context? Context is mediated, that is: how do nation, profession, class, religion, and other domains constitute a particular context? (154)

These factors are at play in all our students' lives in and out of our classrooms and writing centers. Characterizations of students as only international or even as only multilingual potentially overlook opportunities to work with students to best help them learn to write and help them recognize the dynamic contexts in which that learning takes place.

Our work has complicated for us the international context of an internationalizing writing program by pointing to the discursive and relationally constructed nature of context. The notion that our writing program is internationalizing must be understood in terms of how the various participants in the work of the program—administrators (both inside and outside the writing program), instructors, students, writing center consultants, and so forth—are constructing and using the concepts of nation and international as contexts for understanding and working with each other.

Notes

1. Northeastern University IRB# 12–08–21.
2. Full survey is available upon request from the authors.
3. We thank our colleague Mya Poe for her help with survey modification.

References

Anzaldúa, Gloria. 2011a. "Entering into the Serpent." In *Ways of Reading: An Anthology for Writers*. 9th ed., edited by David Bartholomae and Anthony Petrosky, 72–84. Boston, MA: Bedford/St. Martin's.

Anzaldúa, Gloria. 2011b. "How to Tame a Wild Tongue." In *Ways of Reading: An Anthology for Writers*. 9th ed., edited by David Bartholomae and Anthony Petrosky, 85–93. Boston, MA: Bedford/St. Martin's.

Bartholomae, David, and Anthony Petrosky, eds. 2011. *Ways of Reading: An Anthology for Writers*. 9th ed. Boston, MA: Bedford/St. Martin's.

Bedore, Pamela, and Deborah F. Rossen-Knill. 2004. "Informed Self-Placement: Is a Choice Offered a Choice Received?" *WPA: Writing Program Administration* 28 (1–2): 55–78.

Blommaert, Jan. 2010. *The Sociolinguistics of Globalization.* New York: Cambridge. https://doi.org/10.1017/CBO9780511845307.

Blommaert, Jan, and Ben Rampton. 2011. "Language and Superdiversity." *Diversities* 13 (2): 1–21. www.unesco.org/shs/diversities/vol13/issue2/art1.

Canagarajah, A. Suresh. 2006. "The Place of World Englishes in Composition: Pluralization Continued." *College Composition and Communication* 57 (4): 586–619.

Canagarajah, A. Suresh. 2013. *Translingual Practice: Global Englishes and Cosmopolitan Relations.* New York: Routledge.

Chiang, Yuet-Sim D., and Mary Schmida. 1999. "Language Identity and Language Ownership: Linguistic Conflicts of First-Year University Writing Students." In *Generation 1.5 Meets College Composition: Issues in the Teaching of Writing to U.S.-Educated Learners of ESL,* edited by Linda Harklau, Kay M. Losey, and Meryl Siegal, 81–96. Mahwah, NJ: Lawrence Erlbaum.

DasBender, Gita. 2012. "Assessing Generation 1.5 Learners: The Revelations of Directed Self-Placement." In *Writing Assessment in the 21st Century,* edited by Norbert Elliott and Leslie Perelman, 371–84. New York: Hampton.

Ferris, Dana, and Chris Thaiss. 2011. "Writing at UC Davis: Addressing the Needs of Second Language Writers." In "WAC and Second Language Writing: Cross-field Research, Theory, and Program Development," edited by Michelle Cox and Terry Myers Zawacki. Special issue, *Across the Disciplines* 8 (4). https://wac.colostate.edu/atd/ell/ferris-thaiss.cfm.

Griffin, Susan. 2011. "Our Secret." In *Ways of Reading: An Anthology for Writers.* 9th ed., edited by David Bartholomae and Anthony Petrosky, 335–82. Boston, MA: Bedford/St. Martin's.

Horner, Bruce, Min-Zhan Lu, Jacqueline Jones Royster, and John Trimbur. 2011. "Language Difference in Writing: Toward a Translingual Approach." *College English* 73 (3): 303–21.

Jarratt, Susan C., Elizabeth Losh, and David Puente. 2006. "Transnational Identifications: Biliterate Writers in a First-Year Humanities Course." *Journal of Second Language Writing* 15 (1): 24–48. https://doi.org/10.1016/j.jslw.2006.01.001.

Lewiecki-Wilson, Cynthia, Jeff Sommers, and John Paul Tassoni. 2000. "Rhetoric and the Writer's Profile: Problematizing Directed Self-Placement." *Assessing Writing* 7 (2): 165–83. https://doi.org/10.1016/S1075-2935(00)00020-9.

Lippi-Green, Rosina. 1997. *English with an Accent: Language, Ideology, and Discrimination in the United States.* New York: Routledge.

Matsuda, Paul Kei, and Tony Silva. 1999. "Cross-Cultural Composition: Mediated Integration of U.S. and International Students." *Composition Studies* 27 (1): 15–30.

Powell, Farran. 2016. "10 Universities That Attract the Most International Students." *U.S. News & World Report,* July 5. https://www.usnews.com/education/best-colleges/the-short-list-college/articles/2016-07-05/10-universities-that-attract-the-most-international-students.

Royer, Daniel, and Roger Gilles. 1998. "Directed Self-Placement." *College Composition and Communication* 50 (1): 54–70. https://doi.org/10.2307/358352.

Royer, Daniel, and Roger Gilles, eds. 2003. *Directed Self-Placement: Principles and Practices.* New York: Hampton.

Saenkhum, Tanita. 2016. *Decisions, Agency, and Advising: Key Issues in the Placement of Multilingual Writers into First-Year Composition Courses.* Logan: Utah State University Press. https://doi.org/10.7330/9781607325482.

Vertovec, Steven. 2007. "Super-Diversity and Its Implications." *Ethnic and Racial Studies* 30 (6): 1024–54. https://doi.org/10.1080/01419870701599465.

Wideman, John E. 2011. "Our Time." In *Ways of Reading: An Anthology for Writers*. 9th ed., edited by David Bartholomae and Anthony Petrosky, 657–94. Boston, MA: Bedford/ St. Martin's.

5

CONTENDING WITH DIFFERENCE
Points of Leverage for Intellectual Administration of the Multilingual FYC Course

Tarez Samra Graban

INTRODUCTION

In the five years I had oversight of the multilingual composition curriculum at Indiana University (from 2007 to 2012), the university-wide international student population grew by an estimated 75 percent—due in part to an international growth initiative by the university president, with an emphasis on recruiting undergraduate students from competitive secondary schools in the People's Republic of China (Indiana University 2007; *Indy Star* 2015; IU News Room 2008). While the international student population provided the university with an explicit metric to track, in my first few years on campus it became apparent that there was also a growing population of academically bilingual and resident multilingual students, whose language statuses and backgrounds went unnoticed by enrollment and matriculation records.

As a result, what characterized my work as coordinator of multilingual composition was navigating an interplay of assumptions, resistances, and beliefs surrounding *difference* as both a pedagogical and programmatic approach, including whether that term should (or could reasonably) be subsumed under the university's broader vision to internationalize and how the term informed expectations about which students on campus required (or deserved) linguistic support. Because of significant efforts to retain first-year composition as a foundational requirement during the campus's move to a general education curriculum, my course—ENG W131ML, or Elementary Composition Multilingual, previously known as ENG W131NN, or Elementary Composition Non-Native—was positioned at the center of several debates about the viability of enacting a multilingual approach within a composition curriculum that had historically been based in US-centric assumptions about writing. My role as course coordinator quickly became that of a strategist, identifying and productively involving the assumptions of multiple stakeholders across the university in writing program development.

DOI: 10.7330/9781607326762.c005

I argue that navigating these assumptions led me to a kind of "systems thinking," an approach described by Dan Melzer (2013) for transforming writing programs by looking toward problems that are unstructured and somewhat unstable (90). This transformation is perpetual and can occur across any system whose agents locate and negotiate "points of leverage" (75) and whose "attention is on the ways [its structure] will construct behavior" (78). While these leverage points can reflect significant shifts in a program's ideologies (86), they take time and reflection to discern, and they require an understanding of how best to involve the system's multiple agents. In my own work with multilingual composition, I found three such points of leverage through working with institutional agents, department agents, and disciplinary agents, whose reactions or responses helped me not only to focus on reshaping the program's most critical aspects but also to conduct its most critical conversations about difference.

LEVERAGING THE INSTITUTION: MAPPING MICROPROBLEMS ONTO MACROCONTEXTS

The question of difference has been paramount to recent conversations about whether translingualism should be considered the new norm in and for US-based college composition. On the one hand, it is important for WPAs to attend to students' fluctuating linguistic and cultural needs. In a 2011 article in *College Composition and Communication*, Bruce Horner, Samantha NeCamp, and Christiane Donahue argued for the field to take a less "additive" approach to composition scholarship in order to better support "a translingual model of multilingualism [that] emphasiz[es] working across languages" (Horner, NeCamp, and Donahue 2011, 270); at the same time, Horner et al. (2011) argued that working toward "a translingual approach" could enable teachers of composition to "develop alternatives to conventional treatments" of linguistic and discursive difference (304), thereby avoiding unproductive debates about who has the right to what language, as these debates often overlook the fluidity of language practices. The following year, Jay Jordan (2012) observed the various academic and social juxtapositions commonly experienced by L2 writers and their instructors and argued for "intercultural communicative competence" over "lingualism" as the guiding paradigm for FYC because it values (rather than devalues) the linguistic and cultural "baggage" that makes language users flexible and dynamic composers (121).

On the other hand, WPAs are cautioned from promoting discussions of difference over discussions of learning. While the "translingual" conditions described by Horner, NeCamp, and Donahue (2011) focus on forging a relationship between fluctuating languages and achieving mutual intelligibility over fluency (287), Jordan (2015) reminds us that the nomenclature typically associated with the "translingual approach" might still "seek to replace one set of linguistic heroes . . . with another" (365)—that is, the nomenclature assumes a composing process in which teachers expect their students to become conscious experts of their own linguistic negotiation. Either perspective assumes that language and difference are stable categories (Jordan 2015, 369), in spite of evidence to the contrary.

Finally, WPAs are encouraged neither to overlook nor to overemphasize the various negotiations that occur when students bring multiple language resources to the composing process. Paul Kei Matsuda (2014) argues that constructing arbitrary and false binaries between terms like "second language (L2)" and "translingual," and between "code-switching" and "code-meshing" (480), flattens or conflates the very linguistic nuances that should be raised when we attend to students' composing processes. And in an open letter to the field published in *College English*, Dwight Atkinson, Deborah Crusan, Paul Kei Matsuda, Christina Ortmeier-Hooper, and Todd Ruecker propose that journal editors and organization leaders retain a productive distinction between "L2" and "translingual" writing since "translingual" is only one of several orientations toward language difference (Atkinson et al. 2015, 385). Settling this discussion—and hence, settling on the best term (*multilingual, translingual,* or *L2*) to describe the kinds of interventions we should make and the kinds of outcomes we should assess among language learners in first-year composition—is outside the purview of this chapter. Instead, this chapter considers the usefulness of taking up contentions about difference to initiate discussions about programmatic change, neither promoting difference as an ideology nor limiting its contentions only to discussions of linguistic transformation but simply accepting it as the program's critical problem.

In systems thinking, the critical problem of a particular course or program is applied toward the workings of the system itself (Melzer 2013, 93). For example, though it seemed justifiable *ethically*, a regular course release was not *institutionally* justifiable for my role as coordinator of multilingual composition since the director of composition's role earned only one release a year, and there was no mechanism in place to offer release time for a lesser position in duties and scope. Thus, the first point of leverage in contending productively with difference occurred institutionally through liaisons with the professional advising team and the academic advisors in the music and business schools (two schools within the university that had separate requirements from other undergraduate majors across campus). These liaisons did not result in release time for coordinating ENG W131ML, but they served to make the role of coordinator more visible as a first point of contact on decisions regarding course eligibility, advising, and placement and on the establishment of curricular partnerships that would be critical to sustaining the longer-term goal of teacher development (Canagarajah 2016).

These liaisons also created a shared activity through which differences between assumptions about multilingualism and multilingual approaches to FYC programming could be more usefully exposed through a more informed placement process. When I first arrived on campus, there was neither systematic nor directed self-placement of students into ENG W131ML, although there was an internal testing mechanism, managed by the intensive-English program (IEP), that sought to identify most students whose visa, immigration, and/or linguistic statuses matched a perceived need for the course. There was also an office of university advisors, a handful of whom were informally designated as ESL-student advisors due to personal background or professional interest and who directed students to the course one week before each semester began in response to their results on the internal exam. Finally, most outstanding queries about placement eligibility fell into the hands of the composition secretary or composition scheduler and were typically resolved on an individual basis. Through this combination of activities, student-placement decisions were inconsistent at best, as there was no systematic way to differentiate between international and resident multilingual students as language users or composers without conducting a personal interview.

In my five years working with the course, I sought to map or recreate the institutional pathways by which students made their way into the course, eventually linking together what had been several disparate policies informing the matriculation and enrollment of international and/or resident multilingual students, each hosted by a different office on campus. Figure 5.1 depicts the placement pathways identified or recreated by the end of 2012 that would support the revised curriculum. Such mapping in turn exposed tensions among various "actors in the system" by "painting a rich picture" of both the actual system in which they participated and their ideal notions of how such a system should operate (Melzer 2013, 77). For example, making ENG W131ML's placement pathways more visible helped me identify a multifaceted placement strategy by mapping the narrower context of the course onto the more

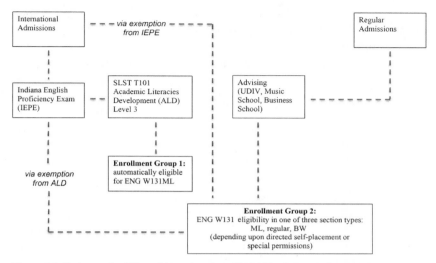

Figure 5.1. Pathways for ESL and L2 writers into ENG W131ML at Indiana University, AY 2011–2012.

vital context of deriving placement decisions informed by students' core language background (Indiana University n.d.b).[1]

Whereas prior placement decisions had been made on the basis of students' visa status or nationality, I consulted with the IEP as they revised their internal placement exam and with the director of Data Services in university advising so as to better understand the constellation of factors I should and could reasonably attend to in making this determination. Ultimately, we found that students' home or resident countries and "first" languages were insufficient for predicting how they would progress through a series of linked courses in academic literacy development and for flagging them to receive special advising, especially among academically bi- and trilingual students who had difficulty identifying which language was their "first." Instead, the nature and class of their secondary schools (e.g., regional, urban, private, public), the principal language(s) in which they performed their education or attained their degrees, and the methods by which their instruction in reading or writing English was delivered (i.e., the kind and frequency of tasks they had been asked to perform in English, including standardized language testing) provided a more coherent picture of students' language competencies and their exposure to learning in a multilingual environment. While not all these factors could be quickly assessed on the basis of students' applications or placement exams alone, it was possible for Data Services to generate a report prior to the start of each term that coalesced several data points, helping to direct various populations of ESL/L2 learners into one of two enrollment groups: students automatically eligible and appropriate for placement into ENG W131ML through the IEPE process, or students whose academic linguistic background prior to IU gained them exemption from either the Indiana English Proficiency Exam (IEPE) or the Academic Literacies Development course taught by IEP instructors and allowed them to choose self-placement in ENG W131ML or another section of English composition.[2]

The pathways map depicted in figure 5.1 also aided the course's instructors in predicting the disparities they might witness among a classroom of otherwise homogenous students and in counseling students who questioned their placement. Even with enrollment groups in place, consultation was still necessary in many cases in which students weren't sure of the best course to select. Indeed, the goal in creating enrollment groups was not to attain an accurate linguistic profile but to better predict the curricular options and advising services we should be prepared to offer, in accordance with FYC placement guidelines articulated by the "CCCC Statement on Second Language Writing and Writers" (CCCC 2014). At best, these measures helped initiate conversations about placement eligibility among several groups of stakeholders on campus. I still required instructors to make an early assessment of students' writing competencies during the first week of the semester, and all instructors still asked students to voluntarily report data about their English instruction, language preferences, and literacy habits on a questionnaire, which I systematically collected and transcribed so as to determine the efficacy of our enrollment groups over time. Admittedly, these data-gathering activities were time consuming even for the 250–400 students we served in ENG W131ML each year and might be unsustainable for a larger program. However, they represented one critical step in identifying the kinds of information sources that were available at Indiana University and that could be reasonably consulted in the interest of fulfilling the placement recommendations offered by CCCC.

LEVERAGING THE DEPARTMENT: GETTING BEYOND "ACCOMMODATION"

Bruce Horner (2015), Matsuda (2014), and John Trimbur (2016), among other scholars, suggest it takes more than one epicenter of intellectual activity to bring a fuller perspective on the teaching and learning of multilingual composition in any program. Specifically, they remind us that any praxis requires an instantiation of political and institutional activity to help change the very nature of our expectations of what such courses can and should do. Furthermore, they remind us that the motivation for these courses, if not already based in an understanding of multilingual aims or a desire to promote them, cannot fully escape the set of monolingual assumptions surrounding them.

Thus, the second point of leverage occurred departmentally through renegotiating teachers' and students' roles in light of several monolingual assumptions surrounding ENG W131ML at the time I renamed the course. The name change from NN to ML was motivated by a core commitment to multilingualism as a pedagogical approach as opposed to a label or a statement of identification, yet the curricular emphasis underlying the course was on broadening discussions of difference to include discursive and academic identification more often than not. Thus, even though the ML designation necessarily broadened our approach to language—as *language identity*, comprised of expertise, inheritance, and affiliation (Leung, Harris, and Rampton 1997)—that designation was easily mistaken for statements against fluency. Ultimately, ENG W131ML tried to make a space for multilingual writers to "negotiate and renegotiate their senses of themselves as language users" (Shuck 2010, 117) beyond a native/nonnative dichotomy.

Yet even as instructors understood the need to develop a pedagogy that simultaneously targeted academic literacy and English fluency, the broader context of the university was still rooted in the assumption that students' "other" languages constituted "problems to be solved" (Hall 2009, 37)—thus, it was rooted in contentions that the most important differences occurred only linguistically. In addition, while all sections of the FYC course emphasized students' being able to make critical arguments through secondary texts, many instructors had historically felt unable to persuade their peers, and in some cases their major professors, that offering specially designated sections of the course for language learners still had critical value and did not involve "remedial" instruction. Finally, where instructors *did* succeed in overcoming the first two assumptions, they found it challenging to persuade their students of the benefits of an FYC approach based on agential difference when the students' academic upbringing often occurred in systems that celebrated homogeneity— economic, social, and sometimes cultural or linguistic. Instructors often became skeptical of this agential approach because their students were operating under a more dichotomous understanding of difference, which we wanted to disrupt, yet our disruptions in turn were perceived as a threat to students' ability to attain linguistic fluency. Students were choosing to see themselves as "traditional ESL" (Lawrick 2013, 29), and hence as monolinguals, in spite of the fact that their performance on most tasks reflected a complex mixture and mixing of literacy practices.

As a result of these assumptions, much of this renegotiation of teachers' and students' roles in the course involved persuading departmental agents, first and foremost, that the principal goal of ENG W131ML was not merely to accommodate L2 writers by providing them a safe space for linguistic deviance but rather to equip them to learn the analytical and rhetorical demands of academic literacy alongside increasing their confidence in using English. Like Christina Ortmeier-Hooper (2010), I wanted to invite both students and instructors to "wrestle with divergent discourses" as they worked out alternate discourses and literacies that better represented their values and interests (15).

In practical terms, I spent much of my first year on campus teaching the curriculum, surveying students and instructors across multiple sections, and keeping track of the critical or pedagogical lenses they said had determined their curricular success. When I first arrived on campus, instructors' concerns centered on three dominant challenges: (1) how—or whether—to mark students' papers toward the dissolution of error; (2) how to teach and assess reading comprehension; and (3) how to improve classroom management with a group of learners that seemed unresponsive or disengaged. Part of this concern stemmed from their lack of coursework in L2 writing issues, but much of it stemmed from their sensitivity to the dualism their students often faced: on the one hand, students legitimately required the scaffolding such a course provided and expressed strong desires to perform as proficiently as their peers; on the other hand, giving extra attention to students' linguistic needs put instructors at risk of either placing undue weight on some aspect of the learning process over others or flattening (or ignoring) difference altogether. In sum, instructors reported feeling caught between the desire to accommodate multilingual writers and the repercussions of identifying them as a discrete group of learners (Ferris 2009; Horner, NeCamp, and Donahue 2011; Ortmeier-Hooper 2010; Tardy and Swales 2008).

In response, I focused on identifying programmatic ideologies—specific to this course—that had historically posed obvious barriers (Tardy 2011, 653) to its reconstruction based on contentions about how (or whether) to attend to cultural and linguistic difference in FYC. The course was housed in the composition program within the English department, not formally linked to the campus writing center, not formally linked to the intensive-English program, and unsupported in terms of preservice training or a formal practicum, although most instructors electing to teach it had had some experience teaching English conversation, had a stated interest in the course, or had completed a semester's practicum for teaching college composition to native English speakers at Indiana or elsewhere. With few exceptions, the teaching staff consisted of English MFA, literature, or composition doctoral students who rotated out after one year or, in some cases, after a single semester, although a handful of instructors taught repeat sections of the course, either in consecutive semesters or intermittently throughout their career at Indiana. While their stake in the course was most visible and immediate, even the most motivated instructors often felt at a loss about how to justify the presence of ENG W131ML within their home department if the end goal of the course was not to achieve complete accuracy in English.

I also focused on articulating through our own instructional challenges what we thought we were loyal to in certain notions of multilingualism and what compelled us to approach the course and the students in the ways we did. My best strategy in that first year was conducting a series of roundtables on specific topics and holding regular one-on-one meetings after observing instructors' classes and syllabi. Indeed, during several of those one-on-one meetings, instructors reported neither wanting to be "marked" as L2 writing instructors nor wanting the investment of their emotional and intellectual energies in the course to be perceived as an intellectual distraction, especially if their principal area of study was in a field other than composition or ESL. To move our curricular imperative beyond a paradigm of accommodation in the longer term, I proposed a trial practicum for the course and began seeking other incentives or rewards for ENG W131ML instructors, inviting them to view the practicum as a deliberate response to their concerns and an opportunity to "produce and test strategies for negotiating the gap between a system of higher education that was founded in the previous America, and the one that needs to work in the next America" (Hall 2009, 36).

Over the course of the next four years, the sum total of visible changes would consist of a two-day preservice training for first-time instructors each semester, a credit-bearing practicum for first-time instructors each semester (although others opted to join occasionally as well), regular classroom observations for first-time instructors, and the opportunity to teach in one of two specially outfitted open-concept classrooms equipped with both moveable and fixed technologies, as well as multiple meeting and projection spaces for various kinds of small- and large-group collaborations. By and large, instructors responded well to the practicum, finding pathways through our readings for their own scholarship on matters such as academic identity, authorship, ownership, and critical literacy and eventually for the construction of syllabi in other classes beyond ENG W131ML when those courses incorporated discussion about marked discourse, multiculturalism, identification, or transfer. Knowing a successful curriculum would need to be coherent both *among* its informal and formal assignments and *between* major assignments and learning outcomes, I built a small library of L2 writing resources and kept a catalog of instructors' preferred in- and out-of-classroom activities as well as their motives for assigning them. In the majority of cases, I ended up adopting or co-opting (with their permission) these activities and making them available through our shared course-management site, not least because these activities often reflected instructors' critical or pedagogical strengths and because they were borne of instructors' earnest attempts to engage with a population of students they might not know how to teach.

Less visibly, I collaborated with instructors who wanted more guided experience designing multilingual syllabi or keying our shared approach to a handful of different texts. I began collecting, tracking, and interpreting student data from various sources—from international admissions to student questionnaires to performance on some of our assignments—so as to report more concretely to the instructors who our students were in terms of university metrics, to monitor that population as it evolved, and to raise questions about how little or much the metrics could reasonably inform our teaching practice. I did these things primarily to re-present ENG W131ML as a site for instructors to develop some of their own scholarly interests and secondarily to invite their participation in the internationalization of the university's curriculum, which would necessarily include identifying resistances and anticipated barriers in both the short and long terms. Such a sustained level of engagement with instructors enabled me to write evaluative letters in support of their teaching portfolios and job dossiers, to nominate them for teaching awards on the basis of their work in the course, and to mentor them in providing peer observations and peer feedback to one another at any stage of their course design.

In addition to helping instructors understand and predict those future tensions and barriers in their work, it was important to enable other departmental agents to watch the work as it unfolded and to understand it as a viable and worthwhile endeavor. Thus, in addition to keeping the director of FYC apprised of these changes, much of this negotiation occurred in conversations I had with the department chair and associate chair, the director of graduate studies, and a few other faculty colleagues concerned about the naming of the course or its placement in the English curriculum. During these conversations, my focus broadened from supporting instructors' pedagogical journeys through difference in FYC to demonstrating my willingness to contend with it myself, as institutional labels tended to shift. For example, I became aware that my role on campus tied me to the perception of promoting certain language ideologies, whether or not those ideologies explicitly underscored the course. When I argued for our curriculum on the basis of its rhetorical soundness or its attention to both broader outcomes as articulated by the CWPA and specific outcomes as articulated by our critical-foundations requirement on campus, I also noticed a perception that ENG W131ML curriculum and instructors were more concerned with student advocacy than with critical literacy, and this perception prevented some instructors from investing in the course. I later discovered that these assumptions were motivated by a suspicion from faculty or administrators outside the program that ENG W131ML promoted the idea that fluency in English was unattainable and unimportant. While this perception may have contributed to instructors' hesitation to claim a personal stake in the course, it eventually provided a useful opportunity for me to engage more explicitly with departmental concerns about English proficiency, within and without FYC, and to begin delineating fluency and accuracy as complementary but distinct curricular goals for language learners.

LEVERAGING BETWEEN THE DISCIPLINES: FINDING TURBULENT CULTURAL WEBS

In light of recent urgings to promote "translinguality" in US college composition (Guerra 2016; Lu and Horner 2016), it may seem unlikely that an FYC approach identified as *multilingual* can help promote *both* students' attainment of English fluency *and* the transformation of US-based composition pedagogy (Atkinson et al. 2015; Canagarajah 2002; Horner et al. 2011; Jordan 2012; Matsuda 2014), or that it can do more than simply promote a nonnative "adaptation" of a US-centric or monolingualist orientation to writing. While these paradigms—multilingual and translingual—do not and need not work against one another, this central disagreement about the constraints of multilingualism not only motivated much of my work at Indiana but also indicated a significant and "turbulent cultural web" (Antram 2006) for negotiating leverage in programmatic redesign: the interdisciplinary spaces between multilingual approaches to FYC and pedagogical approaches to L2 studies and between compositional and library approaches to information literacy.

Like Rebecca Lorimer Leonard (2014), I approach multilingual composition as a kind of "attunement"—"a tuning toward . . . difference or multiplicity" (228) or adaptation of expectations (229)—and less than one month into my first semester on campus, the opportunity for attunement emerged. I was contacted by the (also new) coordinator of the English-language instruction program (ELIP) and assistant professor in second language studies, who requested a meeting and suggested that we had aligning missions: correcting misperceptions about English fluency and English proficiency; overturning functional literacy models that promise a linear transience from "novice" to "expert" composer in the space of a single semester; and shaping the culture of constraint surrounding ML curricula into one of resource (Ewert 2011). As she renovated her program over five years, we worked together on mine, each involving the other in decisions about testing, placement, and curriculum and visiting each other's practicum on a semiregular basis. While neither our courses nor our practica were formally linked, we constructed our guidelines for language testing and composition placement in such a way as to benefit both curricula, to create more teaching and learning opportunities for our instructors, and to argue for how an improved placement process better aligned with the university's goal to marshal more resources into its programs supported under Title VI of the 1972 Higher Education Act. For that reason, it became necessary to engage in each other's disciplinary discourses and to carve out an interdisciplinary space from which to justify pervasive change.

As a result, several instructors of ENG W131ML applied for quarter-time positions as raters on the university's internal language and literacy exam (the Indiana English Proficiency Exam), creating a cross-fertilization of perspectives among teaching and testing but also affirming for them some critical and unresolvable differences between an SLA (second language acquisition) orientation to academic literacies and a multilingual approach to college composition, including the precise nature of *scaffolding*—a term that implied topical sequencing in FYC but more sheltered instruction in SLA. In fact, we never sought to resolve these differences but rather to bring into deeper relief the paradigms within which we worked.

Gail Shuck (2010) has argued that language identity "is neither unified nor stable nor a singular entity to be arrived at only once, but rather shifts in relation to multiple layers of context" (118) comprised of language expertise, inheritance, and affiliation. Moreover, it is situated in larger ideological contexts, familial contexts, gendered practices, and immediate as well as past educational backgrounds, all of which themselves have histories (119) and some of which "become more or less salient as the individual negotiates the various discourses in which she participates" (119). I would add departmental, institutional, and disciplinary to these contexts, extending that multilayered identity building to the relationship that transpires between students and other program agents, for that relationship is established as much from their previous beliefs or experiences as it is within the immediate context of the course. In other words, while I embraced the multilingual nomenclature and program-building model as a way to strive for a transformative approach to FYC, I had to remain cognizant of how this approach intensified (rather than mollified) the translingual dilemma, often amplifying students' "supposed cultural presuppositions" (Hall 2009, 39) rather than problematizing those stereotypes. I began to draw on rhetorical identification as a way of justifying our attempts to increase students' English fluency, and this raised two questions for me anew: Could those cultural presuppositions be tied less to disagreements about ESL pedagogy and more to uninterrogated beliefs about linguistic privilege? What could be disciplinarily contentious about linking language identity to composition pedagogy?

Shuck (2010) employs Aaron Antram's web metaphor to note when and where institutional practices "impose identities on multilingual students, placing only international students into ESL courses, for example, or determining curricula based on simplistic native-speaker/nonnative-speaker distinctions" (118). While second language studies research encourages us to move away from institutional and programmatic practices that reinforce binaries (e.g., "ESL" versus "regular" composition, "native" versus "nonnative" speakers), there are disciplinary reasons for why some of those binaries persist, in turn illuminating the "points in the system that have a high level of connection to multiple actors in the system" (Melzer 2013, 78).

The partnership between ELIP and ENG W131ML garnered some attention from the head of Teaching and Learning at the university libraries, historically another untapped actor in efforts to attune institutional conversations toward difference and multiplicity. Prior to 2007, the library's involvement in ENG W131ML had consisted of offering fifty-minute workshops on various research topics or demonstrations of specific databases, yet this format was fairly disconnected from students' learning processes and from our inquiry-based curriculum. Among instructors' chief complaints were librarians' expectations that students would research topics rather than investigate more nuanced issues or questions that emerged from class discussion and students' subsequent expectations that their issues and questions could be realized within the confines of a library database. Among librarians' chief complaints were students' inability to discern what constituted a sophisticated "source" for their projects and their perceived struggles with conversational English during library help sessions. In response, and armed with a better understanding of students' academic literacies prior to matriculating in ENG W131ML, I collaborated with Teaching and Learning to develop a coauthored goal statement, a set of teaching tools, and a series of embedded instructional modules that would more usefully scaffold information-literacy instruction throughout the course without assuming students' ignorance of source value.

Our shared goal was to devise an instructional model that could better account for how students understand information literacies as processes more directly linked to their own experiences with language acquisition, and that was shaped by the rhetorical and analytical processes driving ENG W131ML. These processes were largely determined by students' investigative writing sequence, by the language of our textbooks, and by Joe Bizup's (2008) schema of source interrogation called BEAM. Bizup's schema represents four rhetorical functions guiding how students might use their sources: for providing background, adding exhibits, engaging in argument, and clarifying methodology. While the schema did not directly influence the concepts or units underlying ENG W131ML, Bizup's acronym served as a cross-disciplinary discussion tool for helping composition instructors and librarians work together on devising a sustainable course plan less informed by sheltered expectations of information seeking and less anchored in the discrete processes of the Association for College and Research Libraries' (ACRL) "Framework for Information Literacy" (http://www.ala.org/acrl/standards/ilframework) and more rooted in the critical demands of our course. By 2012, we had devised a library instructional model that closely aligned with how ENG W131ML students negotiated discourses in multimodal and multilingual ways.

Over the course of five years, other formal and informal partnerships evolved between ML composition and ELIP, and between ENG W131ML and the department of Teaching and Learning, in the interests of rebuilding our programmatic cultures in tandem. Eventually, some of these partnerships enabled us to conduct roundtable discussions for faculty in the College of Arts and Sciences who wanted more information about how to draw on language as a resource in order to teach disciplinary reading or writing to the multilingual learners in their various courses. While these roundtable discussions did not often result in our seeing eye to eye, they became useful spaces for developing and rehearsing a shared vocabulary for describing vital "differences in material and social environment, the timing of disciplinary entry, and general learning/writing patterns" of the students in their classes (Foster 2006, 5).

The most valuable change to come of this leverage point was a shared critical vocabulary that we could easily teach and that our peers could readily learn. Merely arguing from a disciplinary standpoint did not allow me to persuade my colleagues across campus of the importance of measuring their students' fluency beyond spoken or written accent. However, arguing interdisciplinarily gave me the leverage to promote fluency as a kind of "interdependence-in-difference" (Mao 2010, 194) because I could redirect our discussions away from assuming English as a lingua franca and toward understanding English as a set of competencies that function on a sliding scale between conserving and extending knowledge (Hyland 2003, 39). My reticence to promote ENG W131ML as a site for mere English proficiency, for the mitigation of accents, and/ or for the remediation of "foreignness" was informed by my knowledge that much of our students' language learning prior to FYC had involved the reproductive tasks of conserving knowledge (e.g., summarizing, describing, identifying types, and applying formulae and information). It was also echoed in Stephanie Vandrick's (2010) argument that students' sense of being "fluent," "monolingual," or "multilingual" relies as much on their own sense of class privilege as it does on any actual linguistic measure. Thus, the optimal FYC and SLA environment would need to be generative and transformative in order to push students' performance toward extending knowledge on Hyland's scale. It would need to situate students where they could understand how analytical processes help them learn ways of seeking new information, regardless of their linguistic abilities.

When presented in this way, the language-management strategies (Tardy 2011, 650) of faculty across campus could be better informed by the following set of shared concerns:

- If there are more nonnative users of English than so-called native users, who becomes the native speaker in the context of any course?
- What rhetorical resources help a student communicate across the language boundaries apparent in a specific course?
- What are the principal genres driving that course, and how might they evolve in the linguistic contact zone?

- What pedagogical strategies facilitate productive engagement with multilingual texts?
- How should our assessment rubrics, rhetorical norms, and writing standards be revised to accommodate language diversity and multiculturalism?

CONCLUSION

David Foster (2006) has argued in defense of a strong cross-national perspective in educational systems (and, by default, in writing instruction throughout those systems), which gradually diminishes as international students matriculate into programs based solely on US or English-speaking views (2). Critical to Foster's research is the correlation between students' learning/writing activity and the program's potential for promoting a kind of activism that "constructs its significance within limited spheres of local and specific institutional contexts" (23). While courses that offer language support and writing instruction for multilingual learners have historically been created out of the need to solve local problems, they make ready sites for disrupting outmoded notions of fluency and identification throughout the institutional cultures in which they reside. These disruptions, in turn, make ready sites for the growth and professionalization of instructors, tutors, librarians, and academic advisors—all participatory agents in a multilingual FYC activity system.

For the multiple stakeholders in the multilingual FYC program, it became key to identify benefits in our mutual professionalization and development. It was also important that we highlighted the contentious and ongoing nature of our work—more specifically, that we grounded our work in very real critical dilemmas about what it means or could mean to enact a multilingual approach to US college composition among unstable notions of difference. This chapter has sought to demonstrate how those critical dilemmas about multilinguality and the reproduction of language attitudes in US college composition can enable programmatic change by providing an alternative to dichotomies of difference and by negotiating productively the political and institutional forces that act on students' pathways into or out of the ML classroom. Such negotiations, when initiated by writing program administrators, may be able to gradually shift institutional leanings away from the "center-periphery model" of English composition instruction (Richardson 2010, 97) toward a model that looks critically at how linguistic imperialism can travel through policies of matriculation and placement. Furthermore, given more recent calls for less flattening assessment of second language writers (Perryman-Clark 2016, 208), such negotiations may soon become the writing program administrator's imperative.

Notes

1. The language of the revised *Placement Guide* ultimately described the course in this way: "ENG W131ML is designed for those students whose core educational backgrounds occurred in languages other than English. Like other sections of ENG W131, this course offers rigorous instruction in understanding college-level writing and research as a multivocal process. It bears the same amount of credit, requires the same amount of writing, and places the same emphasis on critical thinking, analytical writing, and synthesis as does ENG W131; but it encourages students to gain lexical knowledge in a particular issue or topic area, equips them to become more independent writers of English, and provides them with the opportunity to focus on specific linguistic concerns" (Indiana University n.d.a).
2. Data points included some of the following: secondary school or IB secondary program; personally identified language(s) on university application; date matriculated at IU; results of IEPE in terms of recommended academic literacies levels (i.e., special courses offered by the intensive-English program in eight-week modules); number of academic literacies levels completed prior to requesting ENG W131ML; length of time at IU prior to requesting ENG W131ML; and scores on TOEFL, iELTS, or equivalent testing measures upon matriculation. However, enrollment groups were not formed simply by gathering and combining this institutional data; rather, an enrollment group was identified on the basis of an algorithm determining when certain factors were true at one time.

References

Antram, Aaron. 2006. "There I Am: Writing and Identity in the University Classroom." Master's thesis, Boise State University, Boise, ID.

Atkinson, Dwight, Deborah Crusan, Paul Kei Matsuda, Christina Ortmeier-Hooper, Todd Ruecker, Steve Simpson, and Christine Tardy. 2015. "Clarifying the Relationship between L2 Writing and Translingual Writing: An Open Letter to Writing Studies Editors and Organization Leaders." *College English* 77 (4): 383–86.

Bizup, Joe. 2008. "BEAM: A Rhetorical Vocabulary for Teaching Research-Based Writing." *Rhetoric Review* 27 (1): 72–86. https://doi.org/10.1080/07350190701738858.

Canagarajah, A. Suresh. 2002. *Critical Academic Writing and Multilingual Students*. Ann Arbor: University of Michigan Press. https://doi.org/10.3998/mpub.8903.

Canagarajah, A. Suresh. 2016. "Translingual Writing and Teacher Development in Composition." *College English* 78 (3): 265–73.

CCCC. 2014. "CCCC Statement on Second Language Writing and Writers." Accessed May 1, 2015. http://www.ncte.org/cccc/resources/positions/secondlangwriting.

Ewert, Doreen E. 2011. "ESL Curriculum Revision: Shifting Paradigms for Success." *Journal of Basic Writing* 30 (1): 5–33.

Ferris, Diana. 2009. *Teaching College Writing to Diverse Student Populations*. Ann Arbor: University of Michigan Press. https://doi.org/10.3998/mpub.263445.

Foster, David. 2006. *Writing with Authority: Students' Roles as Writers in Cross-National Perspective*. Carbondale: Southern Illinois University Press.

Guerra, Juan C. 2016. "Cultivating a Rhetorical Sensibility in the Translingual Writing Classroom." *College English* 78 (3): 228–33.

Hall, Jonathan. 2009. "WAC/WID in the Next America: Redefining Professional Identity in the Age of the Multilingual Majority." *WAC Journal* 20:33–49.

Horner, Bruce. 2015. "Rewriting Composition: Moving Beyond a Discourse of Need." *College English* 77 (5): 450–79.

Horner, Bruce, Min-Zhan Lu, Jacqueline Jones Royster, and John Trimbur. 2011. "Opinion: Language Difference in Writing: Toward a Translingual Approach." *College English* 73 (3): 303–21.

Horner, Bruce, Samantha NeCamp, and Christiane Donahue. 2011. "Toward a Multilingual Composition Scholarship: From English Only to a Translingual Norm." *College Composition and Communication* 63 (2): 269–99.

Hyland, Ken. 2003. *Second Language Writing.* Cambridge: Cambridge University Press. https://doi.org/10.1017/CBO9780511667251.

Indiana University. 2007. *iStart.* "University-Wide Enrollment Trends." https://istart.iu .edu/Dashboard/index.cfm?graph=Studentenrollmenttrends&CFID=30414&CFTOK EN=26899305&isloaded=yes.

Indiana University. n.d.a. "Composition at IU." Accessed May 1, 2015. http://www.indi ana.edu/~engweb/composition/courses.shtml.

Indiana University. n.d.b. "Undergraduate Composition: Choosing between ENG W131 and ENG W131ML." Accessed 1 May 2015. http://www.indiana.edu/~engweb/re sources/w131ml_self-placement_2011.pdf.

Indy Star. 2015. "Chinese Student Population Surges at Indiana University." August 30. http://www.indystar.com/story/news/2015/08/30/chinese-student-population-surg es-indiana-university/71425740/.

IU News Room. 2008. "IU Bloomington, More International Than Ever." 18 November. http://newsinfo.iu.edu/news-archive/9301.html.

Jordan, Jay. 2012. *Redesigning Composition for Multilingual Realities.* Urbana, IL: CCCC/ NCTE.

Jordan, Jay. 2015. "Material Translingual Ecologies." *College English* 77 (4): 364–82.

Lawrick, Elena. 2013. "Students in the First-Year ESL Writing Program: Revisiting the Notion of 'Traditional' ESL." *WPA: Writing Program Administration* 36 (2): 27–58.

Leung, Constant, Roxy Harris, and Ben Rampton. 1997. "The Idealized Native Speaker, Reified Ethnicities, and Classroom Realities." *TESOL Quarterly* 31 (3): 543–60. https://doi.org/10.2307/3587837.

Lorimer Leonard, Rebecca. 2014. "Multilingual Writing as Rhetorical Attunement." *College English* 76 (3): 227–47.

Lu, Min-Zhan, and Bruce Horner. 2016. "Introduction: Translingual Work." *College English* 78 (3): 207–18.

Mao, Lu-Ming. 2010. "Why Don't We Speak with an Accent? Practicing Interdependence-In-Difference." In *Cross-Language Relations in Composition,* edited by Bruce Horner, Min-Zhan Lu, Paul Kei Matsuda, 189–95. Carbondale: Southern Illinois University Press.

Matsuda, Paul Kei. 2014. "The Lure of Translingual Writing." *PMLA* 129 (3): 478–83. https://doi.org/10.1632/pmla.2014.129.3.478.

Melzer, Dan. 2013. "Using Systems Thinking to Transform Writing Programs." *WPA: Writing Program Administration* 36 (2): 75–94.

Ortmeier-Hooper, Christina. 2010. "The Shifting Nature of Identity: Social Identity, L2 Writers, and High School." In *Reinventing Identities in Second Language Writing,* edited by Michelle Cox, Jay Jordan, Christina Ortmeier-Hooper, and Gwen Schwartz, 5–28. Urbana, IL: NCTE.

Perryman-Clark, Stacy M. 2016. "Who We Are(n't) Assessing: Racialized Language and Writing Program Assessment in Writing Program Administration." *College English* 79 (2): 206–11.

Richardson, Elaine. 2010. "'English Only,' African American Contributions to Standardized Communication Structures, and the Potential for Social Transformation." In *Cross-Language Relations in Composition*, edited by Bruce Horner, Min-Zhan Lu, and Paul Kei Matsuda, 97–112. Carbondale: Southern Illinois University Press.

Shuck, Gail. 2010. "Language Identity, Agency, and Context: The Shifting Meanings of *Multilingual*." In *Reinventing Identities in Second Language Writing*, edited by Michelle Cox, Jay Jordan, Christina Ortmeier-Hooper, and Gwen Schwartz, 117–38. Urbana, IL: NCTE.

Tardy, Christine M. 2011. "Enacting and Transforming Local Language Policies." *College Composition and Communication* 62 (4): 634–61.

Tardy, Christine M., and John M. Swales. 2008. "Form, Text Organization, Genre, Coherence, and Cohesion." In *Handbook of Research on Writing: History, Society, School, Individual, Text*, edited by Charles Bazerman, 565–81. New York: Lawrence Erlbaum.

Trimbur, John. 2016. "Translingualism and Close Reading." *College English* 78 (3): 219–27.

Vandrick, Stephanie. 2010. "Social Class Privilege Among ESOL Writing Students." In *Reinventing Identities in Second Language Writing*, edited by Michelle Cox, Jay Jordan, Christina Ortmeier-Hooper, and Gwen Schwartz, 257–72. Urbana, IL: NCTE.

6

IT'S NOT A COURSE, IT'S A CULTURE
Supporting International Students' Writing at a Small Liberal Arts College

Stacey Sheriff and Paula Harrington

In the summer of 2012, as we were redesigning the website for the Farnham Writers' Center at Colby College, we brainstormed about a tagline that would signal the college's shift from what we called the *inoculation* to the *life practice* model of writing across the curriculum (WAC). As Colby moved from a one-course first-year English composition requirement to a tiered WAC program, we sought a phrase that would encapsulate this important change. "Write for life?" Too vague. "Write WAC-ky?" Too cute. We eventually came up with one we thought blended our commitment to drafting and revision with a collaborative, socially oriented approach. The tagline we chose was "a culture of writing," and we highlighted it in tangerine italic font on the banner of our website. Little did we know how much that phrase would come to encompass a year later, when Colby, like so many other small liberal arts colleges, saw a sudden increase in its enrollment of international students. Between 2012–2013 and 2013–2014, the number of international students at Colby nearly doubled, from thirty-six to sixty-five, or from 7.3 percent of the entering class to 13.5 percent, and the mix of students' home countries and languages changed as well. We hope this narrative of our challenges, changes, and collaborations will prove useful to other small colleges that are redesigning and adapting their own systems of writing support for international students.

Initially, of course, we intended the phrase *a culture of writing* to signal Colby's lively, developing WAC model and the writers' center essential role in it. With Colby's new internationalization, we also found ourselves, like many writing programs and writing centers, at the forefront of other important curricular, pedagogical, and research initiatives brought on by demographic changes in our student body.

To those at large public universities, the numbers involved in doubling Colby's international student population will seem small. Yet,

DOI: 10.7330/9781607326762.c006

proportional to our size and academic support resources, they were significant—especially as we were not aware of nor prepared for this development. In 2013, our international first-year students increased from about thirty-five to about seventy. With only 450 students in Colby's entering class, this represented a jump from what had been typically 6–7 percent international students to 14 percent in 2014 (Colby College 2015). In fact, if international students are defined as all non-US citizens, then the proportion was 22.1 percent of first-year students in 2014.[1] At the same time, the national background of Colby's international students shifted. The largest group now has Chinese as a first language, and the students often have no previous educational experience in the United States—a significant change as, formerly, most international students had completed some high-school immersion study in English or an international baccalaureate in English at a United World College (UWC).[2] The response among faculty was swift and telling. Even though Colby's faculty are excellent teachers, many had limited experience teaching writing, nevermind to L2 students. "I have a young man from China in one of my courses, and I can see he is bright and hard-working. The problem is, *I don't know how to teach him* how to write essays in English," a well-respected senior professor in the Government Department stood up to explain at a faculty meeting (italics ours).

In identifying the situation as a call from faculty for change and development—rather than solely from international students themselves—he voiced a position held by many of his colleagues. We took it as an acknowledgment that Colby, like all institutions of higher education, needed to embrace the global interconnections of the twenty-first century. Yet we had to do so with few second language (SL) or English-language learner (ELL) trained faculty and staff and without the structural support of initiatives and offices for international students common at larger universities. Our response, therefore, had to be at once global and local. We had already started a mindful partnership as writing program and writers' center directors, one we saw as key to building a WAC program, and we decided we also needed to think holistically about supporting international students' writing. If the new goal for Colby was to admit at least 15 percent international students each year, how could we reconsider our programs and open channels of communication to the offices creating this change? We agreed incoming students should not be the only ones who would have to adapt and change. We, too, should have to change and think intentionally about creating an environment more supportive of linguistic and cultural diversity, less reflexively monolingual and US-centric. We would need to collaborate with colleagues in admissions as well as in student and academic affairs. From first-year advising to course selection, tutoring, and faculty development, we would need to send a consistent message: college writing in English is not just one required composition course; it's an academic culture of writing.

IDENTIFYING STAKEHOLDERS IN SUCCESSFUL INTERNATIONALIZATION

With the influx of international students in 2013–14, the Colby Writing Program and the Farnham Writers' Center experienced two effects almost immediately. First, worried faculty members, particularly those teaching first-year writing courses (W1s), sought help from the writing program on how to respond to what many writing studies and second language scholars might call simply students' "accented language" (Zawacki and Cox 2011), only some of which actually impeded comprehension. Many particularly conscientious faculty wanted suggestions and resources for developing writing assignments and grading rubrics. Some expressed frustration with admissions for "letting in" students with weak English writing and speaking skills. Second, many more first-year international students began coming to the writers' center and asking to register for our one-credit, individual tutorial course (WP112). Many, perhaps directed by faculty, asked specifically for grammatical lower-order-concern assistance, which the tutors had been trained to downplay in favor of a focus on higher-order concerns like argument and organization. These developments made it evident that we would need to build a shared internationally focused pedagogy before we could best educate our new international students.

Our first move was to set about creating a network of stakeholders across the campus invested in making Colby's internationalization work. While that might seem an obvious step, to do so meant reaching across institutional barriers to share information that had until then remained in-house within a particular office. After reflecting on Colby's existing programs and services, we identified five stakeholders: (1) the first-year writing WAC faculty, (2) the associate dean of students for international affairs, (3) the international dean of admissions, (4) the provost's office, and (5) the institutional research office. Each called for separate outreach; together, however, they presented us with the opportunity to make cohesive, collaborative advances in our pedagogy, curriculum, and institutional planning.

At the same time, we considered our existing writing sites and support services and began to conceptualize how we might implement small changes that could have an important impact for our new international students within a short timeframe. These sites we identified as the tutor-training course offered each spring; the one-credit tutorial course that matches individual students with dedicated writing tutors for a semester; and the new first-year W1 courses. These, we thought, allowed for some more immediate adjustments to support the writing work of international students. We have also found it is especially useful to think of any program development or revision as part of a continuous cycle—in our case between the writing program and the Farnham Writers' Center—in which changes in one inform and affect programs and services in the other. Through examining our collaborations with these stakeholders and in these writing sites, we have gained insight not only into our processes but also into directions we expect to take as Colby continues to internationalize.

WAC FACULTY: DEVELOPING THE WRITING PROGRAM WITH INTERNATIONAL STUDENTS IN MIND

Starting in 2009–10, Colby began a long-desired WAC initiative to develop faculty's knowledge of writing pedagogy and to create a menu of first-year writing courses. In 2012, Colby hired Stacey Sheriff as the first WPA. She was tasked with helping faculty develop new W1s and determining an approach to writing in upper-level curricula, assessment, and faculty development around writing pedagogy. Stacey and Paula both teach courses in the writing program and in the English department, and we work collaboratively to build the program on both the faculty and tutoring ends. The increase and shift in our international student body began the year after Stacey started, which proved both challenging and fortuitous. On one hand, it meant doing more faculty and tutor development specifically for international students than we had expected. On the other, it allowed us to weave international pedagogy immediately into our new program development.

As the inaugural writing program director, Stacey immediately sought to build faculty-development offerings. She queried faculty as well as the writing committee about desired topics for faculty-development workshops and about potential guest speakers, and she found that teaching international students more effectively was near the top of everyone's list. Indeed, one of Stacey's first faculty-development events featured an outside second language studies expert, Michelle Cox, who introduced disciplinary faculty to the basics of SL writing pedagogy and strategies for responding to students' writing. Stacey's first year of working with faculty made it clear that there was also a need for ongoing, lower-stakes (i.e., shorter) workshops and discussions about writing pedagogy and international students' backgrounds. She decided to create a writing-pedagogy lunch series during the 12:00–1:00 p.m. hour, which she treated like forty-five to fifty minutes to account for faculty coming from and going to classes. This flexible strategy was challenging for her but welcoming for faculty, and it yielded a diverse cross-section of faculty from different departments and levels of seniority. Over time, Stacey has developed an overarching strategy for workshop planning—one that assumes all potential topics intersect with research, writing pedagogy, and teaching international students. Reading from the literature on WAC and second language writing confirms the large area of productive overlap among all three of these categories (see, for instance, Ferris 2009; Matsuda 2006; Severino 2006). Every year, Stacey plans faculty-development events that address assignment design and responding to student writing, and supporting international students is always a relevant aspect of these foundational topics. Faculty who might be reluctant, for instance, to create detailed written guidelines for their assignments are often more receptive when she explains its utility for many international students and all students who seek help at the writers' center or from a course tutor.

Another important aspect of her outreach to WAC faculty was Stacey's work to introduce colleagues to the scholarship (and, in some cases, the existence) of fields such as composition/writing studies, second language studies, rhetoric, writing program administration, and writing center pedagogy. Lacking access to graduate students or writing program majors, she applied for summer research-assistant funding from the provost. She hired a strong junior writing tutor, who was interested in multilingual pedagogy and writing centers, to review recent literature relevant to international students, writing pedagogy, second language studies, and WAC. Together, they produced an annotated bibliography for a faculty audience and a research poster summary her student presented at the summer research symposium. The poster was organized around effective writing pedagogies/assignments for faculty to consider and effective strategies for multilingual international students to further develop their English writing. As we hoped, this framing drew attention from many faculty and students while shifting the conversation away from the unproductive lament, "What do we [faculty] do about international students?" Stacey posted the bibliography as a program resource and shared it with faculty in course-development consultations. Paula, in turn, incorporated some of the resources to inform her approach to international/SL pedagogy and tutoring in her Tutoring Writing course.

CROSSING THE STREET: WORKING WITH THE
INTERNATIONAL DEAN AND ADMISSIONS

In her first few years as writers' center director, Paula had built a relationship with our associate dean for international affairs through consultations about individual students who had struggled or dropped out of courses because of writing-related concerns. At Colby, the international dean is the only official point of contact for orienting, advising, and supporting international students, but she had not traditionally had ongoing communications with faculty or academic administrators like WPAs/WCDs. As is the case in many institutions, while student and academic-affairs professionals do work that overlaps, consultation and reciprocal professional relationships are not the norm. When Stacey arrived, she also reached out to this dean to expand the path Paula had opened and to learn the rationale for a few long-standing policies, such as the criteria behind the ESL designation given to a few incoming international students each year. Our relationship with this dean has helped us understand the flow of communications new students receive and the myriad ways student-affairs professionals advise international students. It meant, for instance, that the dean thought to contact both of us when she revised her annual introductory letter for new international students, part of which contained specific information about writing courses and support resources. We had not known about this letter, and we were able to update some information and suggest that the required W1 courses and the writers' center be presented together as resources open to all students. We now touch base each year on this welcome message, using it as a reminder to inform each other on programmatic or curricular changes. This dean also has a sense of international students' networks and social and communal dynamics of which faculty might not be aware. She has regular communications with all our international students, nearly two hundred in any given year, and knows many well. We have learned to reach out to her early when struggling students come to our attention, and we have been successful, in part, because we frame our conversations as wanting to contribute to the support network for students rather than "red flag" anyone.

In addition, conscious of the usefulness of her knowledge and the communication channels she has eased for us, we consistently think about ways we might, in turn, help with her work. One of us always participates in international students' orientation, for instance, and we make a point of recommending her counsel to faculty who might otherwise not be aware of her role. We have also positioned ourselves as a kind of bridge between her office and the Office of Admissions and Faculty Aid, which were traditionally quite siloed. This position-ing emerged from two things: (1) our desire to better understand the criteria for international admissions and (2) the realization that our curricular and academic-support knowledge gave us a connection to both offices that professionals in each did not see as existing solely between themselves.[3]

As we began to envision a writing program to serve the greater number of international students, we realized we did not know enough—in either an individual sense or a data-driven way—about their educational, linguistic, and even cultural backgrounds. We were not certain, for example, what precise criteria the Office of Admissions and Financial Aid was using to admit international students. Why were a few students designated ESL and placed in the pre-first-year writing course (Writing Program 111) Paula teaches, for instance, while the vast majority went directly into a section of the first-year writing course required of all Colby students? The international dean did not know and suggested we reach out to the Office of Admissions and Financial Aid. It turns out, as is likely the case at other small liberal arts colleges, that the criteria were based on test scores, grades, application essays, personal contact with admissions representatives (when possible), and participation in international baccalaureate programs. But these criteria had not been revisited in many years, and there was little com-munication about developments in admissions to faculty or Academic Affairs. Indeed, the physical road that separated the admissions building and the administrative and academic buildings paralleled a metaphorical one separating these areas in most people's minds and day-to-day practices.

Opening lines of communication with both the international dean and the admissions office was not a fast or simple process. While there is often an intimacy to the educational experience and community/campus interconnections at Colby, silos persist even on a small cam-pus (Gladstein and Regaignon 2012), and the traditional separateness of the admissions and academic sides of the college had not kept pace with the increasingly interconnected world of our incoming students. We wanted to find a way to begin collaborations with these offices much earlier than communications had happened in the past. Ideally, having data from admissions about incoming international students' schooling, test scores, languages, and previous instruction in English would help us prioritize our recommendations for limited course space and tutor-ing resources. But we also wanted—when considering decisions about student writing—to do so based on *actual* student writing. We knew the pitfalls of creating a timed writing prompt to measure something as complicated as writing ability (Johns 2001; Kroll 1990; Matsuda 2006). The provost's office also maintained that Colby's preferred approach was to mainstream, providing supplemental support as needed, versus test and place students into separate basic writing or specially designed cross-cultural composition classes.

BRINGING STAKEHOLDERS TOGETHER TO READ

Stacey contacted the new director of international admissions to find out what kinds of writing samples they might have from students. Their office had students' common application essays, as we'd assumed, but they also told us about an online, short-answer survey about students' academic, cocurricular, and career interests (administered by Student Affairs) that students complete shortly before course registration in the summer. Though it was an imperfect sample, we thought the combination of typically heavily revised and edited application essays and informal, individual online surveys might provide enough material to identify some students with weaker sentence-level English proficiency and/or self-identified concerns about writing and reading.

This reading became a nexus for learning about each other's processes and concerns. We learned about the international admissions director's goal to find more financial aid for international students, and we were able to tell him about the writers' center's programs, its one-credit tutoring course, and the importance of our staying apprised of big changes in the numbers or demographics of international students. This gathering then became a springboard for individual e-mails to advisors and students. Our objective has been to contact these students by e-mail *before* they enroll in their fall courses in order to avoid sending the message after the fact that their English wasn't "good enough" for the courses they selected. Last year, we were able to achieve this goal, and international students came to Colby with our advance recommendations for writing courses and services to guide them. Having this institutional conversation before students arrive and establishing a basic record to consult in the future have created goodwill among our offices and common ground upon which to build other developments. For instance, when we decided to pilot a research survey about our international students' English-writing preparation and experiences at Colby, the international dean helped us distribute the survey, and both Student Affairs and admissions offices are interested in learning about our findings.

WORKING WITH THE PROVOST'S OFFICE

Because the increase in Colby's admission of international students coincided with large-scale changes in the college's approach to the teaching of writing, we found ourselves at a juncture at once promising and unfamiliar, especially for faculty who would be taking on the new first-year writing-across-the-curriculum courses. Stacey needed to both inspire and reassure these faculty, which she continues to do through various faculty-development programs. While on the surface these WAC courses did not pertain directly to international students—because *all* students at Colby take them—they did connect to internationalization in two ways. First, many WAC faculty were uncertain, as we've said, about how to teach L2 students, especially those with Asian-group first languages. Second, these new W1 courses combined with the increase in international students to highlight our need for a multilingual writing specialist on campus.

For both these developments, the support of the provost's office was indispensable. From her arrival on campus, Stacey began to work closely with the provost to build campus-wide support for the new program. At faculty meetings and departmental events, the provost reiterated the importance of developing an excellent writing program at Colby. Her explicit support lent immediate credibility to Stacey's efforts and allowed Stacey to implement a range of initiatives without first having to overcome institutional hurdles.

More specifically, when it came to the need to hire a multilingual writing specialist to work with the greater number of international students, the provost put her money where her mouth was. After meeting in planning sessions, she agreed to pay a multilingual specialist an hourly rate as a consultant—an unusual arrangement we hope will lead to a full-time position. Although this measure was stopgap, it has allowed us to demonstrate (and begin to document) the need for a permanent specialist in this area.

WORKING WITH THE INSTITUTIONAL RESEARCH OFFICE

Our real work with the fifth stakeholder, the Office of Institutional Research (IR), grew from ongoing, intermittent communications into an emerging partnership concerning our international student survey research project. Stacey had met with the IR director, who was an office of one, as is common in small schools, to learn about student demographics and annual survey results from instruments like NSSE. Similar to our initial experiences with admissions, we learned that sharing data had not been the norm, and our requests for data about international students' performance in W1 classes over time, for instance, met with some hesitation. Moreover, to manage the demand, all requests for information or interpretation assistance from IR also go through the provost's office. As with most program-development or resource requests, we found it necessary to connect explicitly to Colby's mission and priorities. For instance, we gained traction for adding the writing module to the annual NSSE survey at Colby by connecting it to writing program and college-assessment efforts. When we began designing our survey of international students' writing preparation, self-assessment, and experiences at Colby, we were familiar with these dynamics and constraints and were able to emphasize the due diligence we had done in our field to prepare even this internal, pilot survey.

At the suggestion of writing program steering-committee members, we consulted with the IR director to find out if their office already asked students some of the basic demographic (like home country/languages) and academic questions (like majors/minors) we had included. Our exchange helped us trim a number of duplicative survey questions, clarify IR definitions of terms like *international student* and, perhaps most important, identify areas where our research could add texture and provide information that might not have seemed essential to IR but was of interest to us. For example, while IR documented students' home addresses and, usually, citizenship, we also wanted to ask, "What is your home country? (Please feel free to note if you have been raised and educated in more than one country.)" This question allowed a few students to explain complex multinational backgrounds and others to note they had been partially raised or educated in countries that did not match their current home country. IR had some information about students' home or native language, but we decided to include a question that asked students to self-identify their first language(s), and 18 percent of students identified two.

In keeping with our collaborative approach to developing writing programs and services that would benefit international students, we wanted to learn—from international students themselves—about the effects of our changes to existing sites of writing and the ongoing needs for development. We also wanted to direct students' attention to a holistic conception of the sites and resources for writing at Colby, that is, to consider everything from first-year writing classes, the writers' center, faculty feedback on student writing, the experience of English immersion, and more as part of this process. Our pilot survey has just closed, so we are not yet able to report our findings here.[4] But even an initial look at the data from some questions indicates this avenue of research will be helpful. For instance, anecdotal conversations and our review of the literature showed mixed results in terms of students' preferences for and experiences with "mainstream" versus "basic" or ELL writing courses, and little existing research addresses small liberal arts colleges (Braine 1996; Costino and Hyon 2007; Silva 1994). So we were not totally surprised to find that students' responses were split fifty-fifty for the short-answer question, "Many colleges offer first-year writing courses specifically for international students for whom English is not a first language. Do you think this is a good idea? Should Colby consider this? Why or why not?" What was surprising was the way so many students responded with nuanced reasoning (both for and against this idea), contextualized in terms of academic discipline, college reputation, equity, and student self-confidence in a way that would make any writing teacher proud. Moreover, a third of students reported they did *not* feel their high-school academic experience had sufficiently prepared them for their first-year writing course, a proportion that surprised faculty with whom we shared this example. This finding reiterates not only the importance of multilingual writing support and faculty development but also follow-up conversation to plumb the complexities of students' responses.

WORKING WITH EXISTING SITES OF WRITING

As we reflected on the existing sites of writing at Colby that we might expand or enhance to support international students, the natural starting point was our writing center. Colby is fortunate in having the well-established Farnham Writers' Center, which has been in continuous operation since 1984. Its services and programs were already among the best-known resources for first-year students, including first-year international students. Typically, the international dean provided them with information about writers' center tutoring services at an annual orientation. When the number of international students grew, Paula began to make a more formal presentation about writers' center courses and programs. Beyond providing this information and answering students' questions directly about writing support at Colby, she sees the benefit of offering a warm, sincere welcome at orientation to make clear how much Colby values their presence and potential for contribution. Among our many small changes, this personal welcome may be the most basic, but it is also one of the most important at the moment when new international students may be feeling most overwhelmed by the cultural transition they have undertaken.

In terms of the writers' center itself, Paula also saw opportunities to adjust existing programs and services in several targeted ways. While Colby's tutoring courses and programs no doubt differ in their specifics from those at other small liberal arts colleges, we suspect comparable small changes with big payoffs may be possible at similar institutions. At Colby, we are fortunate to have a semester-long, full-credit course that prepares students to become tutors: English 214: Tutoring Writing in Theory and Practice. Since a student cannot become a writing tutor without first taking this course, it provides a key site for developing tutoring strategies to meet the needs of international students. That is, working with SL students requires rethinking the higher-order-concern versus later-order-concern dichotomy (HOCs versus LOCs) made by Gillespie and Lerner (2000) among others. Here, the annotated bibliography of scholarship on teaching writing to multilingual students proved especially useful and demonstrated again the importance of synergy between the writing program and the writers' center.

After reviewing current scholarship in that area, Paula reconsidered her pedagogy to address the issue of training tutors to focus more on LOCs with international students. She began to instruct the tutors in training more in identifying patterns of "error" that derive from linguistic differences, explaining the usage conventions involved and directing international students to grammar handbooks. At the same time, she continued to emphasize that, as A. Suresh Canagarajah (2005) notes, "The obsession with errors in the field of ESOL writing leads to the danger of conveying a sense of failure and handicap" (51). She brought Terry Myers Zawacki and Michelle Cox's notion of "accented language" (Zawacki and Cox 2011) into class discourse, supplementing the earlier perspectives of Judith K. Powers's (1993) "Rethinking Writing Center Conferencing Strategies for the ESL Writer," Susan Blau and John Hall's "Guilt-Free Tutoring: Rethinking How We Tutor Non-Native English-Speaking Students" (Blau and Hall 2002), and Sharon A. Meyers's (2003) "Reassessing the 'Proofreading Trap': ESL Tutoring and Writing." Moreover, because English 214 combines theoretical and empirical approaches, it includes a practicum in which students perform a scaffolded sequence of four activities: (1) they are tutored themselves in the writers' center, (2) they observe another student's tutoring session, (3) they tutor a tutor, and (4) they tutor students themselves while being observed. To help students prepare for this practicum, Paula asked an international student to discuss the challenges L2 students often face during a tutoring session. The most common, of course, involves a situation in which an international student wants help with grammatical "errors" but the tutor's orientation is to focus on organization or argument. After the international students' comments in class, Paula followed up with an activity in which students practiced in pairs with sample L2 writing. This training has grown into a crucial component of our tutoring pedagogy as the usage of our writers' center by multilingual students has continued to rise. Currently, approximately 40 percent of the center's total annual tutoring sessions are with nonnative English speakers,[5] a number substantially higher than even three years ago.

These changes in pedagogical training for tutors brought another matter into relief: the need to recruit international students as tutors in the writers' center. Before Paula's recruitment effort, the center's culture had been primarily one-way when it came to L2 students; they were there to *be* tutored, not to tutor. Not only does having international students as tutors inspire other international students, but it also offers the possibility of a more fluid exchange in a first language—currently often Mandarin-to-Mandarin with some code switching in English—that enhances the learning that occurs. Because of the existing writing sites in our W1 courses, Paula has been able to solicit faculty recommendations for first-year international students whose writing in English is particularly strong, and she invites those students to take the tutor-training class. Last year, in a class with an enrollment of thirty-five, 20 percent (seven) were nonnative English speakers.

Paula has also recruited international students as tutors through our Writing Program 111 course (WP111). When Stacey and Paula began working with the international dean in Student Affairs and admissions on guided placement for new students, this course was, in effect, a holdover from the days of ESL designations. It was a three-credit, nongraded class a student took in the first semester with a one-credit, nongraded course known as Writing Program 112 for four credits, the number required for a single course at Colby. After completing the Writing Program 111–112 bridge, the student would go on to a traditional first-year writing course. WP111 allows Paula to get to know a small group of international students unusually well, and she now encourages those she thinks would make good tutors down the road to work to become tutors.

After consulting with the international dean, we decided to move WP111 to full-credit status and uncouple the two courses so we could also encourage new international students who did *not* have an ESL designation to take WP112 separately. In 112, a student pairs with a tutor to work in weekly hour-long sessions on writing-related material throughout the semester. Often, they focus on the student's draft papers for a first-year writing class, but they may just as well concentrate on grammar review in English, for example, or on rhetorical approaches different from those in the student's first language. A student may take this course twice for credit, and this now-decoupled course has become one of our most successful resources for international students. More than half of the enrollment in Writing Program 112 is now consistently international students, many of whom choose to repeat it. (The course remains open to any Colby student, and students working on capstone projects, for example, also often enroll).

A final change the writers' center made to benefit international students has been the hiring of our part-time multilingual specialist. This specialist works through the center as our only professional writing assistant, holding several office hours a week with L2 students who schedule tutoring sessions by appointment. Given the greater number of international students who now want to take Writing Program 112, the multilingual specialist also teaches several "112ers" each semester.

SOME REFLECTIONS FOR OTHER SLACS

While we recognize that every institution is different in its history, practices, culture, and challenges, we also see in this narrative of our experience at Colby some trends, changes, and approaches that may prove useful to other small colleges as they assess their own positions during this period of internationalization. First, it is important—at the risk of stepping on some toes—to take the lead in identifying and approaching other institutional stakeholders. Our experience has been that, after acknowledging the common objective of serving international students who, in turn, contribute to our campus, colleagues have seen the benefits in sharing information and collaborating to implement small but important changes. We count these sustained, student-oriented collaborations as one of our greatest advances as Colby becomes more international, and we recommend reaching across institutional barriers wherever possible.

We have also seen the importance of taking stock to see what programs and services, such as WP112, already exist that might serve international students well. Again, this takes a willingness to rethink, revise, and restructure, but those habits of mind are central to our field of endeavor—and part of the fun, we think, of being teacher-scholars and administrators.

In addition, we have not hesitated to shake the trees for financial resources when it comes to international students, who, after all, are paying tuition and need support. Our best example here is the hiring of our multilingual specialist; it took going to the provost and making a unique arrangement with her and with Human Resources, but we were able to take a step forward by doing so. A word of advice: before getting the go-ahead, we were asked to do some research into the local job market to determine the rate of pay. This process required negotiation with Human Resources but in the end proved fruitful. Were we to do it again, though, we would probably have conducted this research in advance and come prepared. We are now pursuing seed-grant funding and position requests to build full-time local expertise.

Finally, having initiated formative, in-house research with our survey of international students at Colby, we emphasize the need for ongoing research tailored to individual institutions that is also capable of benefitting small liberal arts colleges broadly. We are, simply put, in this together, which seems only fitting in our era of global education.

Notes

1. Between 2005 and 2011, the average proportion of international students in the incoming class was 6.9 percent.
2. Since 2000, Colby has enrolled international UWC graduates through the Davis United World College scholarship program, which "provides annual grants in support of need-based scholarships for each matriculated UWC graduate for up to four years of undergraduate study" (davisuwcscholars.org/program/by_the_numbers /how-this-works).
3. This divide reminds Stacey of the all-too-common one between many WAC directors/programs and ESL specialists/programs, described succinctly by Zawacki and Cox (2011) in their editorial introduction to an *Across the Disciplines* special issue on WAC and SL writing (Cox and Zawacki 2011).
4. We surveyed 185 upper-class international students using the official IR definition based on residence and citizenship. Of these, 52 percent completed the survey, which is quite good. We hope for similar response rates from the first-year international students we will query at the end of the year.
5. This figure is hard to quantify precisely because it relies on students' self-identifying, which they sometimes choose not to do.

References

Blau, Susan, and John Hall. 2002. "Guilt-Free Tutoring: Rethinking How We Tutor Non-Native English-Speaking Students." *Writing Center Journal* 23 (1): 22–44.

Braine, George. 1996. "ESL Students in First-Year Writing Courses: ESL versus Mainstream Classes." *Journal of Second Language Writing* 5 (2): 91–107. https://doi.org /10.1016/S1060-3743(96)90020-X.

Canagarajah, A. Suresh. 2005. *Critical Academic Writing and Multilingual Students*. Ann Arbor: University of Michigan Press.

Colby College. 2015. *Fall 2015 Fact Book*. Waterville, ME: Office of Institutional Research.

Costino, Kimberly A., and Sunny Hyon. 2007. "'A Class for Students Like Me': Reconsidering Relationships among Identity Labels, Residency Status, and Students'

Preferences for Mainstream or Multilingual Composition." *Journal of Second Language Writing* 16 (2): 63–81. https://doi.org/10.1016/j.jslw.2007.04.001.

Cox, Michelle, and Terry Myers Zawacki, eds. 2011. "WAC and Second Language Writing: Cross-Field Research, Theory, and Program Development." Special issue, *Across the Disciplines* 8(4). https://wac.colostate.edu/atd/ell/index.cfm.

Ferris, Dana R. 2009. *Response to Student Writing: Implications for Second Language Students.* New York: Routledge.

Gillespie, Paula, and Neal Lerner. 2000. *The Allyn and Bacon Guide to Peer Tutoring.* New York: Longman.

Gladstein, Jill M., and Dara Rossman Regaignon. 2012. *Writing Program Administration at Small Liberal Arts Colleges.* Anderson, SC: Parlor.

Johns, Ann M. 2001. "ESL Students and WAC Programs: Varied Populations and Diverse Needs." In *WAC for the New Millennium: Strategies for Continuing Writing across the Curriculum Programs,* edited by Susan H. McLeod, Eric Miraglia, Margot Soven, and Christopher Thaiss, 141–64. Urbana, IL: NCTE.

Kroll, Barbara. 1990. "The Rhetoric/Syntax Split: Designing a Curriculum for ESL Students." *Journal of Basic Writing* 9 (1): 40–55.

Matsuda, Paul Kei. 2006. "The Myth of Linguistic Homogeneity in U.S. College Composition." *College English* 68 (6): 637–51. https://doi.org/10.2307/25472180.

Meyers, Sharon. 2003. "Reassessing the 'Proofreading Trap': ESL Tutoring and Writing Instruction." *Writing Center Journal* 24 (1): 51–70.

Powers, Judith K. 1993. "Rethinking Writing Center Conferencing Strategies for the ESL Writer." *Writing Center Journal* 13 (2): 39–47.

Severino, Carol. 2006. "The Sociopolitical Implications of Response to Second Language and Second Dialect Writing." In *Second-Language Writing in the Composition Classroom: A Critical Sourcebook,* edited by Paul Kei Matsuda, Michelle Cox, Jay Jordan, and Christina Ortmeier-Hooper, 330–50. Boston, MA: Bedford/St. Martin's.

Silva, Tony. 1994. "An Examination of Writing Program Administrators' Options for the Placement of ESL Students in First Year Writing Classes." *WPA: Writing Program Administration* 18 (1): 37–43.

Zawacki, Terry Myers, and Michelle Cox. 2011. Introduction to "WAC and Second Language Writing: Cross-Field Research, Theory, and Program Development." Special issue, *Across the Disciplines* 8 (4), edited by Michelle Cox and Terry Myers Zawacki. http://wac.colostate.edu/atd/ell/index.cfm.

7

EXPANDING THE ROLE OF THE WRITING CENTER AT THE GLOBAL UNIVERSITY

Yu-Kyung Kang

INTRODUCTION

Over the past ten years, the University of Illinois at Urbana-Champaign (UIUC) has witnessed a dramatic increase in the international student population: the population increased from 12.1 percent in fall 2005 to 23.2 percent of the total student body as of fall 2015. The increase in international undergraduate enrollment, from 1,451 in fall 2005 to 5,400 as of fall 2015, has been the most significant contributor to the overall increase. The university's upper administrators have welcomed the large number of international students as a source of diversity and revenue, but for many of the administrators, faculty, and staff on the front lines, this sudden and unanticipated increase of international students has prompted confusion, exposed deficiencies in the support offered the students, and brought about significantly increased and altered work responsibilities. As one program chair described it, attending to issues arising from the dramatic increase in the international student population was like "putting out fires" (Kang 2015, 91). Units and departments unsure of how to address the language needs of international students often turned to the campus writing center for assistance, prompting the center, despite its limited funding and resources, to develop new relationships with various units across campus. In addition to meeting the demands/needs of literacy support across campus, the writing center, known as the Writers Workshop (WW), has also been pressed to adapt its in-house management and services to the changing student demographics. The rapid increase in the number of international students and the university's underpreparedness in supporting them have heightened and altered the role of the writing center, making it a hub for international student support and a central source for development of faculty and consultation for administrators.

DOI: 10.7330/9781607326762.c007

This chapter draws on my experience as a writing consultant,[1] ESL-services coordinator, and assistant director of the WW and on a longitudinal ethnographic study (conducted between 2011 and 2014) of the literacy and rhetorical practices of Korean undergraduate students, the second-largest nationality among international undergraduate students on campus. With that foundation, I describe how the changing demographics prompted the WW not only to revamp the center's regular in-house services (e.g., one-to-one consultations, workshops, consultant training) but also to explore new services (e.g., short-term writing groups for ESL students, including single-language writing groups) and to collaborate in new ways with units, programs, and departments across campus. Based on our local experiences, I then argue that in the midst of the internationalization of their institutions, writing centers must invent a new rhetoric that reasserts their role of supporting literacy development in both curricular and extracurricular contexts of international students' college experiences. I further urge a reexamination of the role of the campus writing center that not only adapts to changing demographics but also proactively engages with and influences ideologies surrounding language and literacy in the United States and the world.

RESPONDING TO THE CHANGING LOCAL AND GLOBAL CONTEXTS
Adapting Roles to Changing Demographics
The current Writers Workshop (WW) at UIUC was established in 1990 along with the Center for Writing Studies, which also was responsible for the writing-across-the-curriculum (WAC) program for faculty and graduate teaching assistants. Since then, its main function has been to provide "free writing assistance" to "students, faculty, and staff from all disciplines and at all stages of the writing process" (University of Illinois 2016). The writing consultants, both graduate and undergraduate, engage in nondirective, collaborative, and student-centered interactions in one-on-one sessions that align broadly with the typical methods and missions of writing centers in US higher education institutions today. In addition to the individual sessions, the WW has regularly provided special workshops on topics such as personal statements, thesis/dissertation writing, and specific topics requested by programs across campus.

Neal Lerner's (2001) historical research on the beginnings of the Writing Clinic at UIUC shows that the early role of writing centers at UIUC was not nearly so broad. The Writing Clinic, UIUC's first writing center, was established in 1942 in response to the literacy "crisis" of that time, changing student demographics during the Second World War

(WWII). Lerner (2001, 15) quotes the English department's 1948 *Faculty Bulletin*, which described its initial mission in quite narrow terms, very different from the current functions of the Writers Workshop.

> The clinic, designed for students whose written English is unsatisfactory, will have three major objectives. They are to analyze the writing difficulties, to provide the advice necessary to remedy them, and to determine the effectiveness of remedial efforts. . . . The clinic will not supervise writing or provide tutoring. However, it may, in some cases, advise a student to enroll in some particular course or to employ a tutor. ("English Department Clinic Re-established" 5, quoted in Lerner 2001, 15)

Since then, for writing centers at Illinois and across US higher education institutions, change in the student population has repeatedly served as the impetus for institutional change, as was the case with the enrollment of large numbers of WWII veterans in the 1940s and of previously excluded underrepresented minorities during the open-admissions era in the 1960s and 1970s. Although initially charged with a remedial mission and expressing a deficit attitude toward students, the history of writing centers in general, and of writing support at UIUC in particular, highlights what Peter Carino has described as "the multiple forces in play at various moments . . . demonstrat[ing] that writing centers and those who work in them are always imbricated in the history of writing programs, higher education, public debates, as well as in local and even personal imperatives" (Carino 1996, 39).

During the past decade, with the globalization and internationalization of US higher education institutions, UIUC has gone through another very significant change in student demographics, comparable to the earlier changes that accompanied the return of WWII veterans and open admissions: the sharp rise in the international student population. From fall 2005 to fall 2015, the number of international students grew from 4,904 to over 10,208. For several years, Illinois even boasted the largest international student population of any US public institution (Institute of International Education 2016).[2] Reflecting the dramatic increase in international students described earlier, so far in 2015–16, almost 80 percent of the visits to the WW were made by students who identified a language other than English as their home language. These changes seem poised once again to shift the mission of the Writers Workshop at Illinois and of many writing centers in the United States.

My administrative, research, and teaching/tutoring experience from 2011 to 2015 took place in the middle of this dramatic increase in the international population at UIUC and thus was a part of the broader pattern across US institutions of higher education. Complaints from faculty and staff working with international students suggested that the amount and adequacy of support available to them was not keeping pace with their increasing numbers. Thus, with my professional commitment as a researcher, teacher, and administrator, and with personal investment as an international student, I became engaged in working to support international students on the U of I campus. In the following section, I elaborate on the expanding role and the work of the university's writing center during this time, drawing on my administrative experience as the ESL services coordinator (fall 2011–spring 2012) and assistant director of the WW (fall 2012–spring 2015), as well as on many years of consulting. As I held these positions during my doctoral studies in writing studies, I was also engaged in researching and publishing on transnational literacy, second language writing, and writing program administration. Thus, I was able to engage in these administrative opportunities and practices to make sense of the theoretical and practical aspects of my study and vice-versa. The conclusions in this chapter then are also based on my two-year ethnographic and autoethnographic (IRB-approved) study on the literacy and rhetorical practices of Korean undergraduate students during this time of change at UIUC. This chapter offers a firsthand account of the changing role of the Writers Workshop as it intertwined with my research, my administrative work, and my own experiences as an international ESL student during this time of global transformation.

Multilingual/ESL and the Writing Center

Despite the presence of both domestic and international ESL/multilingual students and scholars in US higher education from before the first appearance of writing centers in the 1930s, through the emergence of writing center scholarship as a field in the 1970s, to the prominence of multilingual students and scholars in writing centers today, the majority of writing center theory and practice has been developed with monolingual writers in mind. The 1993 article "Tutoring ESL Students: Issues and Options," published in *College Composition and Communication* (*CCC*) by Muriel Harris (writing center scholar) and Tony Silva (second language writing scholar), is one of the first notable pieces regarding how to work with ESL writers in writing tutorials (Harris and Silva 1993). Since then, articles on ESL writers and writing in writing centers have emerged sporadically in journals such as *The Writing Center Journal*, *CCC*, and *TESOL Journal*. Like Harris and Silva's article, most writing center work on ESL has focused on introducing, informing, and training its directors and tutors, the main audience, on issues like various types and characteristics of ESL students, the applicability of second language acquisition (SLA) theories and studies, and effective methods in attending to various linguistic and writing issues with ESL writing (e.g., error correction, plagiarism) while maintaining the core writing center principles for tutorials—that they be collaborative, student centered, and nondirective.

In parallel with composition studies, in the early years of their establishment, writing centers adopted three pedagogical models—current-traditional rhetoric (focus on writer's grammatical correctness), expressivism (focus on writing as a means of self-discovery), and social constructionism (focus on writer's sociocultural and historical settings)—that persisted well into the mid-1980s (Gillespie and Lerner 2008). Since then, as with the field of second language writing, writing center work has been influenced by L1 composition theories including cultural studies, postcolonial, postmodern, and postprocess approaches. Much of the prominent work with these influences is assembled in the first (2004) and second (2009) editions of *ESL Writers: A Guide for Writing Center Tutors* edited by Shanti Bruce and Ben Rafoth. These books, used in writing centers in numerous institutions across the United States, present valuable and applicable work of practitioners and scholars in fields such as writing centers, second language writing, and composition studies (Bruce and Rafoth 2009).

Although there has been increased attention to multilingual writers in writing centers over the past two decades, much of that work has been focused on ensuring that writing tutorials are effective. Interestingly, more recent work, such as *Multilingual Writers and Writing Centers* by Ben Rafoth (2015) and *Tutoring Second Language Writers* edited by Bruce and Rafoth (2016), have begun to go beyond the "how-tos" (i.e., tools and techniques) for helping second language writers by "connecting writing center worlds to multiple relevant worlds outside the center" (e.g., language politics, issues of Othering, research) (Severino 2016, ix). For further advancement in writing center scholarship on second language writers, much theoretical and practical examination is needed beyond the tutorial. Through a case study at UIUC (an institution at the forefront of university globalization), this chapter contributes to these efforts by exploring possible roles for writing centers. Responding to the particular contexts and circumstances of the internationalization of the UIUC campus, the WW not only revamped its work within the center walls (e.g., consultations, workshops) but, more significantly, broadened its function and role to contribute beyond the center walls to the larger university community.

(RE)WORKING WITHIN THE UNIVERSITY'S
INTERNATIONALIZATION

Expanding Within

Although the percentage of students with ESL backgrounds increased from 54.7 percent of WW visits in 2005 to almost 80 percent in 2015, it is important to note the already significant international student population before 2005. Professional-development sessions for consultations attending to ESL/multilingual issues have long existed in the WW. In fall 2006, when I first started working as a writing consultant, I recall international ESL/multilingual graduate students taking up a significant number of the centers' visits.[3] This was also when WW began hiring qualified graduate students (both L1 and L2) from programs like the division of teaching English as a second language, education, and English to work as writing consultants and also to help train/inform consulting staff on ways to work with L2 speakers and writers. Such hiring practices have persisted, as an average of two or three writing consultants specializing in second language education have staffed the workshop since I arrived. As the numbers of the international population started escalating in the mid-2000s, so did the center's attention to the population in its program, policy, and day-to-day duties. For example, the half day of the two-day orientation for new consultants that had been solely devoted to ESL topics was revamped with more and focused readings and discussions on application of L2/multilingual issues in writing center work. Furthermore, the facilitators and consultants discussed current issues on multilingual and translingual approaches with particular UIUC context (e.g., students, academic and institutional culture) in mind. In the past five years, consultants have been provided with opportunities to meet and converse with leading scholars (e.g., Paul Matsuda, Ben Rafoth) whose work and interests are in L2.

In fall 2011, the increased number of international students led to the development of a new position, ESL services coordinator, that I was recruited to fill. I was hired to plan, develop, and manage L2/multilingual-related services for tutors and tutees at the workshop. In this position, my responsibility was to, broadly, find ways to better support L2/multilingual writers at the center. Once I was appointed, I had the opportunity to recognize and try to meet a number of previously unmet needs at the WW. The most immediate need was to help consultants working with these writers. However, in addition to professional development for writing consultants, I also began to conduct surveys via e-mail and more informal personal communication to examine tutors' experience working with L2/multilingual writers and to gauge what was needed. Another significant responsibility was to reevaluate and continue to organize and facilitate writing groups for international students, which had just begun the previous academic year. In spring 2010, WW had begun providing two sets of four 1.5-hour workshop sessions (ESL writing groups) each semester, one for undergraduates and one for graduate students. With the WW visits already running near capacity at more than 90 percent, the writing groups were initially created with a goal of providing writing support to more ESL/multilingual students. It was a way to maximize in-house support for students with the already limited resources at the workshop.[4]

As I took up this administrative position in the WW, I was also beginning a study of the literacy and educational experiences of Korean undergraduate students at UIUC. The 697 Korean undergraduate students enrolled in fall 2016 constitute the second-largest international student population, following only students coming from China. According to my research, the majority of the Korean undergraduates at UIUC have had *jogi yuhak* (or ESA—early study abroad) experience in English-speaking countries (e.g., United States, Canada, Australia, Singapore) before enrolling at the university. This precollege transnational educational migration has been very popular in Korea and other East Asian countries. According to the Korean Ministry of Education, in 2006, the number of students that left Korea for *jogi yuhak* peaked at twenty-nine thousand. Although the common goal of *jogi yuhak* is for students to become global citizens and fluent in the "global" language, English, I was finding that many of the students at Illinois had abandoned the pursuit of "perfect English" and were engaged in practices of *localization*, working to redevelop their Korean culture and language (Kang 2015, 87). Because they felt that their English competency lingered way below expectations for early study-abroad students, I was finding that they hid their English (both in speaking and writing) as much as possible and especially around their Korean peers. My research then was suggesting that the particular literacy practices of many Korean undergraduate students, influenced by monolingual language ideologies shaped by their unique educational and language experiences during their transnational journey, were hindering their English literacy development at the university.

Drawing on this research, in my second semester as the ESL services coordinator, I proposed modifying the ESL writing groups for undergraduate students for Korean students (and later Chinese students as well). Going against mainstream L2 scholarship's notion that the target language is best learned and acquired when students are immersed in the target language, I successfully argued that undergraduate groups oriented to students with the same first-language background and facilitated by a consultant in that language—hence the name *single-language writing group* (SLWG)—would be useful in helping students with their US academic writing and English language in general. I saw the SLWG as a space for the students to engage fluently in complex discussions of rhetorical challenges they face and to identify, discuss, and critique self-deprecating language ideologies. The SLWG was a space for students to develop translingual dispositions (Canagarajah 2013; Horner et. al. 2011) that would ultimately contribute to their language and literacy development. The SLWG was also an intervention in the pedagogical approaches to language development, an apparatus for bringing meaningful change within the continuously growing transnational landscape of the university. The establishment of the Korean SLWG acted as both a rhetorical move for the writing center in a transnational context and as a new practice for literacy education in higher education.

Venturing Out

In addition to in-house efforts to support ESL/multilingual writers, the WW paid increased attention to collaborating and building connections with the larger university. As the ESL services coordinator and assistant director (fall 2011–spring 2015) at the WW and someone with training in the fields of teaching English as a second language, writing studies, and writing centers, I spent much time and energy on outreach efforts to communicate and collaborate with programs and units across campus under both Academic and Student Affairs to help support multilingual writers. These measures were prompted by the increasing number of international L2 students, as the WW was the university's only campus-wide, non-course-based, and non-credit-bearing writing support center. They were also prompted by the increasing number of departments, programs, and faculty requesting ESL writing groups or individualized support for the international students in their programs and/or courses. To many students, faculty, and administrators, the WW was still perceived as a place for students to go or faculty to send their international students so their writing and/or language would be "fixed." The two main objectives of my outreach initiatives were to provide more literacy support and to combat common misconceptions of the practices and development of international L2 writers/learners and of the WW's role in the institution.

Initial outreach work was driven by the demand from programs and units under Academic Affairs that had experienced a sharper increase in international students than had others and that had less knowledge and fewer resources to support these students.[5] Thus, in this instance, the WW found itself reacting and responding to external demands. The first notable request for assistance at the WW was from the executive associate director of the School of Art and Design in the College of Fine and Applied Arts (FAA) in fall 2012. His immediate concern was for the growing number of international students in writing-intensive courses like Art History, but broadly his concerns were for FAA as a whole. Throughout the semester, individual and group meetings were held with the assistant dean, faculty/program administrators, and teaching assistants at FAA to address various issues, such as the value of TOEFL scores, cross-cultural communication, evaluation of ESL-student writing, and training for faculty and teaching assistants. For example, the WW, with the writing-across-the-curriculum (WAC) program, co-organized and facilitated a workshop, working with ESL writers in art and design classes, for TAs working with students in writing-intensive courses. Since 2012, the WW has continued to provide consultations and workshops on working with ESL/multilingual writers for various departments and programs across campus (e.g., CITL,[6] the College of Business, the College of Music).

In comparison to the rather reactive stance with units and programs under Academic Affairs, the WW's outreach efforts were more proactive with units and programs under Student Affairs (e.g., the Career Center, the Counseling Center, University Housing, and recreation). Through formal and informal meetings with counterparts working with international students, we were able to brainstorm, design, and implement measures to better support international students. For example, I worked with the campus-wide Career Center to tailor cover-letter workshops to meet the needs of international students' job searches in the global market. Through my conversations with my international counterpart at the campus Counseling Center, we were able to exchange information and experience working with students going through emotional and psychological issues related to language use and learning. This led to a workshop that informed writing consultants on how to better understand and work with multilingual students in tutoring sessions. These outreach efforts were motivated by need and evidence and were reinforced by my ethnographic study that demonstrated that international (and all) students' literacy practices and development happen not only in the classrooms but also in their everyday college experiences.

In the spring of 2013, the WW developed cultural-sensitivity programs for office staff on campus who were responding to a large international student population for the first time. This initiative began when WW administrators recognized the need for its own front-desk staff to get focused guidance on how to work with diverse international populations and found that no such program existed. The WW director decided to take the initiative in developing the training. The WW gathered interested individuals from different programs and units across campus (e.g., International Student and Scholar Services, the Department of Communication, the Intensive English Institute) and, working together with these units and departments, successfully organized, publicized, and administered Working with International Students: A Workshop for Staff. This pilot workshop was so successful that additional departments and units across campus began requesting similar workshops for their staff and academic advisors. The group, with a few more interested members, continued the workshops for one year until the demands became too great for the WW and its group to handle. The workshops are now provided by the Office of International Programs and Studies, an administrative unit serving as a central resource for "all things international" at Illinois (Illinois International 2018).

IMPLICATIONS AND RECOMMENDATIONS
Shaping Discourse through Writing Center Work

For quite a while, the role of the writing center has been focused on developing and providing effective one-on-one writing tutorials. As college and university contexts have reframed their missions around internationalizing and globalizing their institutions, scholars have begun calling for WPAs to "serve as agents in bringing meaningful change for students, faculty, and institutions" in these times of escalating transnational contexts (Martins 2015, 4). At the University of Illinois, the WW has been responding, reactively and proactively, to this call and responding to the needs of the university and its members. It has not only been taking measures to revamp its traditional in-house services (e.g., one-on-one tutorials, workshops) but also has expanded its boundaries by going beyond the writing center walls in communicating and collaborating with departments, units, and programs across campus. These efforts are noteworthy on two levels. First of all, they represent measures that are effective and impactful in providing better and more literacy/writing support not only for the student writers but also for faculty, staff, and administrators who are working with them. More important, these efforts are crucial examples of ways WPAs can shape the views and discourse surrounding international students and their English language and language practices.

At Illinois, as at many other higher education institutions across the United States, there is an urgent need for intervention in the way many students, educators, and administrators view speakers and writers of English as a second (third, fourth . . .) language. Grounded in composition studies' official "affirm[ation of] the students' rights to their own patterns and varieties of language" with CCCC's 1974 *Students' Right to Their Own Language* resolution, and extended by recent translingualists (Canagarajah 2013; Horner et al. 2011), discourse legitimizing language varieties has always had an uneven reception in the field, especially in regard to multilingual writers, and certainly has not proliferated much beyond our discipline's conversations, as is evident in the WW consultations in which students still bring in red-pen-ridden feedback (from instructors who are not willing to see beyond the "errors" to understand the content), noting that their instructors or professors have sent them to WW to get their "bad" English "fixed." It was also evident through my formal and informal meetings with faculty and program administrators across campus who were frustrated with how international students "can't speak English."

In this respect, the writing center, as a "powerful symbol of student support" (Lerner 2001, 14) in colleges and universities, can use its institutional position to educate not only across disciplines but also across administrative and transnational boundaries. There are several examples, through the University of Illinois's WW work, that point to changes in the perception of L2 writers, to creating an institutional discourse and atmosphere that celebrates students of diverse languages and cultures and empowers them to thrive in the US university. One example, the growing presence of L2 writing consultants at the writing center, has sent a powerful message to students (and faculty) in presenting L2 writers as legitimate users of English. The SLWG, discussed earlier, is another good example. This series of sessions provided a space for students to confront their own self-deprecating English ideologies and to restore their self-respect by understanding their own literacy history and ideologies (Kang 2016). Last, I have also witnessed a gradual and striking change in the rhetoric of some of the faculty administrators with whom I have been consulting and communicating with over several years. In a recent conversation with an academic program administrator and faculty member, I noticed his comments were marked by more complexity and sensitivity. For example, as we were looking over one of his Chinese student's written analysis assignments, he pointed to a few "awkward" words and phrasings he wanted to change but hesitated, worried he would "alter the cultural connotations" not evident to his "American eyes." These anecdotes and more serve as examples of the subtle but meaningful impact a writing center can have on promoting a deeper understanding of differences in language use in the university community.

As these examples suggest, the role of the writing center in educating and training could be crucial in changing the discourse of how international L2 students' English is perceived and talked about. The institutional position of the Writers Workshop as a campus-wide academic service unit, so prominently serving international student writers, has enabled the WW to be placed at the center of university conversations about the internationalization boom. Although its growth and expansion in its role is overall positive, the WW must tackle chronic (e.g., lack of resources, lack of recognition) and emerging (e.g., a truncated campus-wide network) challenges in effectively and continuously responding to the needs of the changing university. Most important though, the challenges of this time are about redefining the place of the writing center in the university—not just as a place for student support but also as one of innovation, leadership, policy, and curricula.

Where Do We Begin?

As the University of Illinois at Urbana-Champaign has experienced a dramatic increase in its international student population, its writing center has been both reactive and proactive in forging a new role for itself, both with in-house adaptations and new outreach activities. Although these efforts have been productive and effective given the limited resources, further efforts are needed in sustaining such work and making a difference in the wider university community. The following recommendations are drawn from my research and administrative experience. These basic recommendations aim to build a solid foundation that can foster growth and innovative ideas that can meet the individual needs of a variety of institutions. The creative and thoughtful events, programs, and policies that emerge can tackle the apparent, but also the not-so-apparent, needs that influence the language ideologies of not only international, multilingual, student writers but also of faculty, staff, and administrators in higher education institutions.

Knowing Our Student Writers. Most writing center scholars emphasize the importance of knowing the students we work with. When working with multilingual writers, various questions about the writer and writing should be investigated carefully. Who are the writers? In what contexts (e.g., social, educational, economic) did they learn English? How do they use (or not use) English on the US campus? What other languages and language varieties have they encountered during their lives and education? What language goals do they have, not only for a particular paper but also for their undergraduate/graduate education in the United States? These questions are basic but paramount in effectively engaging with the students as individuals as well as a collective group.

As evidenced through students I have encountered in my administrative work and research, the goals and the educational and literacy trajectories of the international student populations on our US campuses are increasingly complex and diverse. In the case of many Korean undergraduate students at UIUC, it was critical to recognize that many of the students' literacy and rhetorical practices had emerged out of extensive early-study-abroad experience (Kang 2015, 2016). Anecdotally, a number of students from China also have educational trajectories that include international experiences with English (and other languages) before they arrive at the university. One faculty member told me, for example, of a Chinese graduate student who was recalling her challenges in high school in Singapore with working out the differences between Singlish (Singapore English) and the Standard English of school, where Singlish was rejected. For that matter, we should not assume that US students have grown up and gone to school in settled monolingual contexts. The consequences of globalization (cf. Blommaert 2010, on truncated competencies in multiple languages and language varieties) on literacy education are profound.

It was only with in-depth knowledge of the particular and peculiar literacy and rhetorical practices and the language ideologies behind the practices that I was able to argue for and then design the single-language writing group (SLWG) for Korean undergraduate students that addressed the impacts of their transnational literate lives and their language ideologies. Aware of the fact that the students avoided using English among their Korean peers due to the fear/worry of being negatively evaluated for their not-so-"perfect English," I was able create a specific environment for the students to freely discuss their issues with writing in their first language, Korean. Without knowing the students and having insights into how their transnational educational experiences had led to limiting language ideologies, I would never have conceived of SLWGs. It is also clearly a challenge to find other consultants who not only understood the languages but also have a sense of how to stage conversations about not only specific rhetorical and linguistic challenges but also complex language ideologies.

The Need for Ongoing Research: Knowing our students requires more than informal discussion. Noting that writing centers are often insensitive to the issues of their students, Jessica Williams (2006) argues for formal needs analysis, which "has been largely absent from work with L2 writers in WCs [writing centers]" (118). Thus, more ongoing research is needed to keep up with the continuously changing student populations and their educational, cultural, and transnational backgrounds. The SLWG presented earlier is an example of a researched-based initiative that would otherwise have been counterintuitive. For example, in the first chapter of the second edition of *ESL Writers: A Guide for Writing Center Tutors*, Iona Leki (2009) describes common linguistic backgrounds of ESL college students, with a distinction between Generation 1.5 students and international students. Although informative, as demonstrated in my research on Korean undergraduate students with early-study-abroad (ESA) experience (Kang 2016), the categories Leki identifies are too simplistic to capture the complexities of many multilingual linguistic lives today that trace educational paths across the globe. In the Korean SLWG, it was challenging to unpack the way students' limited (sometimes race-based) ideologies of language had developed across the quite diverse experiences represented in one small group of students. The Korean SLWG was an optimal research site to further explore the complex and nuanced linguistic and transnational educational experiences of students with ESA experience in a pedagogical context.

Continuous Training, Communication, and Commitment: Writing centers today have definitely come a long way in their development and in their role in the institutions they serve. However, to not get caught in the trap of being defined as fix-it shops, writing center directors and other WPAs must provide continuous training/professional development in writing centers where, in many institutions, turnover is frequent because consulting staff is composed of graduate or peer (undergraduate) students. Such measures will keep consultants who work with students well informed and trained regarding the language development of students who speak English as a second (third, fourth, fifth . . .) language. For example, in consulting sessions, when student consultants do not know how to teach and practice grammar with the student writers, they tend to fall back on inadvertently "fixing" the grammar errors by suggesting better options for their grammar and/or word choices. Although presenting alternatives can be an effective teaching method for some language learners, consultants also must teach the student writers how to actually work on grammar issues.

In addition to continuous communication internally, as noted earlier, continuous dialogue and collaboration with units and programs across campus is important in keeping a consensus about what the writing center does and how it does it. It is also important administrators stay committed to exploring and experimenting to develop and sustain successful and beneficial programs and measures already in place. For example, despite its successful outcomes, although the ESL writing groups continued, the SLWGs were discontinued as I left my administrative position for a TA position in another unit in spring 2014. They were discontinued primarily due to the challenge of finding consultants/ facilitators of the same first language who also had the translingual disposition the positions called for. The possibility of overcoming this challenge substantially decreased with the absence of an L2 writing specialist focused on and committed to L2 support. This challenge suggests not only the need for specific resources at the writing center but also the need for broader efforts and commitment on the part of the writing center administrator in promoting research and administrative work in order to further adapt, develop, and sustain programs like SLWGs and make them part of the fabric of writing center services.

CONCLUSION

As I noted, historically, writing center missions and practices have evolved as the contexts of higher education, especially the composition of student enrollments, have shifted. Globalization of higher education calls for once again reforming writing centers to raise their institutional profile and to bring their student-centered perspectives more directly into campus instructional and administrative conversations. A key contextual factor, despite efforts by some academics, is that the United States has been one of the countries most resistant to embracing multilingualism. The world has been accommodating the dominance of our monolingualism for decades now, but that era is fading and we must forge a new translingual stance in the Anglocentric world and in our language pedagogies. As US higher education institutions further internationalize, and as scholar-teachers in language and education increasingly value linguistic diversity, there must be practical institutional strategies to communicate the value of multilingualism/translingualism. In many writing centers (and first-year writing programs), second language issues are dealt with on "special" occasions (e.g., beginning-of-the-year orientations, one-time professional development) or as one part of a larger event (usually under the same category with "nontraditional" students). If "linguistic homogeneity" is not the norm of our student population (Matsuda 2006), multilingual issues should be integrated into all conversations by default. One-time workshops, orientations, and events can certainly be critical in informing faculty, students, and staff about multilingual/ESL issues, but these topics must be embedded within the regular programs and curricula continuously and consistently.

The current moment, with US higher education institutions experiencing an unprecedented increase in the number of international undergraduate students, is a pivotal time. As an administrator, researcher, instructor/tutor, and mentor at the university, I believe it is now critical for scholars, teachers, and administrators to take note of and embrace the complexities our students bring with them to the university. The efforts in attending to the needs of our international students must move away from a rhetoric/discourse of deficit or of the international student population as a "problem" that needs to be solved. In this regard, writing centers in particular and WPAs in general must take an active role in reshaping the institutional rhetoric surrounding what writing centers do and shaping representations of multilingual students. In this moment of transition, we have the opportunity to create a new rhetoric, new practices, and new or expanded institutional missions in our centers and across campus, ones that celebrate and embrace international students, their literacy histories, and their rhetorical and linguistic practices.

Notes

1.   Writing centers in the United States are still widely described as offering tutorials, and the staff is typically tutors. The Writers Workshop, like many writing centers across the United States, adopted the term *consultant* early to try to shift the framework. While tutors typically tell people how to do things one on one (and often, in the United States, help students who are struggling with the material), as in the case of math tutors, *consultant* pushes the reframing, as it signals that the interaction is for any writer (anyone can use the services of a consultant) and that the interaction is more dialogic.

2.   UIUC kept first place amongst public higher education institutions until the 2014–2015 academic year. In the 2015–2016 academic year, Arizona State University's international student population increased approximately 30 percent from its previous year, making it the institution with the largest international student population (Institute of International Education 2016).

3.   Writers Workshop data on international student visitation numbers do not exist until academic year 2005–2006.

4.   As a common narrative for most writing centers across US higher education institutions, the WW has been coping with limited resources in serving over forty-five thousand students with an average of twenty to twenty-five consultants at the center, which averages approximately six thousand hours/sessions a year.

5.   Departments and programs in the College of Business and College of Engineering, financially more stable sectors, had been responding to the increase with their own resources. For example, the College of Business created extra tutoring sessions with new hires for its required Business 101 courses.

6.   The Center for Innovation in Teaching and Learning (CITL) supports academic units with varieties of services including tools for teaching and learning success (CITL 2018).

References

Blommaert, Jan. 2010. *The Sociolinguistics of Globalization.* Cambridge: Cambridge University Press. https://doi.org/10.1017/CBO9780511845307.

Bruce, Shanti, and Ben Rafoth, eds. 2009. *ESL Writers: A Guide for Writing Center Tutors.* 2nd ed. Portsmouth, NH: Boynton/Cook.

Bruce, Shanti, and Ben Rafoth, eds. 2016. *Tutoring Second Language Writers.* Logan: Utah State University Press. https://doi.org/10.7330/9781607324140.

Canagarajah, A. Suresh. 2013. *Translingual Practice: Global Englishes and Cosmopolitan Relations.* London: Routledge.

Carino, Peter. 1996. "Open Admissions and the Construction of Writing Center History: A Tale of Three Models." *Writing Center Journal* 17 (1): 30–48.

CITL (Center for Innovation in Teaching & Learning). 2018. University of Illinois. http://citl.illinois.edu/.

Gillespie, Paula, and Neal Lerner. 2008. *Longman Guide to Peer Tutoring.* 2nd ed. New York: Pearson.

Harris, Muriel, and Tony Silva. 1993. "Tutoring ESL Students: Issues and Options." *College Composition and Communication* 44 (4): 525–37. https://doi.org/10.2307/358388.

Horner, Bruce, Min-Zhan Lu, Jacqueline Jones Roster, and John Trimbur. 2011. "Language Difference in Writing: Toward a Translingual Approach." *College English* 73 (3): 303–21.

Illinois International. 2018. University of Illinois. http://international.illinois.edu/about/index.html.

Institute of International Education. *Open Doors.* 2016. https://www.iie.org/Research-and-Publications/Open-Doors.

Kang, Yu-Kyung. 2015. "Tensions of the Local and Global: South Korean Students Navigating and Maximizing US College Life." *Literacy in Composition Studies* 3 (3): 86–109. http://licsjournal.org/OJS/index.php/LiCS/article/view/99/129.

Kang, Yu-Kyung. 2016. "English—Only When Necessary: Literacy Practices of Korean Undergraduate Students at a 'Global' University." PhD dissertation, University of Illinois at Urbana-Champaign.

Leki, Ilona. 2009. "Before the Conversation: A Sketch of Some Possible Backgrounds, Experiences." In *ESL Writers: A Guide for Writing Center Tutors,* edited by Shanti Bruce and Ben Rafoth, 1–17. Portsmouth, NH: Boyton/Cook.

Lerner, Neal. 2001. "Searching for Robert Moore." *Writing Center Journal* 22 (1): 9–32.

Martins, David. 2015. *Transnational Writing Program Administration.* Logan: Utah State University Press. https://doi.org/10.7330/9780874219623.

Matsuda, Paul Kei. 2006. "The Myth of Linguistic Homogeneity in U.S. College Composition." *College English* 68 (6): 637–51. https://doi.org/10.2307/25472180.

Rafoth, Ben. 2015. *Multilingual Writers and Writing Centers.* Logan: Utah State University Press. https://doi.org/10.7330/9780874219647.

Severino, Carol. 2016. "Beyond the How-To's: Connecting the Word and the World." Forward to *Tutoring Second Language Writers,* edited by Shanti Bruce and Ben Rafoth, ix–viii. Logan: Utah State University Press.

University of Illinois at Urbana-Champaign, Center for Writing Studies. 2016. "Writers Workshop: About the Workshop." http://www.cws.illinois.edu/workshop/about/.

Williams, Jessica. 2006. "The Role(s) of Writing Centers in Second Language Instruction." In *The Politics of Second Language Writing: In Search of the Promised Land,* edited by Paul Kei Matsuda, Christina Ortmeier-Hooper, and Xiaoye You, 109–26. West Lafayette, IN: Parlor.

PART III

Curricular Development

8

"I AM NO LONGER SURE THIS SERVES OUR STUDENTS WELL"
Redesigning FYW to Prepare Students for Transnational Literacy Realities

David Swiencicki Martins and Stanley Van Horn

INTRODUCTION

Rochester Institute of Technology is a private university situated in western New York with over eighteen thousand students. With several key programs in the fine arts and design alongside its engineering, science, and computing programs, RIT sees itself as a STEAM institution. RIT also has international locations in Croatia, Kosovo, and Dubai, with partnership programs in China and the Dominican Republic. On RIT's Rochester, New York, campus, there are more than two thousand international students, with the largest numbers from India, China, Saudi Arabia, and the Dominican Republic.

As the first-year writing program director at Rochester Institute of Technology, Martins received an e-mail from a faculty member in Dubrovnik, Croatia. Rebecca Roja Charry was teaching FYW at RIT Croatia, the oldest of RIT's international locations. In the e-mail, Rebecca wrote, "I am no longer sure that this [curriculum] serves our students well." Although Martins had never met Rebecca, her statement highlighted the significant changes in the contexts of students engaged in RIT's FYW curriculum and raised questions about how well the course prepared students in Rochester for the transnational realities of twenty-first-century literacy practice. In this chapter we describe our efforts to internationalize the FYW curriculum and offer our reflection on the redesigned curriculum.

Prior to this internationalization project, Martins had helped design an FYW class with a writing-about-writing (WAW) approach (Downs and Wardle 2007) in which students were assigned readings on language use and academic writing. In order to highlight the richness and breadth of literacy learning in students' lives, well beyond the often narrow scope

DOI: 10.7330/9781607326762.c008

of schooling, Martins also regularly assigns a literacy narrative intended to engage students in an autoethnographic analysis of their literacy acquisition (Brodkey 1996; Eldred and Mortensen 1992; Young 2004) in which students' own literacy experiences and the experiences of their classmates are the focus of deliberate reflection.

As director of RIT's program of English as an additional language, Van Horn began to collaborate with Martins on linking learning outcomes of his English for academic purposes (EAP) courses for international students with those of the RIT FYW courses. Within the subfields of applied linguistics, the EAP perspective draws from the strands that emphasize the study of context and discourse community (e.g., Firth 1952; Halliday 1978; Rose and Martin 2012) and that have been advocated for as a "socially realistic linguistics" (Kachru 1981). As RIT engaged in the project of globalizing its curriculum, Van Horn saw opportunities to integrate the intercultural learning students experienced in the English-language program into FYW. That intercultural learning engages students regularly in the metacognitive exploration of layered patterns: from linguistic word- and sentence-level language patterns to cultural patterns of organizing spoken and written discourse. This teaching and learning was informed by studies in cross-cultural pragmatics and interactional sociolinguistics (Goffman 1974, 1981; Gumperz 1982, 1992; Tannen 1984, 2007) and the ethnography of communication (Cazden 1994, 2001; Hymes 1974; Saville-Troike 2003). For international students, the need to understand and interact with culturally unfamiliar texts seemed to be a given, and the metacognitive exercise seemed useful in adapting to new cultural and academic environments. In the context of an FYW course delivered across global campuses, we wondered whether adding elements of cultural exploration would noticeably enrich the metacognitive toolkit of the writing-about-writing curriculum.

Our belief is that contextual and cultural awareness offers a way for students to become more flexible thinkers through repetition of experience-reflection-response. The FYW curriculum we designed for this project attempted to enrich a cross-cultural awareness in students for whom it was already nascent or encourage a sense of cross-cultural awareness in those for whom it was not. With adequate tools, we believe, people can complicate their notion of communication by discovery through and with others. With these motivations in mind, and the desire to highlight the social and cultural processes in writing, two new student learning outcomes (SLOs) were added to those common to FYW in the university writing program.

- Students understand that difference in language is a resource for producing meaning in writing, speaking, reading, and listening.
- Students become aware of the influences—social, linguistic, cultural, and national—that have shaped them as writers, students, and individuals.

After redesigning the FYW curriculum to include these SLOs, we recruited two experienced instructors to each teach one section of the course. Asking that they retain the WAW approach and assign a literacy narrative, we encouraged the two instructors to make the course their own based on their interests and experiences. We then worked with the two instructors to assess the learning outcomes through a range of practices including an examination of students' awareness and abilities pre- and postinstruction. We also collected a final portfolio of each student's written work that included a reflective cover letter. Finally, we asked both instructors to prepare a reflective teaching journal on the materials they created for the class and the pedagogy they developed while teaching the course. After a brief description of the curriculum, we offer our analyses of these assessment activities.

CURRICULUM DESCRIPTION

In 2011, when we developed the new curriculum, Joseph Harris's (2006) *Rewriting: How to Do Things with Texts* had recently been adopted as one of three possible textbooks for use in the ten-week Writing Seminar course. This text had been selected to provide students with a conceptual toolkit for how to read other writers' texts and how to use those texts in their own writing. As another part of the shared experience, both instructors selected articles by Bronwyn T. Williams (2008), Gloria Anzaldúa (1987), and Cynthia L. Selfe and Gail E. Hawisher with Oladipupo (Dipo) Lahore and Pengfei Song (Selfe et al. 2006). The instructors sought to introduce students to a specific way of understanding and practicing the moves of academic *conversation* in writing at the same time as they explored issues in literacy studies: language variety, identity, and technology in international or global contexts.

Two of the assignments were designed to introduce students to a project-based approach to reading, writing, and using sources (Harris 2006, 16–19). The "Coming to Terms" assignment asked students to analyze an author's "purpose, evidence, and MOVES." Students started their analysis with writing in class, and then, after working through peer review, revised their writing into a formal essay. The "Forwarding" assignment, as described in the course syllabus, asked students to integrate their experience reading an article with their own experiences: "Begin with a clear reference to the Selfe essay . . . before you add your own 'case study' to the discussion that has begun and will continue. Your 'case' may refer to your own literacy story, whether that is in a first language or another language." While students were practicing this way of using another's writing in their own, they were also writing about their past literacy experiences.

The "Literacy Writing Project" included a sequence of writing tasks that culminated with the students writing "an autobiographical narrative of a meaningful literacy event [they had] experienced." In addition to the literacy narrative, students interviewed a classmate and wrote a "literacy profile" of their peer. That profile was intended to give the class "a clear picture of some of the influences that shaped how [the peer] learned to write" and also to "highlight some of the interesting or significant features of [the peer's experience]." The final research paper in the course then asked students to take a position regarding "some aspect or issue related to the Internationalization of English and its impact on literacy, writing, teaching, etc." Students were expected "to consider [their] own 'stake' and moves [they wanted] to make, to forward and/or counter a claim or position so that [they were] adding to the discourse on this topic." Students were asked to use at least one of the essays read for class and at least two sources found online, conduct a survey to use as evidence, and "consider the literacy and language experiences of [their] own and of people in [their] research group." The culminating writing project integrated aspects from each of the other activities in the class. Along the way, each essay assignment included in-class writing, collaborative discussion, and peer review.

COMMUNICATION REFLECTION TASK

Alongside course readings on language and identity and on world Englishes, Van Horn offered one lecture-workshop on the linguistic study of cross-cultural communication. The workshop had two purposes: (1) to collect a baseline of how students were thinking about difference in culture and communication, in their own terms, through a written reflection task, and (2) to present some core concepts drawn from interactional sociolinguistics and ethnomethodology that might be used to triangulate notions of identity, interaction, and observable features of language. The lecture portion discussed language variation from micro-linguistic features (phonology and dialect, word choices) to features of discourse (e.g., order of information, cultural and situational variation in interpreting context and goals).

In the communication reflection task, students were asked to recount and reflect on two past communication experiences: one in which communication had been satisfying or fun and one in which communication had been difficult or frustrating, with cultural or linguistic variation in mind. Through analysis of this open-ended task, we aimed to gather information from the thirty-one students in the two sections.

- What kind of experiences do students have interacting with a variety of people? Do students demonstrate a favorable, explicit value in getting to know people with different backgrounds?
- What ways of thinking do students bring to their interactions?

In terms of pedagogy, a goal of examining the students' on-the-ground concerns about communication was for us to be able to select relevant readings and topics that would be optimized to reach them where they are as a platform for deeper critical thinking on culture and communication. In terms of defining learning outcomes, we also wanted to see what concepts students already used when thinking about interaction across difference.

By asking students to reflect on their emotional stances and on the problem solving required of troubling interactions, we borrow from cross-cultural communication studies in which communication problems or "critical incidents" are examined to uncover hidden cultural patterns (e.g., Ramsay, Barker, and Jones 1999, drawing from methods proposed as early as Flanagan 1954) and from interactional sociolinguists, who actively seek cross-talk and misalignments (e.g., Gumperz 1982) as way of shedding light on how interaction is organized to make inferences about participants' interactional goals.

One preliminary question for us was, what if the answer to our first question is simply yes—that our students were already experienced, reflective global citizens with much experience, confidence, and positive curiosity? If so, perhaps there is no point in explicit efforts to internationalize the curriculum. This was not the case, but two of the thirty-one students set the bar for demonstrating an active interest in learning about others in their comments:

- I prefer when I talk with people who are not from my country since they have many differences in their way of thinking.
- I work on campus at Ben and Jerry's. I love being able to communicate with those from all different backgrounds. In the few minutes it takes to ask the customer what they would like, you learn a lot about them—the language they speak, the people they are with, their body language, and the small talk conversations.

Students' written reflections were compiled, and a broad qualitative content analysis was carried out to identify recurrent or dominant themes. We identified social and interactional factors that guided their assessment of the communicative event, emotional stances toward communication, and any reference to formal features of language, style, or discourse. Student reflections sorted into two major themes: *belonging* and *meeting interactional goals*. In addition two minor themes also emerged: *power and competition* (winning arguments and debates) and *affective stances* such as communication anxiety or the pure joy of writing.

On the theme of belonging, the majority of students discussed positive interactions with family and friends: talking with parents, friends, boy/girlfriends. Although collectively the thirty-one students had the experience of living in at least eight countries, culture did not emerge as significantly as family and friendship roles. Of those who brought up culture, a Korean American student mentioned, "Communicating in two languages with my friends from Korea was satisfying because we are from a similar background and culture"—though he does not break down which aspects were particularly satisfying. Another student with family members from India and the United States commented, "Family vacation to the south. . . . The culture itself was so different it made it seem like I was attempting to contact extra-terrestrials"—but we don't come to understand in which ways the culture is so alien. The most elaborated answer came from a US-born student who discussed her family background.

> My family are a big large group of Italians, so for family dinner all you do is talk and eat. Sometimes it's hard to get a word in! But the best part about dinner is when most people head home and there's about half of us left. Most of us listen to stories about my aunts, uncles and mom growing up. We laugh so hard that we cry! The way they tell the stories makes it even more entertaining because they're all arguing at once about who's telling the story wrong.

This latter response connected a cultural style, a communication activity and situation (family narratives, at dinner), and features of discourse (cooperative overlap—"arguing all at once"). There did not seem to be an emergent pattern in which students with more experience living in multiple countries had more descriptive and analytical tools to articulate their experience.

When they were asked about satisfying or frustrating situations with different groups of people, students predictably focused on interactional goals. What we did not predict, however, was that half the responses centered on access to a language—being able to speak it or not. Even so, the communicative event remained largely unanalyzed. When describing frustrating situations, international students brought up examples of feeling unable to use English "in a way that native speakers understand." US and Canadian students brought up frustrations of not being able to use their classroom-learned Spanish with native speakers. In adapting to life on a university campus with a college for deaf and hard-of-hearing students, several students brought up examples of not being able to communicate or interact with deaf and hard-of-hearing classmates because they did not know American Sign Language. One student elaborated:

> We have a deaf volleyball player here on the team, she knows a little bit of sign and speaks OK but at times it is hard to communicate with her because she doesn't always understand our interpreter. The most difficult times are when the interpreter is not present and we have to try and make her understand a drill or what the coach is saying with what little sign we know. Volleyball is mainly a sport about communication so this is a constant struggle to understand each other.

Even in this elaborated response, which describes the communicative scene in some detail, the main question is about access: do we speak the same language or not? Where students discussed communicative success, there was a focus on shared language—or in succeeding despite limited or lacking shared language. Students recognized language as a barrier even when optimistically working around it. One student noted,

> I stayed with a host family in Mexico and had to speak Spanish most of the time. . . . I remember speaking Spanish [with host-family brothers] one night and staying up with them playing Halo. I'd never played and was pretty bad, but we had a good time anyway. We couldn't always speak but we'd get points across with gestures as well. I was proud of myself for being able to talk with them and have a good time.

Where students turned to discuss language and difference in language, they cited discrete surface features of language as factors in intelligibility and comprehensibility: "accents," "appropriate words," "sentence structures" as items that either helped out, got in the way, or might be accommodated. One student wrote, "A time that communication was satisfying was when I was able to get over the accent of an Israeli friend. Between the accent and his sometimes different usage of words, he was difficult to understand. However we learned to communicate anyways which led to a rewarding friendship." This statement evidences exactly the interaction experience we hope students as global citizens may come to have; this student is demonstrating an awareness that difference does not need to become barrier. At the same time, in this example, barriers take the form of "accents" and "words," and the communicative effort seems unilateral, as the friend was "difficult to understand."

Identifying the various themes in student reflections on the lecture helps identify "key words" for future versions of the course and helps instructors encourage students toward richer reflection. For example, because access to language seems to be a ground-level consideration for students, instructors can ask students to reflect on specific aspects of a communicative event. If students comfortably sit with the conclusion that it is nice to know languages but are not given opportunities to reflect on contexts and situations that may have multiple interpretations, or to reflect on how situations and texts are organized culturally, the course falls short. Writing projects in which students examine their own verbal repertoire and think about the degree to which it overlaps with others pose important questions: Is someone beating around the bush or being polite? Is someone simply getting to the point, or is the behavior perceived as out of bounds and pushy? Was it that "accent" and "words" were in the way or a cultural pattern? Is my accent just as hard for the others as theirs are for me?

INSTRUCTOR REFLECTIONS

During the preparation for and then delivery of the course, the two instructors wrote reflective journals. Their reflections were invaluable to our understanding of the curriculum. In their journals, instructors acknowledged a range of awareness of cultural diversity among the students in the class and reflected on the opportunities for and barriers to learning in this *internationalized* class. The teaching journals are filled with anecdotes highlighting how language variety is experienced in direct relation to others and how awareness is based on seeing how external forces impact and shape internal cognition. Throughout the course, the instructors created spaces for students to be challenged by reading and writing critically, reflecting on experience, and analyzing their own and others' writing.

One key issue raised by the instructors' reflections was the role of the literacy narrative, a writing task that is complicated, reiterative, and personal. Early in her journal, one of the instructors wrote,

> Honestly I am wondering how we can ask for a literacy narrative? Whose literacy and in what language? That almost seems very Western/white academic to ask. Are we talking about how we learn to communicate in any language? Or are we talking about multiple literacies and many languages?

This instructor initially saw the literacy-narrative assignment as a barrier to learning. By the end of the course, the instructor was convinced that reading classmates' literacy narratives "helped [the students] broaden their perspective." Initially concerned about how students would respond to and be able to learn from the literacy-narrative assignment, the instructor's reflection demonstrates the degree to which writing assignments can play a variety of roles in the class. In addition to serving as an opportunity for students to reflect on their own language-learning and -using experiences, it also offers students a chance to learn about their peers' prior learning experiences. This kind of social learning highlights how interactional spaces can impact students' understanding of their own learning, development, and language proficiency.

Another barrier to learning posed by the literacy-narrative assignment was the struggle students had deepening their understanding of the connections among language, literacy, and identity. One instructor described how students often seemed to be "drifting toward making generalizations about literacy rather than using their experience and perspectives as a guiding force of the essay." The other instructor observed that students had difficulty articulating "how their experiences have molded their literacy development" and establishing "connections" between their own and others' experiences. In one case, the instructor explained how a student talked about a multidimensional experience in class only to write about a different experience.

> [The student] revealed to me that 1) her parents still can't speak much English, 2) while she speaks Chinese fluently, she cannot read Chinese, and 3) when she returned to China a few years ago to visit family, many of her relatives teased her for her American accent. Although we talked about all of these experiences in class, she chose an experience that turned out to be more one-dimensional, at least in the way that she described it.

When the instructor reflected more on what might be a barrier to students' exploration of their own and their classmates' personal literacy experiences, she wrote,

> Students are somewhat hesitant to point out the challenges and obstacles they have experienced in their multilingual backgrounds. . . . Perhaps it is also an effect of the self-consciousness they feel as a result of being in a class with Americans. Perhaps they assume the Americans will see these experiences as a sign of weakness or that discussing them will somehow put them at a disadvantage. On the other hand, it's also possible that they simply lack awareness of their own experiences as they view them as so mundane that they are not worth mentioning or exploring further.

Although the instructor's reflection reveals the complexity of the instructional space, a number of factors clearly impact the students' work on this writing task. Students do not want to appear vulnerable in front of their classmates, especially when issues associated with accent or language proficiency might be at work. In addition, when students are enrolled in multiple classes, they may periodically avoid challenging reflective work because it is difficult. Likewise, the curriculum includes a large variety of linked learning tasks that encourage a particular process, and students may not yet trust in a long-term process.

A second key issue was students' experience of *authority*. Along with the literacy narrative, the curriculum included critical reading of articles and peer review of student writing. The readings, along with peer-review tasks, raised questions about who has authority to write, how assumed proficiency impacts notions of authority and identity, and how writers "find their own voice." Instructors worked to understand the cause of the students' experience of authority. For some students, instructors thought, peer review "may violate certain cultural rules," and some international students "may be unwilling to express criticism [of US students' writing]." One instructor wrote that peer review might also be understood as being "further manifestation of their [students'] lack of authority and confidence in their own writing."

A third key issue raised in the instructors' journals was the importance of designing interactional spaces where students work together in meaningful ways and where differences in interpretation, experience, or perspective could be explored together. For example, because both instructors elected to teach many of the same readings, we were able to see how different groups of students responded to the same text. According to the instructor, the class that was less explicitly multilingual did not appear to take up ideas from Gloria Anzaldúa's article. The other, more internationally diverse class described Anzaldúa's writing as "angry writing" but found it to be an interesting example of expression. In fact, it produced something of a breakthrough moment for some members of her class who began to see that writing with a point of view was different from the writing they had seen previously. This experience suggests that instructors can try to elicit responses from students, but infusing a learning environment with specific concepts does not easily or simply translate into predictable learning.

Another example of the importance of designing deliberate interaction among students comes from the journal of an instructor who noted differences in background between US students and international students in her class and what she had observed in classes that didn't include US students.

The American students in the class had minimal, if any, exposure to other cultures prior to this class. All of them came from predominantly white suburban or small town communities with little diversity. This obstacle faced by the American students was matched by the obstacle faced by the international students—the intimidation factor. Most, though not all, of the international students had never taken classes with American students prior to Writing Seminar. The result was a hesitance that was not characteristic of their communication style inside my [English as additional language] classroom.

Based on the instructor reflections, the importance of creating opportunities for diverse groups of students, who happen to be enrolled in a class for a semester together, to develop interpersonal connections and feelings of trust cannot be underestimated.

CASE STUDIES

Internationalized curricula require both a broad range of interactions among students and opportunities to deepen or complicate understanding of those interactions. Below, we discuss the written work of the two students we call "Craig" and "Noorah," whose work included twenty-six drafts of five different assignments.

Craig's case reveals multiple opportunities to engage in a broad range of interactions but also shows the degree to which that breadth may have also made it more challenging to deepen his reflection. We highlight Craig's story not as a critique of the instructors or the student but because in analyzing his materials, we identified a possible weak spot of the curriculum.

In his final research paper, "The Internationalization of English," Craig takes up an issue he first explored in the first-day diagnostic essay. On that first day of class, students read a short article by Steve Meacham entitled "One Global Tongue," which appeared in the *Sydney Morning Herald* on March 30, 2011. In the article, Meacham describes a Eurovision Song Contest in which only three of the thirty-eight songs representing the various countries in the competition were sung in languages other than English. This is evidence, Meacham suggests, that "we seem to be heading toward a shared language—English." In Craig's initial exploration of the topic, he describes a situation in which "the growing number of countries that are using English as a second language is so that when they go to places with English as their primary language, they are able to easily converse with them. There are advantages and disadvantages for that." In his characterization, following one of the ideas from the short article, the main concern for native speakers of English is competitiveness for jobs against others who are multilingual: "I think in the sense of a job market it would be wise to have the ability to converse in multiple languages." For Craig, access to language is something of a polarity, you have it or you don't. People who have access to more than one language have more power.

By the end of the ten-week term, Craig shifted his focus to whether it is even possible to create one homogeneous global Standard English. He concludes his final paper arguing that creating one World English is not possible because of social networking technology and the influence of individual speakers' accents and cultural backgrounds, which he sees as intimately connected to speakers' sense of identity and individuality. Influenced by his engagement with perspectives offered by Min-Zhan Lu (via Bronwyn T. Williams [2008]) and Gloria Anzaldúa, a classmate from Australia, and two articles he found while doing database research, Craig concludes his essay: "Although it may be difficult at times to inter-act with people from different cultural backgrounds, it is an individual choice to make whether you are willing to adapt to their style of speech or if you are proud to maintain your own cultural identity and speak your own way." Craig seems to have changed some of his thinking as a result of engaging with the course readings.

However, exploring Craig's writing, two observations raise questions for us about what the curriculum accomplished and how we might mod-ify the course activities. First, although two subsequent iterations of his paper revealed the addition of two developed paragraphs introducing perspectives by Min-Zhan Lu and Gloria Anzaldúa, those additions did not alter his introduction and did not produce any change in the conclu-sion, which remained the same across all drafts. Second, although one added paragraph introduced statements by Min-Zhan Lu, we noticed that those quotations were different from those in an earlier assign-ment that were more directly relevant to the issues of adaptation he raised in his final paper. In his final paper, Craig quotes from a source: "'Americans are not great thinkers . . . I mean I love the American peo-ple, but if you don't say things the way they're used to hearing them, they don't understand' (qtd. in Jones 1076)." Craig forwards this idea to express the "need for adapting to a particular culture's word, phrases, and accents." In his "Coming to Terms" essay, in which he is tasked with identifying Williams's "aims," "key ideas," "moves," and "uses and lim-its," he highlights one key idea by quoting Lu, who talks about taking "'a dual approach to reading such texts and consider[ing] how we read them against our cultural experience and expectations for standardized English writing as well as how and why the individual writer may have composed a text with features different than we expect' (512)." Both quotations speak directly to the impact on understanding of a listener/ reader's expectations for another speaker/writer's language use, but in the shift from the task of coming to terms to the task of forwarding ideas from others in the service of his own project, Craig chooses not to use an idea he had earlier identified as important and misses an opportunity to work his way through the implications of communication across language variety that might impact the creation of one World English. Still, Craig's attention to these issues was exactly what we had hoped for in designing the course.

In his writing, Craig reveals opportunities for rich interactions with a variety of perspectives and ideas. That breadth of interaction, however, does not necessarily produce a depth of interaction. Indeed, in his end-of-term reflection, Craig describes what he learned most about writing: "The most important thing for any paper, regardless of the course it is for, is the formatting." He learned this not from the course, however, but when he "talked to a graduate student at the start of this year about school and any tips he has on writing a paper." Craig is looking for useful communication models. In internationalized courses, the breadth of communication opportunity must be accompanied by a depth of reflection that can help students move beyond the conceptual understandings they have before the class to develop new tools for communicating in a complicated, multicultural, and multilingual world. We believe it is important to design activities that specifically ask students to develop practices and tools for complicating their thinking more directly.

The second case we discuss here focuses on Noorah, who came to RIT from Saudi Arabia on a scholarship and studied English at RIT before entering the first-year writing class. Noorah's case reveals the development of a new affective stance toward language—the value of confidence and expression over form—and the rejection of the need to adopt a new accent and identity. From the beginning of the writing course, Noorah reflected openly on her experience of language and her affective stance to language-learning situations. In writing her literacy narrative, she remembered her enjoyment at playing with the sound of words before she knew what they meant. In her communication reflection task, she fondly recalled retelling stories she had read to her family, reinterpreting them to insert herself as the protagonist. She also remembered neutral or less positive experiences: her parents' compelling her to read things in formal (classical) Arabic rather than allowing her to read popular materials written for children in the regional colloquial variety and attending special private-school classes in English, which she felt to be frustrating and artificial because students did not use English to speak to one another but only to answer questions on their papers. Arriving to study in the United States, Noorah struggled with language, and she described that struggle with a paradox: she felt she knew English well, but in her interactions in the United States, she still felt she could not make herself understood. Consequently, she came to her initial hypothesis, which was that she might need to adopt an American identity in order for Americans to understand her.

As Noorah completed her "Coming to Terms" assignment, based on her reading of Gloria Anzaldúa's (1987) "How to Tame a Wild Tongue," Noorah focused on the shame Anazaldúa experienced because of her accent. "Accent" appeared throughout many of Noorah's writings as she examined ideas of identity and the ideology of language correctness. Noorah struggled with Gloria Anzaldúa's use of code switching but found the writing to be powerful. In her writing, she drew heavily on Anzaldúa's insights on the topics of voice, overcoming silence, soul, and friendship.

In the literacy-profile assignment, in which Noorah interviewed another international student, she goes somewhat beyond the descriptive nature of the profiling task and develops an explicit ideology of language learning: it takes encouragement, self-motivation, and interaction. Learning is not, in her words, "the property of the instructor." She uses the literacy profile as a tool for constructing an epistemology for lifelong language learning. Observing Noorah's efforts was inspiring, making us want to find ways to encourage all instructors to recreate the conditions that might make it possible for all students to take ownership of learning in similar ways.

As Noorah developed her final research paper for the course, the paper, despite the multiple revisions, remained rough; there were many ideas that were inchoate and implicit but nonetheless rich and interesting. In one theme, Noorah worked to reconcile something that was bothering her about the Anzaldúa piece, the connection between accent and identity, and the conformity of accent and the suppression of identity. She ultimately concludes that trying to adopt someone else's accent is not only a loss of identity but is also unnecessary since most people can understand across accents. She notes that accents are on the surface and "not the first obstacle [to learning]" and that we must be clear about "who we are and what we want." She also argues that attaining a "native speaker" accent is an unclear goal because there are regional accents. Noorah returns to the notion that motivation and the ability to "understand what we want" are key. She resolves her paradox: one doesn't need to lose an identity or feel ashamed of an accent in order to express an idea. In focus-group interviews at the end of the course, Noorah reiterated this point: "The most important is that we have confidence"—the point of view is the identity, not the accent.

Noorah's writings across the course show a narrative arc: from a girl who loved playing with language as a child, to a student in the United States frustrated that she could not make herself understood despite studying English for many years, to a person trying to adapt her way of speaking "in a way that native speakers could understand," to a confident communicator rejecting Anzaldúa's "problem" of sacrificing or reconciling accent and identity. Where Craig seems to have settled with the notion that everyone has their own language, and is entitled to it, Noorah seems poised to communicate across language and cultural difference in sophisticated ways. Craig does not deny that he must deal with language variety, but he doesn't seem to engage with it much, either. Noorah seems ready to express herself with confidence, aware of the ways that accents, word translation, and other social and cultural processes are at work in any communicative situation.

CONCLUSION

What does it mean to internationalize a first-year writing course? We believe internationalizing FYW must extend beyond business as usual focused on topics like World Englishes, the global digital divide, and identity. Our experiences have us focused on (1) designing opportunities for students to interact in socially diverse activities and reflect deeply in writing on their communication experiences and (2) identifying key concepts instructors and students can use to make sense of the complex communication experiences in those contexts. The kinds of opportunities we have in mind include collaborative, conversational experiences with peers of different linguistic backgrounds and exploring situations that are culturally mixed or have some form of hybridity. For example, when one instructor described how international students felt intimidated by native speakers, peer review could be seen as a prime opportunity to explore those affective experiences rather than work past them in order to conduct a review. Doing so shifts the focus of peer review away from *process*, per se, toward meaningful exchange between writers. The keywords we have in mind include *language variety*, *verbal repertoire*, *literacy*, and *interaction*. Our hope is that with these strategies in class, students will develop tools for and an interest in cross-cultural communication that will flourish into the future. Such a curriculum, we believe, will serve students well.

References

Anzaldúa, Gloria. 1987. *Borderland/ La Frontera: The New Mestiza.* 2nd ed. San Francisco, CA: Aunt Lute.

Brodkey, Linda. 1996. *Writing Permitted in Designated Areas Only.* Minneapolis: University of Minnesota Press.

Cazden, Courtney B. 1994. "Language, Cognition, and ESL Literacy: Vygotsky and ESL Literacy Teaching." *TESOL Quarterly* 28 (1): 172–76. https://doi.org/10.2307/358 7207.

Cazden, Courtney B. 2001. *Classroom Discourse: The Language of Learning and Teaching.* 2nd ed. Portsmouth, NH: Heinemann.

Downs, Douglas, and Elizabeth Wardle. 2007. "Teaching about Writing, Righting Misconceptions: (Re)Envisioning 'First-Year Composition' as 'Introduction to Writing Studies.'" *College Composition and Communication* 58 (4): 552–84.

Eldred, Janet Carey, and Peter Mortensen. 1992. "Reading Literacy Narratives." *College English* 54 (5): 512–39. https://doi.org/10.2307/378153.

Firth, John Rupert. 1952 (1968). "Linguistic Analysis as a Study of Meaning." In *Selected Papers of J.R. Firth 1952–1959,* edited by Frank Robert Palmer, 12–26. Bloomington: Indiana University Press.

Flanagan, John C. 1954. "The Critical Incident Technique." *Psychological Bulletin* 51 (4): 327–58. https://doi.org/10.1037/h0061470.

Goffman, Erving. 1974. *Frame Analysis: An Essay on the Organization of Experience.* Cambridge, MA: Harvard University Press.

Goffman, Erving. 1981. *Forms of Talk.* Philadelphia: University of Pennsylvania Press.

Gumperz, John J. 1982. *Discourse Strategies.* Cambridge: Cambridge University Press. https://doi.org/10.1017/CBO9780511611834.

Gumperz, John J. 1992. "Contextualizing and Understanding." In *Rethinking Context: Language as an Interactive Phenomenon,* edited by Alessandro Duranti and Charles Goodwin, 229–52. Cambridge: Cambridge University Press.

Halliday, Michael A. K. 1978. *Language as a Social Semiotic: The Social Interpretation of Language and Meaning.* London: Edward Arnold.

Harris, Joseph. 2006. *Rewriting: How to Do Things with Texts.* Logan: Utah State University Press.

Hymes, Dell. 1974. *Foundations in Sociolinguistics: An Ethnographic Approach.* Philadelphia: University of Pennsylvania Press.

Kachru, Braj B. 1981. "Socially Realistic Linguistics: The Firthian Tradition." *International Journal of the Sociology of Language* 3 (1): 65–89.

Ramsay, Sheryl, Michelle Barker, and Elizabeth Jones. 1999. "Academic Adjustment and Learning Processes: A Comparison of International and Local Students in First-Year University." *Higher Education Research & Development* 18 (1): 129–44. https://doi.org/10.1080/0729436990180110.

Rose, David, and James R. Martin. 2012. *Learning to Write, Reading to Learn: Genre, Knowledge and Pedagogy in the Sydney School.* Sheffield: Equinox.

Saville-Troike, Muriel. 2003. *The Ethnography of Communication.* 3rd ed. Oxford: John Wiley and Sons. https://doi.org/10.1002/9780470758373.

Selfe, Cynthia L., Gail E. Hawisher, Oladipupo Lahore, and Pengfei Song. 2006. "Literacies and the Complexities of the Global Digital Divide." In *The Norton Book of Composition Studies,* edited by Susan Miller, 1499–531. New York: W. W. Norton.

Tannen, Deborah. 1984. *Conversational Style: Analyzing Talk Among Friends.* Norwood, NJ: Ablex.

Tannen, Deborah. 2007. *Talking Voices: Repetition, Dialogue and Imagery in Conversational Discourse.* 2nd ed. Cambridge: Cambridge University Press. https://doi.org/10.1017/CBO9780511618987.

Williams, Bronwyn T. 2008. "Around the Block and Around the World: Teaching Literacy Across Cultures." *Journal of Adolescent & Adult Literacy* 51 (6): 510–14. https://doi.org /10.1598/JAAL.51.6.7.

Young, Morris. 2004. *Minor Re/Visions: Asian American Literacy Narratives as a Rhetoric of Citizenship.* Carbondale: Southern Illinois University Press.

9

"HOLDING THE LANGUAGE IN MY HAND"
A Multilingual Lens on Curricular Design

Gail Shuck and Daniel Wilber

A MULTILINGUAL LENS

A common institutional response to the influx of international students into US colleges and universities is to raise English-proficiency test scores for admission. However, working toward an inclusive campus requires us to consider how such a response highlights an ideology deeply embedded in the very structure of many educational institutions—an ideology of monolingualism as the norm (Matsuda 2006; Shuck 2006). This ideological stance suggests that a student with a high enough score would no longer need support for their language development after being admitted.

We have seen this assumption play out in a widespread lack of faculty preparation in teaching multilingual populations. International students are seen to bring "diversity" and "culture" to our campuses, as long as their English is at near-native proficiency. Dana Ferris (2009) recounts a panel discussion in which an audience member expressed the assumption that English learners are someone else's problem, saying, "I don't *want* to know how to work with ESL students. I have enough work to do. I need to know how to get them *out* of my classes" (136). Within such an ideological model of the world, language difference is seen as a burden unless it is barely visible.

The increase in international student populations in the United States gives us an opportunity to reenvision campus-wide structures in ways that can construct an institutional ethos that fully recognizes, values, and systematically supports multilingual students. What we need is a new lens—a multilingual lens—for viewing the goals of writing programs; the responsibility for supporting faculty across the curriculum in learning linguistically inclusive pedagogies; the criteria for measuring writing proficiency; and the readings, writing projects, and classroom activities we develop.

DOI: 10.7330/9781607326762.c009

That is, viewing all of our work as though linguistic diversity were simply the unquestioned norm would mean accounting for the presence of multilingual students, addressing their needs, and developing culturally and linguistically inclusive practices at the outset. Such a multilingual lens on our work, we argue, is wholly preferable to retrofitting a set of pedagogical and administrative practices that were meant for monolingual, monocultural students. If educators saw the everyday work of education through multilingual lenses, what would that work look like?

TOWARD INSTITUTION-WIDE SUPPORT FOR MULTILINGUAL WRITERS

Barbara Kroll (2006) uses the metaphor of the "Promised Land" to describe institutions where a multilingual lens might color everyday institutional practice. She describes an ideal in which "each and every NNES [nonnative English speaking] student at an English-medium campus would have access to programs of student and support systems that are designed to promote mastery and excellence in academic English, in ways that address the local and specific needs of those students" (298). Recent discussions of language difference as a resource (Canagarajah 2013; Cox 2014; Shapiro et al. 2016) have guided us toward that ideal, highlighting the need to embrace linguistic diversity as fundamental to educational processes that prepare all students for life in a globally interconnected world.

Kroll describes a number of institutional challenges, including assessment, placement, and curricular structures, each of which will take a well-coordinated, campus-wide effort to overcome. Dana Ferris (2009) recommends five principles that can guide how we address these challenges (see also Conference on College Composition and Communication 2009):

1. writing program structures that offer choices of multilingual or mainstream sections;

2. appropriate and nuanced methods for identifying L2 learners and tracking their progress at an institutional level;

3. fair and equitable assessment methods that account for linguistic diversity;

4. faculty preparation across the curriculum for developing knowledge of the teaching of writing and the needs of L2 writers;

5. support programs with tutors prepared to work with L2 writers.

However linguistically inclusive such institutional practices may be, we must also grapple with a new reality: a rapid increase in students admitted with low English-proficiency levels, preventing them from being able to read academic texts, understand assignment prompts, or participate in class discussions. In addition, at our institution we are seeing a combination of factors that are exacerbating this problem. These include

1. rapid increases in the number of international students, primarily from Saudi Arabia and Kuwait;

2. cultural differences between Middle Eastern and US educational norms, which have led to increased reports of academic dishonesty among international students;

3. strict demands from their scholarship sponsors, including pressure to finish their degrees in four years and to avoid courses specifically for English learners;

4. lower L1 literacy levels.

The combination of these factors is making students' difficulties with academic language highly visible.

A NEW COURSE OPTION: ACCELERATED ENGLISH

The new first-year writing (FYW) option we are piloting offers a response to these pressures. It also presents a model that recognizes the presence of multilingual writers and addresses their need for language support without requiring a long sequence of ESL courses. Such sequences of preacademic courses perpetuate the "myth of transience" (Rose 1985), which imagines that language and literacy difficulties can be solved with a series of nonacademic courses, after which those difficulties are thought to disappear (Zamel 1995, 510). Although our two levels of ESL courses (English 122 and 123) are credit bearing and effective in preparing students for FYW courses, they do not fulfill the FYW requirement. The courses remain among our offerings, however, because many students place into one or the other ESL level because they lack the knowledge of English and/or academic literacy needed to participate fully in the reading and writing tasks of English 101.

Our small step toward becoming a "Promised Land" institution is a six-credit, one-semester course temporarily called Accelerated English 101 for Multilingual Students (hereafter, Accelerated English), which fulfills the first-semester FYW requirement.[1] Adapted from the accelerated learning program (ALP) (Adams et al. 2009), this course is held six hours per week, has only fifteen students and an embedded tutor, and is currently only open to multilingual students. Unlike ALP, this course does not have two groups of students in the same class, with one taking English 101 plus a one-hour studio and one just taking English 101. All students in a section of Accelerated English are together for the full six hours per week. Accelerated English bypasses the second ESL level and uses the English 101 curriculum but provides more time and language support. In doing so, Accelerated English helps alleviate the pressure some multilingual students face and offers them a choice between two curricular paths: ESL level II (English 123) and then English 101 for six credits over two semesters, or Accelerated English for six credits in one semester.

Until recently, multilingual students with lower overall English proficiency took one or both courses in the two-semester, pre-FYW sequence. After being admitted to the university based on English-proficiency exams (primarily IELTS or TOEFL), international students write a single-draft essay for our ESOL (English for speakers of other languages) placement test. While this method is hardly ideal (see Hamp-Lyons 1991; Peckham 2006), we believe it offers a more complete picture of students' academic literacies and English fluency than either a standardized test or our online placement tool, The Write Class, which does not yet include a sufficiently sensitive mechanism for identifying English-language proficiency.

The ESOL test places some English learners directly into English 101 or 101-Plus (101P)—a four-credit version of English 101 modeled more directly on the accelerated learning program. Approximately 10–20 percent of new international students receive a high enough placement score to have that choice. Students with lower placement scores had few choices before we created Accelerated English. Because of the perceived barrier to academic progress presented by the English 122/123 sequence, we discovered that some students were actively trying to resist following their placement results. Several had discovered it was possible to enroll in an online FYW course at another institution without a placement test, while others would wait as long as two years to retake the placement exam in the hope of getting a higher score.

If Boise State had two parallel FYW sequences—a "regular" FYW course and a requirement-fulfilling FYW course for multilingual students, which is a common structure at many institutions—students would have the choice of multilingual-specific courses, and we would be better able to offer officially designated cross-cultural composition courses. However, without the convenience of a parallel course structure, these courses were difficult to administer. Enrollment in these sections had to be administered by individual permission codes for online registration.

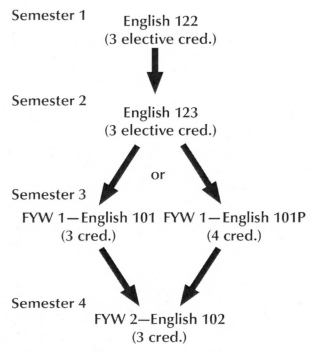

Figure 9.1. Fewer options before the curricular change (Source: Shapiro et al. 2016).

The result was an uneven rate of success in achieving a balance of native and nonnative English speakers. Rather than continuing to rely on a clunky registration process for systematically cross-cultural sections, we have offered more opportunities for faculty to develop a greater understanding of second language writing pedagogy. In this way, students can be supported even after they complete English 122 and 123.

In the last few years, Boise State's FYW program developed English 101-Plus (101P) as well as The Write Class, the online course-match system described earlier. We have found, however, that the support available to English learners within English 101P has not been sufficient for replacing the language-learning opportunities afforded by the pre-101 ESL courses. A different option for multilingual students that would offer access to the FYW curriculum was becoming increasingly important to develop.

The two figures below illustrate the paths Accelerated English opens up for students. Let us take the example of a student who places into English 122. Without Accelerated English as an option, that student

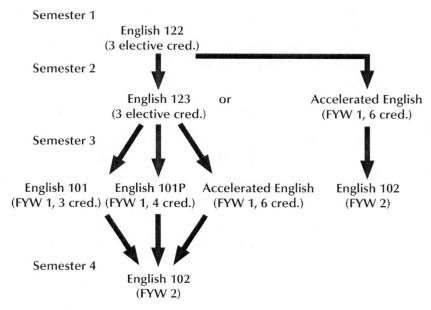

Figure 9.2. After the addition of Accelerated English (Source: Shapiro et al. 2016).

would take the following path, with one juncture for making a deci-sion—whether to take English 101 or 101P after passing English 123 at the end of their first year in college:

With the addition of Accelerated English, that same student could jump from English 122 to a 101-equivalent course, enrolling in English 102 in their third semester, as in the figure below:

A student who passed English 122, then, could choose from two paths after the first semester. A student who passed English 123 (or placed directly into English 101) would be able to choose from three paths: a three-credit, four-credit, or six-credit course to fulfill the first-semester FYW requirement. This set of options also allows students to choose a multilingual-only section if they wish. Students thus have a new opportu-nity to make agentive decisions about different levels of integrated sup-port, mainstream or multilingual classroom environments, and control over their time to degree.

IDENTIFYING THE PRIMARY DECIDING FACTORS

Central to our efforts of creating well-designed, suitable options for students are these questions: How have students responded to these options, and what forces are playing a role in the choices they make? Further, what menu of course options and what degree of agency would create improved conditions for students and their future success (Saenkhum 2012; Shapiro et al. 2016)? Investigating these questions required us to talk directly to the students themselves about their choices. We thus recruited students enrolled in the pre-101 English 123 course and students enrolled in Accelerated English and invited them to participate in an online survey regarding the ways in which they learned about the two options and their reasons behind their decision. The survey also gave them the option of participating in a follow-up interview. During the first two semesters of Accelerated English, we reached out to all students in both courses and received one hundred responses on the survey; of those respondents, we interviewed seven.

The primary survey data we are sharing in this chapter are the students' reasons for choosing the course they were enrolled in. We expected to find that multilingual students often face conflicting pressures that factor into their course choices, and indeed, our data support this hypothesis. We developed the survey response choices based on our previous experiences talking with students in these courses, many of whom privileged peers' over advisers' suggestions and also told us they wanted courses that accelerated their time to degree. In the interviews, we sought more details about how students perceived this new course option, whether it offered a greater sense of agency and whether they felt it appropriately matched their needs. Were students seeing Accelerated English as an option that removed barriers to their academic progress or that presented new barriers to their success? The survey results indicated that students were primarily divided between two competing factors: support and time to degree. The remaining multiple-choice responses were divided among several different options, including an Other category, in which several students essentially repeated a concept in one of the predetermined options. For example, one student clicked on Other but then typed, "The test score showed I am on level 4, which is 123," which effectively repeats the content of a predetermined answer option. In such cases, we have included their text-based answer with the other answers to the corresponding multiple-choice option.

As we see below, students enrolled in Accelerated English were split between choosing faster academic progress and finding support for their English development. We also see that, of the respondents taking English 123, two would have preferred Accelerated English. Similarly, of the students taking Accelerated English, eight were eligible for English 101 but chose to take a six-credit course rather than waiting to take

Table 9.1.

Primary Reason for Taking Accelerated English				
I wanted to finish the English composition requirements faster.	I wanted the extra time and support.	I needed at least 12 credits.	A friend or advisor told me I should take it.	All the English 101 classes were full.
25% (n = 21)	24% (n = 20)	15% (n = 13)	11% (n = 9)	9% (n = 8)

Primary Reason for Taking English 123				
The test said I needed it.	I didn't feel confident to take English 101 yet.	It comes after English 122.	All of the Accel. English classes were full.	My advisor told me I had to take it after English 122.
36% (n = 5)	14% (n = 2)	14% (n = 2)	14% (n = 2)	7% (n = 1)

English 101 the following semester. Their motivation could be either to progress through the required course sequence faster or to get the support they thought would be helpful for them.

We were particularly interested to learn through interviews how varying pressures and motivations impacted students' decisions and how residency status, financial support, and personal needs might be creating competing pressures. In order to establish a better understanding of what our students need, we asked the students open-ended questions revolving around the following topics:

1. What are the advantages and disadvantages of these two course options—English 123 and Accelerated English?

2. What pressures and motivations guide students' curricular decisions?

COMPETING FORCES: EXPEDIENCY AND SUPPORT

Expediency

Information gathered from these interviews supports scholarship that argues students are better served through multiple course options aligned for a multiplicity of student needs (Silva 1994) and that these options should be part of a curricular structure that allows for optimal conditions for agency (Saenkhum 2012; Shapiro et al. 2016). One argument for multiple options stems from the fact that many students make decisions based on expediency. Many of our students are financially supported through government sponsorships that impose restrictive time frames that do not always support student success. Short of arranging a series of meetings with the ministries of higher education in Saudi Arabia and Kuwait to protest such restrictions, we must recognize the reality that many students—from all national backgrounds—are pushed or push themselves to move more quickly through FYW requirements than taking the two pre-101 courses would allow. When we asked students about the motivations that drove their course preference, several indicated time constraints as the number one concern driving their decision, as the following excerpts from different interviews reveal.

> *Fahad:* I am already late. I'm twenty-one years now. And I need to finish my studies faster. So I chose [Accelerated English][2] as an option.[3]
>
> *Abdul:* Lots of pressure. I have bad luck, honestly . . . I don't want to be like out of track because you know I'm sponsored by Kuwait Cultural Office and I have like four years to finish engineering classes and get my degree.
>
> *Chantara:* I want to finish, because I want to find a job. My friend they graduate already and they have a job. . . . Because maybe I use my parent's money, I don't have my own money . . . and [I want to] help them too.

These students' experiences echo what we hear from many international students. In fact, some interviewees shared that they would be willing to take any course that might expedite their time to degree. We find our students actively seek out programs that meet that need, even if it requires looking outside the scope of our course menu and finding another institution. These same students might ignore the advice of the placement test or their advisors and choose a route that would not provide the support Accelerated English does. Because most of the Saudi and Kuwaiti-sponsored students at Boise State are under similar pressures, they share information with each other on which trajectories are going to get them to finish faster. These tensions between expediency and available options makes it difficult to create optimal conditions for greater student agency when students are willing to do anything to get through the degree faster.

Support

Another motivation students in our study expressed, seemingly contradictory to their desire to push quickly through their degrees, was the desire for support for their language development and their academic success. In fact, some of the same students who were at first primarily motivated by the desire for a shorter time to degree described the benefits of Accelerated English—particularly in the kinds of support it provided. Chantara, for example, came to understand that that course provided considerable support, although she had some initial reservations about the impact on her time to degree and indicated she would have chosen an English 101 section if one had been available. However, as she said approximately four or five weeks into the course, "I get used to it. . . . The second [hour] we have an activity to work on our homework or assignment, and if we don't understand we can ask [my teacher]. I feel relaxed." Even Fahad, who was willing to take any class at all that would accelerate the time to degree, said that he thought Accelerated English would be easier than English 101 and, on reflection, said it was an appropriate level for him. Abdul, who talked about having only four years to finish his BS in engineering, later recognized that for some students, "It is possible to get into 101, but they will have a lot of problems."

The survey results also indicated that, for some respondents, having extra support and extended classroom time took precedence over the need for expediency. Twenty of the students in Accelerated English wanted that time and support, and two of the students in English 123 chose that option specifically to give them more time before attempting English 101. The interviews further revealed that one of the more appealing forms of support was provided by multilingual-only designated courses. In explaining their reasons, students identified working with multilingual classmates and having a trained second language writing instructor as two key benefits of taking either English 123 or Accelerated English over mainstream sections of English 101. Echoing the findings of George Braine (1996) and Kimberly Costino and Sunny Hyon (2007), Abdul expressed this position well.

> Being with international students is much easier than being with native speakers. I'm not afraid [of native English speakers]. I lived with a host family, but it is different to be in a class with native speakers versus hanging out with them.

Chantara shared a similar point.

> With international student, I can talk to them, but if American people, I'm afraid to talk some word. I study economics, not too many international student. I talk with them not too much. . . . But if I talk with international student, I can talk comfortable. Maybe next semester I will can talk more comfortable with American people.

This apprehension to participate with native English speakers was expressed by others we spoke with and reflects the belief held by many multilingual students that their English will mark them as outsiders, indicating that they must contend with a pervasive monolingualist ideology among their professors as well as their classmates (see also Blommaert and Verschueren 1998; Ruecker 2011; Shuck 2006). Students can feel apprehensive even in cross-cultural sections taught by faculty who integrate sound, multilingual-friendly strategies into the course design. Many international students, then, prefer multilingual-only designated sections until they have more confidence that not sounding like a native English speaker is not a deficit. Although other studies have shown some multilingual students prefer to be in classes with native English speakers if they have the option (Braine 1996; Saenkhum 2012), most students in our sample echoed what Fahad said about multilingual-only sections: "There is no disadvantage."

In a similar way, students preferred Accelerated English because they felt the instructor would understand international students better. Abdul, who tested into 101 but chose Accelerated English told us,

> I was more caring about a professor that I want to talk in. Like there are some professors who know I am international, and they, you know, like deal with you differently because they know that you are not a native speaker and there are some words that you can't understand and you know these things. So I was more care about finding a teacher who can . . . who like Arabian people.

Abdul highlighted a concern that some instructors would not account for language difference or provide any support. We do have faculty who actively resist training opportunities, even some who express outright racist beliefs in the classroom. These dispositions do not resonate with the institutional ethos we are calling for, nor do they reflect our university's mission statement to serve local and global communities. Many students, however, have experienced such responses from faculty, which seem to be leading students away from mainstream course offerings when options are available. The same student-created network of information that guides students toward faster routes to graduation also actively shares information about which instructors understand the needs of international students. During interviews, students consistently offered the names of specific teachers, and enrolling in their courses became a primary motivation that would lead them to consider English 123 if Accelerated English was unavailable.

Having pre-FYW courses specifically for English learners offers students opportunities to learn and engage at different speeds. Students who were enrolled in English 123 often saw the course as a stepping stone or as an opportunity to learn at a slower pace. Shadha, a social worker from Iraq, appreciated the encouragement she received from her English 123 teacher and said her goal is to pursue psychology or social work, but only "if I feel comfortable holding the language in my hand." For her, "holding the language in [her] hand" described a level of confidence in her English proficiency. It seemed to us that such an image also captures the kind of care for language development and the acceptance of students' L1 linguistic resources a linguistically inclusive pedagogy would provide.

Jasem, sponsored by his employer in Kuwait, first tried to get into Accelerated English, despite his English 101 placement, since he wanted additional support. When he discovered all the sections of Accelerated English were full, he enrolled in English 123 rather than waiting a semester for English 101. He continued in English 123 so he could take time to learn and be in an environment with fewer consequences for his grade-point average.

> I can do more. I can take English 101 and I can make good papers, but as what I planned, I want to start from the basic. I want to take all the trickies, everything, yeah. . . . For me, in my opinion, there is no disadvantage, I think there are too many benefits of that class, yes. Because it is fail and pass a class, I can do whatever I want. I want to learn. So I can write and getting wrong and getting feedback, so I don't think I will lose points. This is just to practice, practice, practice class.

For Jasem, the lower-stakes learning opportunity created an environment where he felt safe and able to take chances in his work. Developing at his own pace seems to be a primary motivation for him. He also expressed a degree of relief that a different pacing option was available, and because multiple options existed, he recognized his agency in choosing among them. As he described at another point in the interview, a seat in Accelerated English became available just before the semester started, and yet he chose to stay in English 123. As a parent of three children, he felt the six-credit load of Accelerated English created a high-stakes concern that if his children became sick, he might fail the class due to absences and threaten renewal of his student visa.

Students perceived the high stakes of a six-credit course differently. Through these interviews, we noticed how quickly word of mouth spreads among international students, which has highlighted a gap between how we describe these course options and how students perceive them. Several students believed that Accelerated English was equivalent to two courses worth of work rather than three credits of English 101 and three credits of additional support. We have therefore identified new approaches to communicating the unique differences between course options, including better communication with Testing Services and our Advising and Academic Enhancement office. However, as our students have said, even with information, they may be pressured to pursue trajectories that are without support and not appropriate for their current level of English proficiency. Other students shared that they believed Accelerated English would be too much work at first or that taking six English credits might negatively impact their GPA in a single semester, but perspectives seem to be changing. Accelerated English is now in very high demand. As of the first week of classes in this third iteration of the course, we had five students enrolled in English 123 and fifty-seven students enrolled in Accelerated English.

PRELIMINARY PERFORMANCE DATA

In addition to the qualitative data on students' course choices, we also assessed the effectiveness of Accelerated English in preparing students for subsequent courses. In order for Accelerated English to be a viable option, it must be at least similar in success to the alternative path (English 123 → English 101 → English 102). We therefore compared the English 102 grades of the first cohort of Accelerated English enrollees with those of students who took the longer path. As the table below demonstrates, Accelerated English seems to be more than just a viable alternative. While we had a very small sample, which included several students with high enough English proficiency levels to place directly into English 101, we were pleased to learn that 43 percent (n = 21) received an A+, A, or A- at the end of the course. In comparison, students who had taken the track of English 123, English 101, and then English 102 actually had lower success rates, with 37 percent (n = 27) scoring an A+, A, or A- at the end of the course, but with the small sample size, we cannot claim statistical significance, and it is too soon to do more than speculate about why Accelerated English appears to be successful. However, these numbers are encouraging, lending justification to a proposal we are developing to continue offering Accelerated English as a permanent, rather than a pilot, course and confirming our belief that, with appropriate support, students can enter into university work more quickly and be successful.

Although the multilingual students who had taken Accelerated English or English 123 did not do as well overall in English 102 as the entire population of students did (58 percent of all English 102 students received an A or A- or A+ in English 102), this can be explained in part by the fact that most students in Accelerated English and English 123 came to Boise State with significantly lower English-proficiency levels than all those multilingual and monolingual students who begin their

Table 9.2. Grades in English 102, by course sequence.

Accelerated English → English 102		*Engl. 123 → Engl. 101 → Engl. 102*	
Received an A (incl. A– and A+)	43%	Received an A (incl. A– and A+)	37%
Received a D or F	10%	Received a D or F	11%

FYW sequence with English 101 or 101P. It would not be realistic to expect that their English repertoires would, after one or two semesters, have expanded so quickly that they would be up to all the demands of doing research, which is the focus of English 102, at the same pace and effectiveness as much more fluent speakers and writers. Moreover, there is no guarantee every English 102 instructor is fully prepared to be able to assess the students' work fairly or give English learners equal access to the full curriculum, despite Gail's best efforts to increase faculty support throughout the FYW program.

One additional finding that was striking is that thirty-nine students who took Accelerated English in spring 2015 did not choose to take English 102 in a subsequent semester. It would seem to contradict our survey respondents' claims that finishing the requirements faster is their primary motivation. Perhaps if we interviewed the students who have not yet enrolled in English 102, we might discover students are less interested in expediency than our study suggests. However, we have heard from several students outside this study that they waited to enroll in English 102 for two reasons: (1) they wish to make more progress in other degree requirements—especially in math—and (2) they worry their English has not yet improved sufficiently to handle the research requirements in English 102. Our small quantitative assessment shows this latter concern may be unfounded. However, it also suggests that providing a section of English 102 with a higher level of language support would be desirable.

IMPLICATIONS AND CONCLUSION

A multilingual lens requires several dimensions that are both challenging to envision and unsettling to enact. We do not pretend one addition to the FYW curriculum will be the only way toward the "Promised Land." Moving toward a new way of seeing linguistic diversity as an asset requires time, patience, and education, and we hope within our local context that Accelerated English, and more broadly, this multifaceted approach to curricular design, might become a springboard for other educators to consider. Such efforts require an institution-wide, concerted effort to value student contributions at the forefront of the conversation—a conversation that requires us to adopt a multilingual lens and challenge the myth of linguistic homogeneity (Matsuda 2006). Monolingualist practices, sustained by white, upper-class privilege, have impacted second language writers across the globe, limiting the voices we hear in research. If we can challenge such practices by offering a menu of sufficient and appropriate course options, we can begin to account for the complexity—of needs, of linguistic and cultural backgrounds, of motivations, of contexts—that come into play as students chart their own educational paths.

Our study further suggests we should provide systematic ways to consider student voices not only as we design L2 writing research (Cox et al. 2010; Leki 2001) but also as we develop and assess institutional practices that could meet the complexity of student needs more effectively (Crusan 2010; Royer and Gilles 1998). Thus, we have attempted to create campus-wide opportunities for multilingual students to speak to administrators and lend their voices to the larger conversation, shedding light on tensions and opportunities (see also Shuck 2004). A student panel educating faculty about supportive pedagogical strategies can do more to effect ideological change than days of faculty training (see also Howard 2003). Such conversations at our university are engaging new cross-campus partners in thinking about how we might integrate support more broadly throughout the campus and widen the path toward a more inclusive future.

Notes

1. The cumbersome course title is in part an accommodation to the Saudi Arabian Cultural Mission's (the government-scholarship managers') request to have *101* appear on the scholarship recipients' transcripts.
2. Students used the course number, which is a temporary university designation for pilot courses.
3. Excerpts from interviews are unedited from the original transcripts. We support student agency in making language choices as well as course choices.

References

Adams, Peter, Sarah Gearhart, Robert Miller, and Anne Roberts. 2009. "The Accelerated Learning Program: Throwing Open the Gates." *Journal of Basic Writing* 28 (2): 50–69.
Blommaert, Jan, and Jef Verschueren. 1998. "The Role of Language in European Nationalist Ideologies." In *Language Ideologies: Practice and Theory*, edited by Bambi Schieffelin, Kathryn Woolard, and Paul Kroskrity, 189–210. New York: Oxford University Press.

Braine, George. 1996. "ESL Students in First-Year Writing Courses: ESL Versus Mainstream Classes." *Journal of Second Language Writing* 5 (2): 91–107. https://doi.org /10.1016/S1060-3743(96)90020-X.

Canagarajah, A. Suresh. 2013. *Translingual Practice: Global Englishes and Cosmopolitan Relations.* London: Routledge.

Conference on College Composition and Communication (CCCC). 2009. "Statement on Second-Language Writing and Writers." http://www.ncte.org/cccc/resources/posi tions/secondlangwriting.

Costino, Kimberly, and Sunny Hyon. 2007. "'A Class for Students Like Me': Reconsidering Relationships among Identity Labels, Residency Status, and Students' Preferences for Mainstream or Multilingual Composition." *Journal of Second Language Writing* 16 (2): 63–81. https://doi.org/10.1016/j.jslw.2007.04.001.

Cox, Michelle. 2014. "Response to Today's 'Felt Need': WAC, Faculty Development, and Second Language Writers." In *WAC and Second Language Writers: Research towards Linguistically and Culturally Inclusive Programs and Practices,* edited by Terry Myers Zawacki and Michelle Cox, 299–326. Fort Collins, CO: WAC Clearinghouse.

Cox, Michelle, Jay Jordan, Christina Ortmeier-Hooper, and Gwen Gray Schwartz, eds. 2010. *Reinventing Identities in Second Language Writing.* Urbana, IL: NCTE.

Crusan, Deborah. 2010. *Assessment in the Second Language Writing Classroom.* Ann Arbor: University of Michigan Press. https://doi.org/10.3998/mpub.770334.

Ferris, Dana R. 2009. *Teaching College Writing to Diverse Student Populations.* Ann Arbor: University of Michigan Press. https://doi.org/10.3998/mpub.263445.

Hamp-Lyons, Liz, ed. 1991. *Assessing Second Language Writing in Academic Contexts.* Norwood, NJ: Ablex.

Howard, Rebecca M. 2003. "WPAs and/versus Administrators: Using Multimedia Rhetoric to Promote Shared Premises for Writing Instruction." *WPA: Writing Program Administration* 27 (1–2): 9–22.

Kroll, Barbara. 2006. "Toward a Promised Land of Writing: At the Intersection of Hope and Reality." In *The Politics of Second Language Writing,* edited by Paul Kei Matsuda, Christina Ortmeier-Hooper, and Xiaoye You, 297–305. West Lafayette, IN: Parlor.

Leki, Ilona. 2001. "Hearing Voices: L2 Students' Experiences in L2 Writing Courses." In *On Second Language Writing,* edited by Tony Silva and Paul Kei Matsuda, 17–28. Mahwah, NJ: Lawrence Erlbaum.

Matsuda, Paul K. 2006. "The Myth of Linguistic Homogeneity in U.S. College Composition." *College English* 68 (6): 637–51. https://doi.org/10.2307/25472180.

Peckham, Irvin. 2006. "Turning Placement into Practice." *WPA: Writing Program Administration* 29 (3): 65–83.

Rose, Mike. 1985. "The Language of Exclusion: Writing Instruction at the University." *College English* 47 (4): 341–59. https://doi.org/10.2307/376957.

Royer, Daniel, and Roger Gilles. 1998. "Directed Self-Placement: An Attitude of Orientation." *College Composition and Communication* 50 (1): 54–70. https://doi.org/10 .2307/358352.

Ruecker, Todd. 2011. "Challenging the Native and Nonnative English Speaker Hierarchy in ELT: New Directions from Race Theory." *Critical Inquiry in Language Studies* 8 (4): 400–422. https://doi.org/10.1080/15427587.2011.615709.

Saenkhum, Tanita. 2012. "Investigating Agency in Multilingual Writers' Placement Decisions: A Case Study of the Writing Programs at Arizona State University." PhD diss., Arizona State University.

Shapiro, Shawna, Michelle Cox, Gail Shuck, and Emily Simnitt. 2016. "Teaching for Agency: From Appreciating Linguistic Diversity to Empowering Student Writers." *Composition Studies* 44 (1): 31–52.

Shuck, Gail. 2004. "Ownership of Text, Ownership of Language: Two Students' Participation in a Student-Run Conference." *Reading Matrix* 4 (3): 24–39. http://www.readingmatrix.com/articles/shuck/article.pdf.

Shuck, Gail. 2006. "Combating Monolingualism: A Novice Administrator's Challenge." *WPA: Writing Program Administration* 30 (1–2): 59–82.

Silva, Tony. 1994. "An Examination of Writing Program Administrators' Options for the Placement of ESL Students in First-Year Writing Classes." *WPA: Writing Program Administration* 18 (1–2): 37–43.

Zamel, Vivian. 1995. "Strangers in Academia: The Experiences of Faculty and ESL Students Across the Curriculum." *College Composition and Communication* 46 (4): 506–21. https://doi.org/10.2307/358325.

10

INTERCULTURAL COMMUNICATION AND TEAMWORK
Revising Business Writing for Global Networks

Heidi A. McKee

Like many institutions, Miami University has seen a significant increase in international student enrollment, particularly from China. In 2005, international students comprised less than 1 percent of undergraduates; in fall 2015 they were 11.4 percent, or 1,875 of 16,447 students. The majority of undergraduate international students at Miami are enrolled in the Farmer School of Business (FSB). In the FSB, I direct the Howe Writing Initiative (HWI), a center that administers three interrelated programs for the school: WAC/WID, writing center, and business writing.

As of fall 2012, when I was appointed director of the HWI, the business writing program consisted of a one-credit business writing course required of all first-year FSB students (n = ~1,000 per year) that, because of the constraints of such a course, primarily focused on rhetorical concepts and approaches for shorter business communications (e.g., memos, cover letters, short bad news messaging). In this limited curriculum there was no space for in-depth discussion of many essential areas of business communication. In this chapter, I discuss the transformation of this one-credit program into a five-credit, multiyear comprehensive business communication program with an integrated writing and speaking curriculum that, among other things, focuses extensively on intercultural communication and teamwork so as to better meet the learning needs of all students, international and domestic alike.

Given the importance of collaboration and teamwork in all fields—teamwork is often identified as the top skill employers seek in employees (NACE 2014)—and given the increasingly global and intercultural environments in which people live, learn, and work, it is essential that writing program administrators adapt programs so as to better prepare students for working in teams and communicating across cultures. Making the case

DOI: 10.7330/9781607326762.c010

for such changes and then building the networks and support for such changes is tricky, but doable, calling for research and assessment, partnership building, and some fortuitous realignment of institutional priorities.

The influx of international students at Miami has generated tremendous positive impacts on academics and provided the catalyst for making important and much-needed changes to our business writing program. After discussing the data and process of building the new program, I overview intercultural communication competencies, particularly in relation to teamwork, that shape the new curriculum. I close with some reflections and recommendations that may be adaptable for those working in other contexts.

THE CATALYST: DOMESTIC AND INTERNATIONAL STUDENT PERSPECTIVES ON INTERCULTURAL TEAMWORK

Recognizing the changing demographic of Miami and recognizing the importance of research for program design and development (Rose and Weiser 1999), in spring 2013 the HWI assistant directors (Amir Hassan, Kevin Rutherford, Jonathan Rylander) and I designed and sent a survey to all 453 international students enrolled in FSB at the time to gather their perspectives and experiences around business communications. A key finding that emerged from the sixty responses received was that international students struggled particularly with teamwork. Because the international students did not write extensive responses to open-ended questions, we decided to conduct interviews to gather more in-depth understanding of their experiences and perceptions. A graduate student in educational leadership, Han Han, joined our project, and she interviewed nineteen international students, twelve of whom were from China. She interviewed the Chinese students in Mandarin and then translated and transcribed the interviews. Han Han and I shared de-identified results from the interviews and surveys with the International Student Advisory Council, an FSB student committee that at the time reported to the dean. The twenty members of the council who met with us discussed the experiences of international students with teamwork, and they recommended we continue our research to include domestic students because, in their words, "We want to know what American students think about working with us."

This was an excellent and important suggestion. Too often the discussion about the increase of international students at US colleges and universities has focused on the international students—what they need to do to adapt to US educational institutions, what the institutions need to do to support them—without as much discussion of the ways in which we all must change. Our first research design is an example of this tendency—we started our research with a focus on international students instead of thinking of all students. What the international student responses emphasized and now a key point that shapes our revised business communication curriculum is the fact that effective teaching and learning about intercultural communication and teamwork must involve everyone—domestic and international students alike (and faculty as well). We are all global citizens, and we all must reflect on and adapt our communication practices.

Guided by the council's advice, the HWI team adapted the survey and sent it to 850 domestic students (chosen randomly and evenly distributed across all class levels and majors). Of the eighty-three responses received, domestic students also identified teamwork as an area with which they struggled. In particular, domestic students identified that working with international students was challenging. (We chose not to interview domestic students because they wrote such in-depth responses to open-ended questions.)

The student perspectives gathered from the surveys and interviews have been helpful as we have revised writing center and WAC/WID programming, and these responses centrally shaped our revisions to the business writing program.

In their interviews, many students from China discussed how important the early interactions in team meetings were and how they often felt the need to gain domestic students' approval and to show domestic students their "value." I quote extensively throughout this section because as WPAs we must listen carefully and most fully to students, our most important stakeholders. The perspectives of the students quoted here showcase key dynamics at work in intercultural teams, especially in student teams.

- It is very important to get approved at the beginning, let them [domestic students] know your strength, like provide idea, or basic data, get the recognition.
- I think the most difficult part is at the beginning, when others do not know you. I feel like that I need to tell them I am qualified. But after others know you, that would be easy, they will know what you are good at, and let you do what you are good at. When everyone become friend, the teamwork is pretty enjoyable.
- At the beginning, if you didn't speak out, you will be ignored. You have to ask what they are talking about. After a few contributions, your teammates will realize your value.

- At the beginning, as you are international student, the American students may think you can't speak English or not speak English very well. They may feel it would be hard to communicate with you, and [they] do not know what you are good at. There might be some Chinese students who do not speak very much in teamwork, they may be afraid to say something wrong. Then the Americans will think they can't help, and then they are gradually excluded from the teamwork, making the teamwork unpleasant. But if you begin to communicate with them at the beginning, tell them who you are, and what you are good at, and not good at, build the relationship through communication, then it will be much more convenient in the later collaboration.

International students recognize, perhaps more keenly than domestic students, how important those first team interactions are, especially because they feel the domestic students may have biases against international students.

From these insights, colleagues and I took away a number of key points that are also emphasized often in the scholarship on teamwork and on intercultural communication: the importance of team-building activities early in the team process and the importance of ensuring team members know more about and value what each member brings to the collaboration (e.g., Staggers, Garcia, and Nagelhout 2008; Vik 2001; Wolfe 2010). Significantly, such team-building and team- and individual-valuing work is essential not just for intercultural communication across language and country of origin but also across all areas of difference. What often complicates intercultural teamwork, however, is the key point students allude to about cultural bias at work. When someone comes into a collaboration with preconceived assumptions about how someone will be as a team member, that certainly hinders effective teamwork. As Kenneth Burke (1966) noted, we each view the world through terministic screens that limit and shape what we know and how we know it, and Miami certainly isn't alone in experiencing many students and faculty (both domestic and international) who carry cultural biases and misperceptions about people from cultural backgrounds and countries of origin other than their own.

Both domestic and international students expressed frustration at the miscommunication and misunderstandings that often occurred in the teamwork they experienced.

- I have a really hard time understanding their ideas and language. The Asian students especially. They do good work though. They always work hard and try a lot, but I just have a hard time understanding them.—*student from the United States*
- Everyone feels we have really great teamwork. I feel really confused. American students are so weird. —*student from China*

- [International students] act like they do not understand and want to just sit back while everyone else does the work. —*student from the United States*
- They [domestic students] want to exclude us and hang out with their friends. Their attitude is not right. They don't want to know us and don't care about it. If they show a little bit passion, it will help a lot when they communicate with international students. We can speak English well enough to go school here, which demonstrate that we are not idiots. We should learn from each other. —*student from China*
- Sometimes I get a feeling that they don't want to work with me, or other American students. —*student from the United States*
- Some international students have understandably poor communication skills and are often a challenge to work with. I often feel like I have to do more work when I work with an international student. —*student from the United States*

In this representative sampling, student responses reveal cultural biases at work. As I'll discuss below, all English is English with an accent, but many domestic students don't see it that way—they hear or read English with an unfamiliar accent and think, erroneously, that the rhetor isn't as capable a student as a native English speaker.

In addition, cultural misunderstandings occur around the very nature of what it means to work in a team—how teamwork should or could be conducted.

- For every group, everyone has his strength, the point is, you need to know in your group, what is your strength, then play your role. And that would be fair, since everyone contributes. I would tell them I am smart, if you give me the question, I would have a lot of ideas, but I am not good at writing. And then the Americans would say "I will do the writing then." And I was like just let them do it. I think it was a good combination; it offset everyone's shortcomings. —student from China
- It is much harder working with them [international students] because they often do not speak English well. This causes for them doing minimal work, and the Americans getting burdened with the harder, longer tasks. We do this because we have the comparative advantage, and want to get the best grade, even though it means a lot more work for us. —student from the United States
- International students are arrogant and try to tell everybody what to do. They think they know everything and it inhibits the group from learning. It's their way or the highway. —student from the United States
- [American students'] attitude is just so-so. They just assume what I said is nothing. They just assume they don't understand what I am talking about. So in this situation, if you think you are right, you have to insist that you are right. —student from China

When designing writing program curriculum for all students, it's imperative, then, to open up all areas of the curriculum to cultural analysis and scrutiny—why this way and not this way? Is this a "US/Western" thing? Are there other ways to approach a particular process and project? This type of scrutiny and analysis takes work and takes the ability to step outside one's own terministic screen. As one student from the United States described,

- I think my main take-away is that all team members have to be willing to adjust communication styles in order to operate effectively on international teams, but a lot of Miami students (American and international alike) aren't ready to make that commitment.

Given the significant increase of international students at Miami and given the diverse, intercultural environments in which students will work—regardless of field and regardless of geographic locale—clearly more than a one-credit business writing class was needed. But this research data was only one piece in making the case to transform the program. What was also essential was assessment data.

MAKING THE CASE FOR CHANGE: ADDING ASSESSMENT DATA TO THE MIX

Assessment is, of course, invaluable for WPAs. How do we know whether what we're doing is working? How do we know what to change and improve in our programs? How do we showcase to our many stakeholders the value of what we do? Assessment lets us do that.

So, equipped with the valuable, but by itself insufficient, data from the international and domestic students' surveys and interviews, I then set about working with colleagues in FSB to conduct a number of assessments of students' written and oral communications. While these assessments are not centered on international issues per se, I briefly discuss them because without these assessments, revisions to the program may not have happened—or at least not as extensively.

In spring 2013, and again in spring 2015, we conducted a direct assessment of student portfolios from BUS 102, the one-credit business writing course. The portfolios contained all five of the projects students completed in the course. In addition to providing data related to the course outcomes, reading 10 percent of all portfolios highlighted just how limiting a one-credit class is. In the assessment reports we submitted to the dean and associate deans (the writing program in FSB is not in a department but instead reports directly to the deans), we emphasized how inadequate a one-credit course is. Areas we were not able to include in the curriculum or not include extensively enough included writing research-based reports and proposals, writing with quantitative data, working with tables and figures, writing for presentations, and, important, team research and writing. In the 2013 assessment report, we advocated that "we now have multiple data points indicating that writing curriculum and instruction in the FSB needs to be expanded. . . . Further assessment and study of FSB student writing are needed, especially of student writing in upper division courses."

Fortunately (because of the opportunities it created for program revision), the FSB was due in spring 2016 for its accreditation report and review from the American Association of Colleges and Schools of Business (AACSB), and several years prior to the site visit the dean had appointed an assessment director to coordinate program-specific and division-wide assessments. I eagerly accepted the invitation to serve on the assessment committee and worked closely with administrators, HWI assistant directors (Kathleen Coffey, Dustin Edwards, and Bridget Gelms), and faculty in all six departments to conduct direct assessments of student writing and presentations (including team presentations) and indirect assessments of students' teamwork in senior capstones.

A number of interesting findings resulted. The direct assessment of writing showed in part how many teams of students struggled with longer, research-based writing; many of the team reports read like "Franken-reports," individual sections cobbled together without cohesion or consistency. The direct assessment of presentations—members of the assessment team attended classes to view and score presentations in person—showed that of the 149 seniors observed presenting, many, both domestic and international, struggled with how to present cohesively as a team and how to tailor the content and delivery of both team and individual presentations to appropriate business audiences. Given the curriculum, this finding wasn't surprising. Under the then-current curriculum, in addition to the one-credit business writing course, all FSB students were required to take a three-credit public-speaking course, a course not tailored to business taught by the speech communication program (and subsequently by the strategic communication program).

Another important part of the assessment was an indirect assessment in which the instructors of the capstones were asked to rate each student, and all capstone students were asked to rate themselves and their teammates for several criteria related to their ability to engage in some common teamwork and collaboration skills. The criteria, taken from FSB's divisional outcomes for collaboration,[1] were "establish norms," "listen effectively," "generate ideas," "organize and lead," "build

Table 10.1. Instructor and student ratings for ability to negotiate conflict (4 = excellent; 3 = good; 2 = adequate; 1 = poor; 0 = fails).

	Instructor rating of students	Student rating of teammates	Student rating of self
Ability to negotiate conflict	1.53	2.94	3.19

consensus," "give and receive feedback," and "negotiate conflict." The five-point scale used for this rating was 0-fails to demonstrate, 1-poor, 2-adequate, 3-good, and 4-excellent. Bridget Gelms, an HWI assistant director, led the assessment data analysis, providing the assessment team with innumerable spreadsheets aggregating and comparing the data in a variety of ways. Not surprisingly, instructors rated students lower in all areas than students rated themselves or their teammates, and students rated themselves higher than they rated their teammates. But one area of commonality was that for instructors and students, the lowest rated criterion was "negotiate conflict."[2] Table 10.1 shows this criterion and the average of the instructor ratings, the student ratings of their team- mates, and the student ratings of themselves.

Instructors gave the most 0s and 1s in this category, and no instruc- tor gave any person a rating of 4-excellent in this category (whereas instructors did give 4s in other categories). Students had higher ratings in "negotiate conflict" and gave more 4s (43.8 percent for self and 35.7 percent for other), but they also gave more 0s and 1s. In fact, this is the only criterion for which any student (for self or for other) gave a 0 or a 1, demonstrating that students see the ability to negotiate conflict as being a high need area in their peers and themselves.

Given the issues students articulated in the interview and survey research around intercultural communication and differing cultural understandings of how to work in a team, it's not surprising "negotiate conflict" was the lowest rated criterion.

CONFLUENCE OF INSTITUTIONAL INITIATIVES AND OPPORTUNITIES

A number of other factors came into play in the substantial transforma- tion of the FSB business writing program. I don't go into great detail here so as to keep the focus on the discussion of building intercultural communication and teamwork into the new curriculum, but let me mention some of these initiatives because ultimately these were what created the space for the new curriculum—the research and assessment then provided what to do in that space.

In 2013, Miami faculty voted to revise the Global Miami Plan, and part of the revision is that now every student is required to complete an advanced-writing requirement—a 200- or 300-level three-credit writing course that may be selected from an array of options across the disciplines. At the same time, in fall of 2014, the new dean of the Farmer School of Business called for a review of the FSB's divisional core—the required courses all business majors take. Given the need for WPAs to be involved in key decision-making committees, I again accepted the invitation to serve on the core-curriculum committee. Over the course of eighteen months, colleagues from all programs in business discussed and developed new curriculum for FSB's core. In those discussions I shared the research and assessment findings summarized above, especially addressing all the learning needs the current curriculum was not meeting. Fortunately, colleagues in the FSB recognized and valued the importance of communication and supported revising and extending the program. They saw too the pragmatic benefit of having students' Miami Plan advanced-writing requirement be a business communication course in the FSB's core, a "double dipper" so to speak.

Working with students, faculty, staff, department chairs, and deans in both the Farmer School of Business and the College of Arts and Science, we developed a new business communication program that is comprised now of a two-credit BUS 102 Foundations of Business Communication course required of first-year FSB majors and a three-credit BUS/ENG/STC Advanced Business Communication required of second-year FSB majors. BUS 102 is taught exclusively by business communication faculty in the FSB, while 308 is taught by faculty from the FSB and from strategic communications and by faculty and doctoral students from English.

In this scaffolded, integrated program, each of the courses focuses on helping students identify and develop the rhetorical knowledge and strategies (including process-based composing strategies) for business that will be adaptable and transferable to many contexts. To that end, students in both courses write and present in a variety of business genres and for a variety of scenario-based business contexts. As noted, a particular emphasis of the curriculum is on intercultural communication and collaboration, providing students with direct instruction in how to approach written and oral communications in culturally aware and rhetorically appropriate ways, and with direct instruction in how to research, write, and present with others. What our research showed us loud and clear was that all students need opportunities to build their intercultural-communication competencies, and we have tried to develop a curriculum that is responsive to changing institutional demographics and, more important, to the diverse dynamics of academic, professional, and civic communities.

We fully launch our new curriculum in the fall of 2016, but colleagues and I have piloted a number of sections of the new sophomore-level course, and the discussion that follows is drawn from our experiences to date. As with any responsive program, our business communication curriculum is always evolving, especially in these first years of launching the new program. So I don't go into all the ways we're trying to infuse the curriculum with greater opportunities for developing intercultural competencies. Instead I focus on some key concepts and approaches we made and some key elements we included, particularly around team-work, explaining the rationale for the decisions and providing some scholarship that informed and continues to inform our work.

FOSTERING INTERCULTURAL COMMUNICATION AND COLLABORATION: SOME KEY CONCEPTS AND STRATEGIES

Recognize That All English Is Accented English

All English is English with an accent. This is a key point we discuss with all students. For international students, this discussion helps give them confidence that it is okay to speak and write with an accent. Many international students are reluctant rhetors in English, especially for oral presentations, because of concerns about their English-speaking skills. What we emphasize is that speaking with an accent is just fine as long as vocal delivery (e.g., articulation, pacing, volume, etc.) are clear and appropriate for audience, context, and purpose. For domestic students for whom English is their first language (which is most of the domestic population at Miami), emphasizing that all English is English with an accent raises their awareness that the English they speak is accented as well. Too often domestic students in the United States, especially those immersed in all the unrecognized benefits of both white privilege and class privilege, view their language usage as the norm from which all other usage approaches are seen as lacking. One of our goals is to diversify all students' understanding of what is acceptable English in global business contexts.

Analyze Cultural Frames

Recognizing the diversity of English is just one part of recognizing a broader, more essential point: that each of our particular cultural frames shapes what we expect and what we do in our communications and interactions and how we judge and evaluate others. You are not me, and that's especially true if we're from different cultures. Here's where, of course, rhetoric is essential. When students are provided with a variety of communication scenarios and asked to analyze them from multiple perspectives, they have the opportunity to develop greater awareness that their perspective and approach are not the only possibilities. The goal here is to develop what James Neuliep (2012) calls "cultural mindfulness": "To be *mindful,* people must recognize that strangers may use different perspectives to understand or explain interaction. When we are *mindless,* we tend to assume that strangers interpret our messages the same way as we do" (4).

What often happens—and you can see this in the student quotations shared above—is that people bring to all venues expectations shaped by their culture. When their expectations aren't met, they often don't look to their own perceptions as the problem but instead blame the others who aren't working or communicating the way they think they should. This is what Xiaohong Wei (2009) describes as negative cultural transfer, which

> occurs in all processes of intercultural communication and . . . refers to the cultural interference caused by cultural differences, which shows that people subconsciously use their cultural norms and values not only to guide their behaviors and thoughts but also to judge others' behaviors and thoughts. . . . Negative cultural transfer often results in communicative difficulties, misunderstandings and even hatred.

Negative cultural transfer often occurs in teamwork and team communications.

Build Trust in Teams and Teammates

Individual understandings of what a team is and how it should function are very much shaped by our culture and country of origin (Gibson and Zellmer-Bruhn 2001). If your understanding of how a team should function, for example, is different from mine and we never discuss the fundamentally differing understandings that we hold, we're going to have a harder time working as a team, and the opportunity for misunderstandings will be even greater. For this reason, as with the curricula of most professional communication programs, we designed a curriculum to emphasize the importance of team building. You can't engage in teamwork until you've built a team, as so many scholars and researchers have shown (e.g., Staggers, Garcia, Nagelhout 2008; Wolfe 2010) and as one of the students described above: "When everyone become friend, the teamwork is pretty enjoyable." While we recognize that teammates may not necessarily all become friends, they do need to have a level of familiarity and trust with each other, trust that each cares about the project and trust that each has something important and substantial to bring to the collaboration (Zemliansky 2012). Such trust building requires time—significant class time early in the process for students to be able to work and discuss together their ideas for the project. For virtual teams—and we do intend to offer completely online sections of 102 and 308—this trust building is even more important because it is often harder virtually to build that trust, which is so essential for effective intercultural teamwork (Jarvenpaa, Shaw, and Staples 2004; Porter 2017; Rush Hovde 2014).

To provide students the opportunities to build cultural mindfulness and familiarity and trust with each other, we designed a curriculum that focuses a great deal on team building. Spending time in early team-building activities and then later team reflective activities facilitates better communication and understanding not just for differences shaped by country of origin but also for differences shaped by many other areas such as gender, race, class, sexual orientation, intended profession, and so forth. Whether students are engaging in two-person partnerships in 102 or larger team projects in 308, we ask them to complete a self- and team inventory at the outset of a project. Over a couple of class periods, while planning their approaches to the project, students discuss a variety of questions and issues with their team, sharing their perspectives on how an ideal team should function, what roles team members might hold and which ones they prefer, what their working and communication styles are, what strengths and weaknesses they see themselves bringing to the team, and so forth. Teams also develop communication plans, conflict-resolution plans, and work plans. All these activities are, of course, pretty standard stuff in scholarship on what makes an effective team and for classes such as ours that aim to teach how to work as a team.[3] We intend to put a special emphasis on thinking about how one's cultural experiences shape expectations for teamwork. We share insights from research drawn from academic and professional presses so students have more language and frames for thinking about their approaches to teamwork and to intercultural communication. For example, students find it useful to discuss (based on instructor presentation of a synopsis of the study, not reading the whole article) the impact of leadership style on intercultural teams that has been studied by Jolanta Aritz and Robyn Walker, who found that "a more cooperative leadership style leads to more balanced contribution and participation of all members in the intercultural groups consisting of East Asian and US participants. The most commonly observed directive style representative of mixed groups showed a less balanced contribution and participation rate among all participants" (Aritz and Walker 2014, 87).

Develop Strategies for Negotiating Conflict

Learning how to negotiate conflict and leadership issues is key, too, and is an area we are continuing to build out in our curriculum. T. A. Fredrick's (2008) study of what models teams use for decision making and conflict resolution is helpful here and recognizes that one of the cultures in which all students are immersed is classroom culture. Fredrick found that student teams in professional communication courses often relied on two different models—a traditional, hierarchical teacher-student model, in which one member became the more dominant in the group, and a more collaborative, circular model in which all members discussed and shared and reached consensus on the decision. While Fredrick doesn't address intercultural differences directly, how students view the roles of consensus and dissensus in decision making is also important. One of the areas we emphasize to students is that all teams have dissensus sometimes—that's how ideas get generated, developed, pushed further—and it's a matter of finding a way to engage in vigorous discussions in which multiple viewpoints are discussed and debated without silencing anyone and without tipping from productive dissensus to unproductive dissensus. Asking students to reflect on their understandings of how decisions can and should and might be made is very helpful. In fact, reflection and dialogue are essential. Students need the time to pause and consider a number of questions: How are we doing as a team? How am I doing as a team member? What's going well from my perspective? What isn't? What do we and/or I need to change? In these discussions, it's important for instructors to facilitate and encourage so all voices and perspectives are shared because too often minority perspectives are stifled and majority perspectives dominate in group discussions.

There are, of course, other concepts I could discuss, but with the space remaining I turn to closing reflections for WPAs considering ways to adapt programs so as to better prepare all students for participating in diverse, globalized academic, civic, and professional contexts.

CLOSING REFLECTIONS

The increased presence of international students on US campuses should not be approached from a deficit model that looks only at international students (and through a biased lens at that). Changing dynamics and demographics on campus, in the workplace, in the public sphere call for all of us—regardless of our country of origin—to learn and change. As we revise, expand, and sustain our programs, we must be advocates for all students in our communications, our curricular design, our assessments, and our research.

To be such advocates, as WPAs we must engage in assessment and research in our local contexts and learn more about the scholarship around international students and intercultural communication (writing, speaking, digital, etc.). As the director of a writing center, a WAC/WID program, and a communications program, I encounter a fair share of misunderstanding and misperceptions among colleagues and domestic students about international students, so I find it incredibly beneficial to have research and assessment data to draw from and to be able to show, gently or forcefully depending on the context, how the challenges faculty and students (both domestic and international) might be feeling do not point to a deficit in international students but to areas where we all need to change and grow. And in terms of making program changes, having both assessment data and qualitative perception data has been valuable. The voices of the students gathered in interviews and surveys help explain more fully what outcomes assessment data might mean.

And we need to listen to students—listen carefully and continually so as to understand teaching and learning from their perspectives. In those perspectives, when we hear statements that perhaps make us cringe, as some of the statements quoted earlier in this chapter may do, the responsibility to address those statements and the attitudes they represent falls to us as program directors, curriculum designers, and classroom instructors. If students are struggling working with others different than themselves, it falls to us to try to change our curriculum and pedagogical practices so as to better prepare and help students. How can students be expected to communicate and collaborate effectively with others if they've never been taught how? Intercultural communication and teamwork is hard, especially because of the skills and strategies needed to consider ideas and approaches that may be different from the ones we experience in the cultures in which we're immersed. Too often, particularly in non-writing/communication courses, teamwork is assigned to students without direct instruction in how to work together as a team. Direct instruction is essential for any team, but it is particularly so for teams comprised of both domestic and international students. Situated as we are in programs that focus on communication, we are especially well positioned to both provide that direct instruction for students and reach out to help colleagues in that area as well.

We all have much to learn. The increase of international students at US institutions is a fantastic opportunity and a dynamic catalyst for changing our programs so as to better meet the learning needs of all students

Notes

1. The outcomes have since been revised, but in fall 2014 when this indirect assessment of collaboration was conducted, the outcomes were that students in the Farmer School of Business would be able to:

    Demonstrate effective team communication:

    - Establish team norms and set team goals.
    - Listen effectively.
    - Generate ideas and share information.
    - Organize and lead team meetings.
    - Build consensus to achieve goals.
    - Give and receive peer feedback.
    - Negotiate for conflict resolution.

2. Unfortunately, only two capstone instructors rated their students (probably because of the time-intensive nature and the timing of the task, seven criteria for each student at the busy end of the semester). However, 111 seniors did rate themselves and their peers, approximately 10 percent of the graduating class for the FSB.

3. For an excellent book about team writing, especially useful for undergraduate students, see Joanna Wolfe 2010.

References

Aritz, Jolanta, and Robyn Walker. 2014. "Leadership Styles in Multicultural Groups: Americans and East Asians Working Together." *International Journal of Business Communication* 51 (1): 72–92.

Burke, Kenneth. 1966. *Language as Symbolic Action: Essays on Life, Literature, and Method.* Berkeley: University of California Press.

Fredrick, T. A. 2008. "Facilitating Better Teamwork: Analyzing the Challenges and Strategies of Classroom-Based Collaboration." *Business Communication Quarterly* 71 (4): 439–55. https://doi.org/10.1177/1080569908325860.

Gibson, Christina B., and Mary E. Zellmer-Bruhn. 2001. "Metaphors and Meaning: An Intercultural Analysis of the Concept of Teamwork." *Administrative Science Quarterly* 46 (2): 274–303. https://doi.org/10.2307/2667088.

Jarvenpaa, Sirkka L., Thomas R. Shaw, and D. Sandy Staples. 2004. "Toward Contextualized Theories of Trust: The Role of Trust in Global Virtual Teams." *Information Systems Research* 15 (3): 250–67. https://doi.org/10.1287/isre.1040.0028.

NACE (National Association of Colleges and Employers. 2014. "2014 Job Outlook Survey." http://www.naceweb.org/404.aspx?aspxerrorpath=/s11122014/job-outlook-skills-qualities-employers-want.aspx.

Neuliep, James W. 2012. "The Relationship among Intercultural Communication Apprehension, Ethnocentrism, Uncertainty Reduction, and Communication Satisfaction during Initial Intercultural Interaction: An Extension of Anxiety and Uncertainty Management (AUM) Theory." *Journal of Intercultural Communication Research* 41 (1): 1–16. https://doi.org/10.1080/17475759.2011.623239.

Porter, James E. 2017. "Professional Communication as Phatic: From Classical *Eunoia* to Personal Artificial Intelligence." *Business and Professional Communication Quarterly* 80 (2): 174–93.

Rose, Shirley K, and Irwin Weiser. 1999. *The Writing Program Administrator as Researcher: Inquiry in Action and Reflection*. Portsmouth, NH: Heinemann.

Rush Hovde, Marjorie. 2014. "Factors that Enable and Challenge International Engineering Communication: A Case Study of a United States/British Design Team." *IEEE Transactions on Professional Communication* 57 (4): 242–65. https://doi.org/10.1109/TPC.2014.2363893.

Staggers, Julie, Susan Garcia, and Ed Nagelhout. 2008. "Teamwork through Team Building: Face-to-Face to Online." *Business Communication Quarterly* 71 (4): 472–87. https://doi.org/10.1177/1080569908325862.

Vik, Gretchen. 2001. "Doing More to Teach Teamwork Than Telling Students to Sink or Swim." *Business Communication Quarterly* 64 (4): 112–19. https://doi.org/10.1177/108056990106400413.

Wei, Xiaohong. 2009. "On Negative Cultural Transfer in Communication between Chinese and Americans." *Journal of Intercultural Communication* 21. http://www.immi.se/intercultural/nr21/wei.htm.

Wolfe, Joanna. 2010. *Team Writing: A Guide to Working in Groups*. Boston, MA: Bedford/St. Martin's.

Zemliansky, Pavel. 2012. "Achieving Experiential Cross-cultural Training through a Virtual Teams Project." *IEEE Transactions on Professional Communication* 55 (3): 275–86. https://doi.org/10.1109/TPC.2012.2206191.

PART IV

Faculty Development

11

BUILDING THE INFRASTRUCTURE OF L2 WRITING SUPPORT
The Case of Arizona State University

Katherine Daily O'Meara and Paul Kei Matsuda

Arizona State University (ASU) is the largest institution of higher education in the United States, enrolling over eighty-two thousand undergraduate and graduate students in 2015. As of 2015, ASU also has one of the largest enrollments of international students among US universities. The number of international students more than doubled in the last few years—from around five thousand in 2010 to over eleven thousand in 2014; ASU currently has the fourth-largest enrollment of international students among all institutions and the largest among public institutions (Arizona State University 2015). During the same period, the number of L2 writing courses expanded from twenty-one in fall 2010 to one hundred in fall 2014. ASU also has a strong contingency of faculty and doctoral students who specialize in second language writing and writing program administration. The combination of these conditions has provided a fertile ground for identifying and addressing the presence and needs of second language writers systematically.

In this chapter, we describe the process of building the infrastructure strategically to support international students in the writing programs and how it has contributed to various efforts to enhance support for second language (L2) writers both within and beyond the writing programs. We begin by describing the institutional context and opportunities for change that arose. We then describe how we built the administrative team, followed by a discussion of various efforts to build the community of L2 writing teachers as well as to reach out to the wider university community. Our efforts have been guided by the "CCCC Statement on Second Language Writing and Writers" (2001; CCCC 2009) as well as a growing body of scholarship on L2 writing program administration—a subset of research and scholarship on L2 writing that focuses on issues relevant to WPAs, such as curriculum design, teacher professional development,

DOI: 10.7330/9781607326762.c011

and placement options and procedures (e.g., Braine 1996; Costino and Hyon 2007; Matsuda and Silva 1999; Ortmeier-Hooper 2008; Racelis and Matsuda 2013, 2015; Ruecker 2011; Silva 1994; Williams 1995). We have also made conscious efforts to integrate a research component; many of our initiatives involve systematic collection and analysis of data that can help evaluate the program and generate knowledge for WPAs here and elsewhere (Rose and Weiser 1999).

The description we offer here is not necessarily a package that can be adopted wholesale; rather, we hope to show how we built various aspects of the program strategically in response to a series of challenges and opportunities that arose over the years, using the L2 WPA scholarship as our compass.

THE INSTITUTIONAL CONTEXT

Like most other institutions of US higher education, ASU has a first-year writing requirement for virtually all students. The first-year writing requirement consists of a two-semester sequence, including ENG 101 and 102. Students who are advanced writers can enroll in advanced composition, ENG 105, which condenses the first-year writing requirement into one semester. Students who are deemed in need of additional preparation in academic writing are placed into the stretch program, which extends the sequence into three courses—WAC 101, ENG 101, and ENG 102—providing more time to develop writing proficiency (Glau 1996, 2007).

Students for whom English is not the first language can choose to enroll in parallel L2 sections of first-year composition courses comprised of WAC 107, ENG 107, and ENG 108. L2 sections are not available for advanced composition since the assumption is that students who enroll in the advanced-composition course have strong background in both writing and English and are prepared for a mainstream course. The L2 sections of first-year writing courses mirror mainstream sections in terms of the goals and objectives, which are based on the WPA Outcomes Statement, but the courses are taught by experienced writing teachers who are designated as L2 writing teachers. The practice of offering a separate section for L2 writers is in line with many other US college composition programs (Silva 1994).

In 2007, when Paul Kei Matsuda arrived at ASU as a faculty member, the L2 sections of writing courses were already in place. There also was a full-time lecturer who served as an L2 writing coordinator, who provided resources to teachers of L2 sections. In the following year, both the director of writing programs and the L2 writing coordinator took positions elsewhere, and Paul stepped in as the interim director of writing programs, which provided an opportunity for him to get to know the entire program. During his year as the interim director, he focused on gathering information about the program that could be passed on to the next, more permanent writing programs director.

AN OPPORTUNITY FOR CHANGE

In fall 2009, Shirley K Rose came to ASU as the director of writing programs and initiated a self-study of the program as part of a review by the WPA Consultant-Evaluator Service. The resulting external reviewers' recommendations and the ensuing discussion provided some impetus for institutional changes. The overall recommendation was to capitalize on the size of the program and the quality of the program and people to achieve national prominence while also promoting local involvement. Some of the specific recommendations included tenure-track faculty involvement in administering writing programs; research efforts to facilitate data-based decision making; enhanced communication to increase visibility both within and outside the institution.

The external reviewers for the writing programs—as well as a separate group of external reviewers for the department review a few years later—also recognized the growing population of L2 writers and the existence of faculty strengths in the area of L2 writing. As a result, the position of the director of second language writing (DSLW) was created. The job description for the DSLW (Paul), who reports to the director of writing programs (Shirley), included the following:

- Prepare writing teachers to work effectively with L2 writers.
- Support professional development for all Writing Programs teachers.
- Develop and enhance curriculum for L2 writers.
- Promote L2 writing research in the Writing Programs.
- Achieve national prominence in L2 writing instruction and program administration.

In some ways, the DSLW position was an extension of many of the functions Paul had already been performing as a faculty member, but the official position lent more legitimacy and recognition to those activities.

One of the key responsibilities of the DSLW was teacher preparation. Previously, L2 writing courses had been taught by writing teachers who had some background in teaching English to speakers of other languages (TESOL) or linguistics, or by those who were themselves nonnative English users. While some of them were excellent teachers, the hiring criteria did not include specialized experience or expertise in L2 writing, and the program did not offer sustained or systematic professional-development opportunities in L2 writing—other than an online space where writing teachers could share teaching ideas and materials. To recognize and respond to various issues L2 writers face, background in writing instruction or language instruction alone is not sufficient—even when combined with the best of intentions. For this reason, the qualifications were revised to focus on expertise and experience in L2 writing, and a local certification program for L2 writing teachers was developed for those who had not taught L2 writing courses at ASU.

As a member of the graduate faculty, Paul had already created a graduate course on teaching L2 writing (ENG 525). Offered every year, the course provides an introduction to the field of second language writing in ways that connect research insights and classroom practices. Some of the topics include overview and history of the field, demographics, sites of L2 writing, characteristics and needs of L2 writers (both international and resident), curriculum design, placement options, teacher feedback, peer feedback, collaborative writing, language development, the negotiation of language differences, assessment, and the use of technology. In addition, he created a doctoral-level variable-title course in L2 writing (ENG 625) to prepare doctoral students to conduct research on various issues in L2 writing. So far, the topics have included teaching and researching academic writing, practicing theory in L2 writing, history of L2 writing, and L2 writing program administration.

As part of his DSLW duties, Paul also created a practicum on teaching L2 writing (ENG 594) for experienced writing teachers who are teaching L2 sections for the first time. The discussion at the beginning of each semester focuses on an overview of issues in L2 writing instruction and some of the situations teachers may encounter during the first few weeks of teaching. Throughout the semester, the group discusses various topics, such as assignment design, classroom-interaction strategies, reading and responding to writing, facilitating peer feedback, implementing collaborative writing, facilitating language development, and assessing L2 writing. Class time is also devoted to the discussion of issues and questions that come up in the classroom. All teachers keep and share an online journal and conduct peer observations. To eliminate the financial burden for teachers, the course is offered for free to those who do not have tax-free tuition-waiver benefits. The practicum was initially offered once a year, but given the large demand for L2 sections of writing courses and the shortage of teachers with expertise in L2 writing, the practicum is now offered every semester.

The initial plan for preparing teachers for L2 writing courses was a sequence of two courses—the graduate course in teaching L2 writing (ENG 525) and the practicum (ENG 594) during the first semester of teaching. Given the large demand for L2 writing teachers and to reduce the burden for teachers who were interested in pursuing a specialized preparation but did not have the time to take two graduate courses, ENG 525 was made optional, recommended as an additional professional-development opportunity after completing the practicum. As with the practicum, writing programs teachers who do not qualify for a tuition waiver are able to sit in for free. Upon completion of the practicum course, L2 writing teachers are certified to teach any of the L2 sections of first-year composition courses.

BUILDING THE ADMINISTRATIVE TEAM

The creation of the DSLW position was an important step toward developing a stronger support program for L2 writers at ASU. The tenure-track faculty involvement and the administrative title made the L2 writing program more visible in the eyes of the administration and faculty from other academic units. In fact, other academic units, such as anthropology, engineering, and management, began to approach Paul (often through the dean's office) with requests that he design language-support programs for a growing number of international students. The visibility and legitimacy of the L2 writing program increased responsibility and accountability but also led to additional opportunities for research and professional development for graduate students and writing programs teachers who were specializing in L2 writing (Matsuda and Rose 2011). In this section, we describe some of those opportunities.

A major change in the infrastructure that resulted from the increasing demand for L2 writing expertise was the creation of additional positions. One of the positions created was the lecturer in second language writing, an advanced teaching position for an experienced teacher with a PhD in second language writing or a related field. In addition to teaching L2 writing courses, the person holding this position would be expected to provide leadership to the community of L2 writers and to mentor other L2 writing teachers. Although this position was filled once, the person decided to move on after a year, and we are seeking reauthorization for this position. Another important position is the associate director of second language writing, which comes with two course releases per year. This position provides opportunities for an advanced doctoral student specializing in L2 writing to gain experience in L2 writing program administration. As a way of preparing additional doctoral students for this responsibility, Paul also created the position of assistant director of second language writing with the option of receiving internship credits. Currently, a request to grant a course release for the assistant director is being made in response to the expansion of responsibilities.

Because doctoral students who hold TAships are "in the trenches," actively teaching various writing courses and sharing offices with other writing programs teachers, they have been able to connect with the community of L2 writing teachers in ways the DSLW—as tenure-track faculty with his own office and other responsibilities both within and outside the institution—is not able to. The associate director also serves as a member of the Writing Programs Committee and as the deputy chair of the Second Language Writing Committee, playing a leadership role in planning various activities for the L2 writing community and the larger community of writing teachers.

The associate and assistant director positions also provide opportunities for doctoral students who are interested in writing program administration to engage in sustained administrative projects that lead to dissertation projects and publications. For example, Tanita Saenkhum, the first to hold the associate director position, collaborated with Paul and another doctoral student on a survey research project focusing on writing teachers' perceptions of the presence and needs of L2 writers in first-year writing courses (Matsuda, Saenkhum, and Accardi 2013). She also initiated a project to improve placement practices by creating optimal conditions for student agency. Originally, the placement was handled by academic advisors in various units, and international L2 writers who had language-proficiency test scores (e.g., TOEFL, IELTS) were being advised to take L2 sections regardless of their needs (Braine 1996) or preferences (Costino and Hyon 2007). To provide appropriate support for students who actually need it, the placement procedure was changed to allow students to choose between mainstream or L2 sections within each level of placement. Tanita's work in improving the placement practice led to her dissertation project as well as her first book-length publication (Saenkhum 2016). Thanks to her work, academic advisors and L2 writers now have better access to the information about the placement policies as well as their options.

Katherine (Kat) Daily O'Meara, who took over Tanita's position as the associate director, became interested in fostering the community of L2 writing teachers and created various initiatives to add to the list of existing opportunities that engage L2 writing teachers in the writing programs. These activities have also served as the bases for her dissertation project (O'Meara 2016). In the remainder of this chapter, we describe those initiatives in detail.

THE NEED FOR A SENSE OF COMMUNITY

Structurally, L2 writing is well integrated into the larger writing programs. For example, the L2 writing program has a presence at the Fall Convocation—the annual gathering of all writing teachers in writing programs at the beginning of each academic year, where teachers discuss policy issues and participate in professional-development activities. This event includes writing teachers of all ranks (from part-time and full-time instructors to lecturers, teaching assistants, and tenure-track faculty) who teach a wide range of writing courses (from basic writing and first-year writing to professional writing and upper-division electives in writing and rhetoric). The whole-group session in the morning is an opportunity for the second language writing administrative team to address all writing teachers in the program—not just L2 writing teachers. This is important because L2 writers are ubiquitous—they are present in most writing courses, and all teachers need to be familiar with policies and procedures that affect L2 writers in their classes. We discuss L2 writing-related policies and procedures, such as the identification of misplaced students through diagnostic writing and brief oral interactions during the first week of classes. We remind all writing programs teachers to contact the administrative team if any L2-related questions arise and explain the appeal procedure for placement. We also announce various L2 writing-related initiatives.

In the afternoon of the convocation, we typically offer two breakout sessions scheduled concurrently. One of the sessions, designated for new teachers of L2 sections of first-year composition courses, introduces them to the L2 writing practicum. The other session is targeted toward seasoned L2 writing teachers with one or more semesters of experience under their belts. The topics in this session include current issues the teachers are facing in implementing policies and procedures as well as various pedagogical strategies. The meeting also serves a social, community-building function, allowing the participants to get to know fellow L2 writing teachers as they discuss common issues and concerns.

Despite the structural integration of L2 writing into writing programs, and despite the growing number of writing teachers who are certified to teach L2 writing, some L2 writing teachers felt isolated from the rest of writing programs, from the L2-writing administrative team, and from other L2 writing teachers. As a liaison between the L2 administrative team and L2 writing teachers, Kat noticed this tendency and started looking into it more closely. To help L2 writing teachers feel that they belong, Kat started thinking about ways to make teachers *want* to participate in various professional-development activities by developing a community and a culture of participation.

DEVELOPING A SENSE OF COMMUNITY

A key strategy for community building is creating opportunities for involvement. One of the main vehicles for involving teachers is through the Second Language Writing Committee. The committee comprises the DSLW, associate and assistant directors, and a handful of other L2 writing teachers who volunteer, including graduate teaching assistants as well as full- and part-time instructors. This committee discusses issues that affect L2 writing teachers and their students, thus promoting the sense of investment in the program among the teachers. Another function of the committee is to organize workshops and other activities that contribute to the improvement of the L2 writing program and the professional development of its teachers.

Topics for the L2 writing workshops are chosen based on conversations with L2 writing teachers during the Fall Convocation breakout session. Some of the topics have included L1 versus L2 use in the classroom, addressing grammar, assessment of writing projects, using digital technologies with multilingual populations, and differentiation strategies for a class with multiple language-ability levels. To garner interest among non–L2 specialists, we invited teachers from various areas of the writing programs with relevant expertise to present workshops and share their knowledge. We also made these workshops open to all writing programs teachers—regardless of their specialization. To make these workshops accessible to teachers who have busy teaching schedules, each workshop is offered multiple times on different days and at different times of the day.

Another way of encouraging involvement is to facilitate the sharing of resources among members of the community. During the L2 writing teaching practicum, teachers can collaborate on tasks like the selection of readings and assignment design. The practicum is open only to teachers who are teaching L2 writing sections for the first time. Although all teachers who are already certified to teach L2 writing can continue to use the materials from the practicum, they do not always have opportunities for exchanging teaching materials with each other. To encourage the sharing of materials and insights, we revived the online portal for L2 writing teachers and invited teachers to post their teaching materials and share their thoughts. After creating a new space in ASU's learning-management system, we added all L2-certified teachers to the group. In addition to serving as a space for mutual sharing of resources, we also use the site to post announcements about professional-development opportunities.

To further encourage the sharing of insights and materials, and to add an even greater social dimension to the initiative, Kat started an end-of-semester potluck lunch. At the end of each semester, L2 writing teachers are invited to bring a dish to share and digital and hard copies of their favorite pedagogical tools (e.g., assignment handouts, activities they created, readings, and online resources). The event is scheduled over four hours, and participants are encouraged to stop by anytime during this period. We also provide an option of posting the materials online.

To make the contributions of L2 writing teachers to the program and to their students more visible and to recognize teachers for their efforts, Kat created a recognition program, L2 Writing Teacher Feature. Each month, L2 writing teachers are encouraged to nominate a fellow L2 writing teacher or themselves to be featured as a teacher of the month. Once chosen, nominees are encouraged to share what they enjoy about working with the L2 student population at ASU. They are also encouraged to share an assignment, writing project, or other materials that they have created for their L2 writing classes. In addition, the featured teachers have the opportunity to share a little bit about themselves and their lives outside teaching in the writing program (e.g., interests, families, hobbies). Featured teachers' profiles and bio statements are publicized in a number of locations, including on bulletin boards around the writing program floor, in e-mail blasts to the English department, on the ePortfolio technology implemented by the program, and on social media.

BEYOND THE L2 WRITING COMMUNITY

In addition to developing a strong sense of community among L2 writing teachers, we also have tried to increase the visibility of the L2 writing program through outreach projects. One such initiative was participation in NCTE's National Day on Writing (NDOW), a nationally recognized day for celebrating writing, which provides an additional opportunity for L2 writing integration into the larger writing programs. Because the goal of NDOW is to showcase writing in everyday life, it seemed natural to the members of the L2 Writing Committee to solicit participation from interested L2 writing teachers and their students. In 2014, L2 teachers encouraged their students to create PowerPoint slides of an English-language idiom or phrase with an explanation, a visual rendering of the idiom, and a sample sentence. These slides were collected into a single PowerPoint presentation that was streamed all day on campus during the NDOW. Over one hundred undergraduate and graduate L2 writers and their teachers participated.

Another venue for increasing the visibility of the L2 writing community is the annual local conference on teaching writing sponsored by ASU's writing programs. Each year, L2 writing teachers present their pedagogical research and share teaching materials and strategies at the conference. Although members of the L2 writing administrative team and L2 Writing Committee members often contribute to this effort, there has not been a systematic effort to encourage other L2 writing teachers to participate in this event. This is one area where we can strengthen our effort.

In addition to our L2 writing community in the writing programs, ASU is also home to a vibrant community of TESOL specialists. ASU offers master's and undergraduate certificate programs in Teachers of English to Speakers of Other Languages (TESOL). Kat saw an opportunity to create a connection between the two communities by establishing a program that would be mutually beneficial: the L2 writing teaching (L2WT) internship. The L2WT internship pairs a TESOL student intern with an experienced L2 writing teacher who is teaching a section of L2 writing. The intern-tutors sit in on all classes and are encouraged to work with classroom teachers to be as involved as they are comfortable. In addition, they are required to provide oral and written feedback in a one-to-one environment with students for each major writing project and have the chance to create and implement lessons and materials for use in the L2 writing classroom. The L2WT internship has been deemed a success by all parties involved (tutors, classroom teachers, and L2 writing students): it allows for a dedicated L2 writing teacher cohort to share their expertise with ASU's TESOL students. The L2WT internship helps ASU's TESOL students forge a positive relationship with a writing teacher who also specializes in working with multilingual populations and familiarizes TESOL students not only with tangible on-the-ground experiences of being in the L2 writing classroom but also with sustaining connections to a professional in the field.

It is our hope that, by creating these frameworks and offering these initiatives, we are establishing a resilient culture of L2 writing that will continue to change and be improved based on the needs, perceptions, and ideas of the writing programs' constituents. These initiatives have fostered L2 writing teacher participation within the writing program while simultaneously enhancing visibility for the presence of the L2 writing community to the larger writing program and to the whole university campus.

CHALLENGES

One key struggle in maintaining a successful culture of L2 writing is the working conditions of writing teachers. Starting in fall 2015, the workload distribution for over sixty instructors (a rank within non-tenure-track full-time writing teachers at ASU) was changed from 4/4 teaching plus service and professional development to 5/5 teaching with no service or professional-development responsibilities (or 4/4 teaching with a lower salary). The elimination of service and professional development led to a decline in teacher participation and involvement in professional activities. Despite best efforts in planning workshops and potlucks to suit busy teachers' schedules, we have at times experienced low attendance and participation. Such conditions have made it difficult to maintain a sustainable cohort of part- and full-time writing teachers on the Second Language Writing Committee, and currently the majority of active members are graduate teaching assistants.

Another struggle we have experienced is managing the ongoing requests for additional services provided by L2 writing experts and professionals. In the past two academic years, the DSLW and his administrative team have been tasked with the creation of one-credit language-focused add-on classes for international students to enroll in concurrently with first-year writing courses. In addition, we are currently working on developing L2 support for our upper-division business and technical writing courses. The challenges here are related to time management and the participation of already busy teachers.

CONCLUSION

The response to the presence of international L2 writers did not happen as one systematic change but as an incremental process of making small changes in response to challenges and opportunities that arose. That does not mean the initiatives we took were purely reactive; instead, the decisions were made strategically based on our knowledge of L2 writing program administration scholarship. We have also been conducting research on the program and documenting the outcomes. We were fortunate to have some resources to help in this effort. Indeed, we have a faculty member who has expertise in L2 writing and a group of doctoral students who are specializing in L2 writing. Our writing programs director is also supportive of initiatives to enhance the experience of L2 writers. Having these conditions certainly makes it more feasible to create a strong support structure and a culture of L2 writing, although, as we have described above, it is still not easy.

Do these conditions mean it is impossible to develop an infrastructure and culture of L2 writing at institutions that do not already have an L2 writing specialist, graduate students who specialize in L2 writing, or a large number of L2 writers? Not at all. In the age of global higher education, most, if not all, US institutions enroll L2 writers of various types and are financially benefitting from their presence. Providing appropriate support to help these students succeed is no longer a luxury, if it ever was, and many institutions are beginning to recognize the increasing need for language-support programs.

One of the clear indications of this recognition is the increasing number of requests Paul receives for L2 writing workshops for writing teachers at various institutions across the nation. Although these workshops can provide an awareness and some general strategies for recognizing and addressing issues L2 writers face in the writing classroom, they are far from adequate in addressing the variety and complexity of issues students and teachers encounter. In addition to those one-off workshops, useful though as they may be, it is important to develop local resources to build a sustained mechanism for policymaking, program assessment, professional development, and teacher involvement.

Writing programs can start this effort by advocating for an administrative position for an L2 writing specialist who has strong background in writing program administration, writing instruction, language instruction, and teacher education. It is also important to reevaluate hiring priorities in light of the student population; if writing courses include L2 writers, the qualifications should include not just the ability to teach writing but also the ability to recognize and address language-related issues, including not only the use and negotiation of language but also the development of language. The L2 writing student population has been increasing steadily over the last five decades, and it does not seem to be slowing down anytime soon. It is time all writing programs with an L2 writing population commit themselves to serving the actual student population in the classroom.

References

Arizona State University. 2015. "ASU Ranks No. 4 for International Students." *ASU Now*, November 16. https://asunow.asu.edu/20151116-global-engagement-asu-ranks-no-4 -international-students.

Braine, George. 1996. "ESL Students in First-Year Writing Courses: ESL Versus Mainstream Classes." *Journal of Second Language Writing* 5 (2): 91–107. https://doi.org /10.1016/S1060-3743(96)90020-X.

CCCC (Conference on College Composition and Communication). 2009. "CCCC Statement on Second Language Writing and Writers." http://www.ncte.org/cccc/re sources/positions/secondlangwriting.

"CCCC Statement on Second Language Writing and Writers." 2001. *College Composition and Communication* 52 (4): 669–74.

Costino, Kimberly A., and Sunny Hyon. 2007. "'A Class for Students Like Me': Reconsidering Relationships among Identity Labels, Residency Status, and Students' Preferences for Mainstream or Multilingual Composition." *Journal of Second Language Writing* 16 (2): 63–81. https://doi.org/10.1016/j.jslw.2007.04.001.

Glau, Gregory R. 1996. "The 'Stretch Program': Arizona State University's New Model of University-Level Basic Writing Instruction." *WPA: Writing Program Administration* 20 (1–2): 79–91.

Glau, Gregory R. 2007. "Stretch at 10: A Progress Report on Arizona State University's Stretch Program." *Journal of Basic Writing* 26 (2): 30–48.

Matsuda, Paul Kei, and Shirley K Rose. 2011. *The Rhetoric of WPA-ing*. September. Accessed April 21, 2016. https://vimeo.com/29116549.

Matsuda, Paul Kei, Tanita Saenkhum, and Steven Accardi. 2013. "Writing Teachers' Perceptions of the Presence and Needs of Second Language Writers: An Institutional Case Study." *Journal of Second Language Writing* 22 (1): 68–86. https://doi.org/10.1016 /j.jslw.2012.10.001.

Matsuda, Paul Kei, and Tony Silva. 1999. "Cross-Cultural Composition: Mediated Integration of US and International Students." *Composition Studies* 27 (1): 15–30.

O'Meara, Katherine Daily. 2016. "A Community of Second Language Writing at Arizona State University: An Institutional Ethnography." PhD diss., Arizona State University.

Ortmeier-Hooper, Christina M. 2008. "English May Be My Second Language, But I'm Not 'ESL.'" *College Composition and Communication* 59 (3): 389–419.

Racelis, Juval V., and Paul Kei Matsuda. 2013. "Integrating Process and Genre into the Second Language Writing Classroom: Research Into Practice." *Language Teaching* 46 (3): 382–93. https://doi.org/10.1017/S0261444813000116.

Racelis, Juval V., and Paul Kei Matsuda. 2015. "Exploring the Multiple Identities of L2 Writing Teachers." In *Advances and Current Trends in Language Teacher Identity Research*, edited by Yin Ling Cheung, Selim Ben Said, and Kwanhyun Park, 203–16. London: Routledge.

Rose, Shirley K, and Irwin H. Weiser. 1999. *Writing Program Administrator as Researcher: Inquiry in Action and Reflection*. Portsmouth, NH: Heinemann.

Ruecker, Todd. 2011. "Improving the Placement of L2 Writers: The Students' Perspective." *WPA: Writing Program Administration* 35 (1): 91–117.

Saenkhum, Tanita. 2016. *Decisions, Agency, and Advising: Key Issues in the Placement of Multilingual Writers into First-Year Composition Courses*. Logan: Utah State University Press. https://doi.org/10.7330/9781607325482.

Silva, Tony. 1994. "An Examination of Writing Program Administrators' Options for the Placement of ESL Students in First Year Writing Classes." *WPA: Writing Program Administration* 18 (1–2): 37–43.

Williams, Jessica. 1995. "ESL Composition Program Administration in the United States." *Journal of Second Language Writing* 4 (2): 157–79. https://doi.org/10.1016/1060-3743 (95)90005-5.

12

DEVELOPING FACULTY FOR THE MULTILINGUAL WRITING CLASSROOM

Jennifer E. Haan

INTRODUCTION

In recent years, internationalization has played an increasingly important role in higher education. It is frequently mentioned in strategic plans and university vision statements, has led to the development of centers for international programs and overseas branch campuses, and has resulted in greater student mobility than ever before in the history of higher learning. It is widely regarded as beneficial for institutions, faculty, and students alike. Not only have the number and type of internationalization initiatives been used as measures of institutional effectiveness (Maringe 2011), but researchers, administrators, and teachers have also touted the benefits of the internationalized campus: the opportunities to develop global citizens (Barker et al. 2013), the potential to build relationships across cultures (Ryan 2013), and the possibility of increasing tolerance and respect for diversity in the context of a truly intercultural setting (Bevis and Lucas 2007).

Not only universities have emphasized increased internationalization. Scholars in composition studies have called for a shift in focus in the discipline—one that would bring a global perspective (Donahue 2009; Matsuda, Fruit, and Burton Lamm 2006; Schaub 2003) and would be more attuned to the needs of students from around the world (Canagarajah 2006; Horner et al. 2011; Jordan 2009). These calls for increasingly international perspectives can be productive in providing space for the reexamination of curricular practices, allowing faculty the opportunity to build local, intercultural pedagogies. This process, however, is not without its challenges. Often, the process of curricular and pedagogical reform in response to increased internationalization is fraught with tensions as writing faculty with little experience working in multilingual settings adjust to the realities of instruction in culturally

DOI: 10.7330/9781607326762.c012

and linguistically diverse writing classrooms. As internationalization efforts grow, the importance of understanding faculty response to internationalization efforts becomes more apparent, as faculty will be the ones primarily responsible for working with international students and implementing internationalization strategies both in the classroom and in the university as a whole. This chapter seeks to better understand this faculty response to internationalization efforts by studying both beliefs about working with international students as well as the ways working with international students in first-year composition courses complicates pedagogical strategies and professional identities.

LITERATURE REVIEW

Internationalization and Faculty Response

Although the term *internationalization* has enjoyed increased presence in higher education, it remains somewhat "fuzzy" to define (Ryan 2013). The most widely held definition describes it as "the process of integrating an international and intercultural dimension into the teaching, research, and service functions of a higher education institution" (Knight 2004, 6). The operationalization of this concept includes increased student mobility, instructional approaches that emphasize the global (internationalization of the curriculum), and research that crosses national borders (Ryan 2013).

Although different definitions of internationalization emphasize different key ideas, they overlap in a number of important areas. First, they recognize increased student mobility between countries as an important aspect of internationalization. Attracting international students is often the easiest and most quickly implemented strategy for campus internationalization; raising the numbers of international students[1] cannot only be considered a way to diversify the campus, but it is also an increasingly important source of revenue for all types of higher education institutions. Truly transformative internationalization, however, cannot begin and end with the flow of students between countries; rather it must be integrated into the fabric of the university. Jane Knight (2004) notes that this "concept of integration is specifically used to denote the process of infusing or embedding the international and intercultural dimension into policies and programs to ensure that the international dimension remains central, not marginal, and is sustainable" (12). This is relevant not only to internationalization as a whole but also to the internationalization of the student body. It is not enough to simply have diverse, highly internationalized student enrollment, but those international students must be "central, not marginal"; their needs must be both seen and supported. Unfortunately, as Rosemary Clerehan (2007) notes, "With the diversity of the student body, identifying who students are and what they need from their learning experiences now poses sizable and critical challenges for universities" (188).

With the growing numbers of international students in English-medium universities, researchers in a variety of contexts have investigated "what students need" from the international student perspective, including their experiences adjusting to new cultural and classroom expectations (Grayson 2008; Leask 2009), their challenges in adjusting to the literacy demands of the college writing classroom (Haan and Mallett 2015; Leki 2007), and the types of support international students receive both in and outside the classroom (Andrade 2006; Murphy, Hawkes, and Law 2002). In addition, scholars both from the field of L2 writing and from the field of rhetoric and composition have recognized the need for faculty—even those who are not specialists in L2 language or writing—to become comfortable teaching and working with international students in the classroom (Jordan 2009; Matsuda, Fruit, and Burton Lamm 2006).

Despite these calls, studies on faculty response to university internationalization, both within and outside the composition classroom, are relatively limited both in scope and number, with most of the research focusing on faculty views of international student benefits and challenges and far less research examining faculty pedagogical practices in response to student needs. Within the research on internationalization in higher education, a number of research studies have examined faculty response to working with international students by focusing on faculty perceptions of their students. Margaret Robertson, Martin Line, Susan Jones, and Sharon Thomas found that faculty attributed student difficulties to lack of participation, difficulty understanding lectures, inability to learn independently, and limited critical thinking (Robertson et al. 2000). A subsequent study, however, found a wide range of perceptions of international student needs: some faculty found students to be highly problematic in terms of their preparation for the classroom, while others viewed them positively as bringing international perspectives (Kingston and Forland 2008). Andrea Trice (2003) also studied faculty perceptions of international graduate students across four academic departments, noting both benefits and challenges to enrolling international graduate students. The benefits faculty described include high quality of research, building international connections, and developing department reputations; the challenges listed include communicating with students, building connections between international and domestic students, and evaluating and responding to international students' language skills. Maureen Andrade (2010) surveyed ninety-three instructors at a US university, finding that faculty were "sensitive to L2 students' learning needs" and even willing to consider different teaching approaches to better work with international students, but the research also found that faculty had "minimal interest in focusing on improving students' English skills or learning more about pedagogical methods for teaching NNESs" (230). Recent research echoes much of these findings: faculty see both benefits and challenges to increased international student enrollment and display some interest in working with L2 students but also find working with international students to be "burdensome," with many questioning whether they have the appropriate skills to effectively teach in an internationalized classroom (Haan, Gallagher, and Varandani 2017).

A few studies go beyond faculty response to teaching L2 students and examine pedagogical adjustments made by faculty in internationalized classrooms—both in the context of composition and across other areas of the curriculum. Vivian Zamel (2004) provides narratives from faculty across disciplines of their successful pedagogical adjustment practices, and Xiaoye You and Xiaoqiong You looked at instructional practices of faculty teaching in an international setting, finding that faculty adjust writing tasks, provide additional support, and try to tie writing assignments to students' home cultures (You and You 2013). Other studies have looked specifically at faulty response to writing in an internationalized setting (Ferris et al. 2011; Janopoulos 1992; Lindsey and Crusan 2011), finding a wide range of faculty response practices to L2 students in composition classrooms. This study hopes to add to this body of research by examining faculty beliefs about the instruction of multilingual students in composition classrooms and studying how having increased numbers of multilingual students in the classroom affects those beliefs, their pedagogical practices, and their own professional identities.

METHODS

The University

The data for this study was collected over a two-year period at the University of Dayton, a private, comprehensive university located in the midwestern region of the United States. The university is representative of a particular kind of private, religious-affiliated college or university in the United States in that the majority of its student enrollment takes the form of what some would call "traditional" (Deil-Amen 2015) college students: white, upper middle class, eighteen to twenty-two years old. The vast majority of the students enroll directly after graduating from high school, live on campus, and complete their degrees in four to five years. The university has maintained a strong general education curriculum for undergraduate students and requires them to take a variety of courses in the liberal arts and sciences—including numerous courses in the history, philosophy, psychology, English, sociology, art, and religious studies departments.

The motivation for this research came as the administration, much like at other institutions in the United States (Ryan 2013), began to place increasing emphasis on internationalization efforts across the institution. This internationalization effort resulted in the development of numerous strategic partnerships with universities overseas, the development of an international branch campus of the university, and a substantial increase in the recruitment and enrollment of international students on the US campus. This increased international student enrollment was so substantial, in fact, that the number of full-time international undergraduate students increased from 143 students in fall 2011 to 945 students in fall 2015. This increase was not only numeric but also affected the overall composition of the student body, increasing the overall percentage of undergraduate international students from 2 percent in 2011 to 11 percent in 2015. As the international student enrollment grew, discussions began throughout campus concerning the role of the faculty and administration in providing support and instruction for international students, particularly those for whom English is a second (or third or fourth) language. Faculty, many of whom had little or no experience working with international students, were teaching students with different language and cultural backgrounds than they were used to, and many felt unprepared (or underprepared) to respond to these students' needs. In this context, I began working with colleagues to better understand faculty response to internationalization efforts more broadly, and within that, the instruction of international student writers more particularly.

The Research

The research project included an online survey sent to all faculty members across disciplines, a set of interviews with faculty members from the writing program, and a course-length ethnographic study of three writing instructors who were working with large numbers of international students for the first time. Each of these measures elicited valuable information, providing general faculty reactions to increased campus internationalization and allowing me to observe specific instructional responses to a changing classroom population.

The survey was initially piloted with a group of fifteen faculty members, then sent via e-mail to approximately five hundred faculty members across different units of the university. The survey included twelve Likert-type questions, each with an optional open-ended comment box. One hundred and ninety-two faculty responded, from all units of the university, including the colleges of education, health sciences, business, engineering, and arts and sciences. Eighteen of those responses were from English-department faculty working in the first- and second-year writing program, and although interesting responses were provided from faculty across the curriculum, the data included in this chapter stem only from writing program faculty members. In addition to the survey, writing program faculty participated in interviews to respond to additional questions; fifteen composition faculty participated in those interviews. The interviews included semistructured questions and provided ample opportunity for faculty to address self-designated areas of concern. Both the survey and the interview questions broadly addressed four main areas: responses to internationalization, faculty perceptions of international students, current pedagogical practices, and faculty-development opportunities. Finally, I conducted a course-long ethnographic study, following a group of three experienced composition instructors through their first time teaching in a multilingual, intercultural classroom. Two of these classrooms were intentionally intercultural in that they were designed to enroll both international and domestic students in approximately equal numbers. The third course was not intentionally intercultural; it was simply a factor of timing and enrollment patterns that a majority of the students in the class were international. When following these courses, I used classroom observations, stimulated-recall reflections, interviews, and think-aloud protocols to better understand the process of development and adjustment veteran faculty undergo as they respond to a changing student population.

The Writing Program

The writing program at the university involves a two-semester sequence, generally taught over a period of two years. The first course in the sequence (Eng 100) aligns fairly closely with a writing-about-writing approach. Students are asked to read texts about writing, literacy, and rhetoric; write about their own literacy histories and writing practices; and research and write about the discourse practices of particular groups on campus. Instructors for the course design their own assignments, but most make use of a standard course pack including readings from such authors as Mike Rose, Malcolm X, and James Paul Gee. The second semester in the two-course sequence (Eng 200) is a theme-based course, with individual instructors designing course themes based on their own interests and/or areas of research. The themes of the course vary widely, from broad topics such as happiness, vocation, art, or family to more narrow examinations of particular issues (e.g., representations of cancer, food sustainability, human rights), television shows (e.g., *Buffy the Vampire Slayer*, *The Office*), or musical genres (e.g., The Beatles, hip-hop, heavy metal). In each Eng 200 course, regardless of theme, students are expected to write about the course topic from a variety of disciplinary perspectives, and all the sections have the same student learning outcomes.

The Faculty

Every faculty member in the English department is expected to teach one of the writing program courses each semester, and faculty backgrounds vary widely within broader areas of English studies, including those who focus on literature, creative writing, critical theory, rhetoric and composition, and professional and technical writing. There are forty-five full-time faculty members, eighteen of whom are full-time lecturers, and most have PhDs in English or a related field. The faculty is relatively stable—there is not a heavy reliance on temporary, short-term, or adjunct contracts to teach composition courses; most of the faculty members have many years of experience teaching first-year writing, both at this university and elsewhere.

Of the fifteen faculty who participated in focus groups and interviews, nine were full-time lecturers and six were tenured or tenure-track faculty; four had backgrounds in rhetoric and composition, and eleven had backgrounds in literature or creative writing. The three faculty members who participated in the longer, course-based research project also represented these varying backgrounds: all had been teaching writing at the university level for over fifteen years; one was a tenured associate professor, and two were full-time instructors; one had a PhD focusing on literature, one had an MA in English, and one had a PhD with a focus on writing studies.

Two of the three courses I followed were Eng 100 courses. Both of these used the standard writing-about-writing approach and incorporated the standard readings from the Eng 100 course pack. The third course was an Eng 200 theme-based course in which the topic of the course related to music, and the readings related to different disciplinary perspectives on a genre of music. All three of the faculty members who participated in the longer study are well-respected by both students and colleagues in the department, and they have numerous years of experience teaching these composition courses. Before the course I observed, all of them had some experience teaching international students in their composition courses, but it was "only a handful" throughout the years: "Not enough to affect the makeup of the course." For all of them, the course I studied was the first time each had taught a course with more than 50 percent international students. Observing faculty with this combination—having extensive experience in writing instruction while at the same time having little experience teaching international students—allowed me to gain greater insight on how faculty respond to changing student demographics in terms of their beliefs, their pedagogical practices, and their own professional identities.

FINDINGS

Faculty Beliefs about Language Use

The question of language use and language diversity in the composition classroom has played an important role in recent discussions in composition studies and L2 writing. Many have argued that greater attention needs to be paid to multilingual issues (Jordan 2012; Leki 2007), and a number of researchers have called for greater linguistic diversity in the composition classroom (Canagarajah 2006; Horner et al. 2011). As Christine Tardy (2011) notes, however, "These arguments for the recognition of language diversity in the college writing classroom are theoretically persuasive, yet they tend to leave unexplored the perspectives of writing teachers and students" (637). Both survey and focus-group responses in this study, as well as in-depth interviews with the long-term study participants, indicated that concerns about "appropriate language use" quickly become central in an internationalized classroom. In this study, questions surrounding language use seemed to cluster around two primary areas.

First, faculty interview responses centered on issues of English-language fluency and proficiency. Respondents to both the survey and the interview questions commented extensively on the role of language proficiency in relation to their international students' success in the course. Some indicated perception of language as a skill that is being built alongside specific subject-matter concepts: "Their grammar is still in progress, especially when working with course specific vocabulary and theories." Most responses, however, indicated a view of English-language proficiency as something that should be stable and in place prior to the start of the writing course. One respondent noted, "Getting the students where we need them, in terms of language, is just a bridge too far. It can't be done." And another stated, "This stuff—the language stuff— needs to be worked out before they get in my class. We have to be able to move forward with writing. They are still struggling with appropriate grammar." This view represents a commonly held deficiency orientation to language and also fails to recognize the complex relationship between formal language knowledge and other types of knowledge in developing disciplinary expertise (Tardy 2009). It is important to point out, however, that faculty holding these views shared a commensurate interest in working with and helping students improve their English-language skills throughout the courses; most of them discussed spending hours of extra time outside the class working with and responding to students in order to "get their language up to the level where they can succeed."

A second language-related issue that arose during interviews was the role of incorporating multiple languages in the classroom. Five of the fifteen faculty interviewed indicated no space in a writing classroom for the use of languages other than English. Some relied on the common monolingual assumption that using other languages might limit students' abilities to improve proficiency in English: "I think it's important to bring multiple cultural perspectives in the class, and I try to use articles from people of different backgrounds, but if they're always reading in their native language, they won't learn how to read in English." Others worried about the logistic ramifications of using multiple languages: "If they read something in a language I don't know, I won't know if they are summarizing accurately or not." Finally, assessment figured prominently in interviewees' reasoning: "I'm not sure how I would grade a paper that incorporates other languages."

The majority of faculty participants, however, allowed for the use of multiple languages in different settings in their composition classrooms. These ten reported allowing (and sometimes recommending) that students use languages other than English for prewriting and drafting, for readings, and for clarification of materials both in and outside the classroom. One respondent noted, "Sometimes it's helpful for them to talk to their neighbor or read an explanation in Arabic, and if it helps them understand the material, that's okay." This incorporation of multiple languages, however, was invariably accompanied by questions and concerns: "I let them read a translation of the text. Will that keep them from improving their English?" or "Should they translate or use translators? I'm not sure what to do about that." These questions regarding language use in the classroom revealed faculty uncertainties about appropriate practices. Interestingly, eleven of the fifteen faculty members interviewed asked for specific policies addressing this issue—from the department, the university, or from "an expert" in the field. One comment represents these requests: "It would be helpful if there were some sort of department policy on the use of other languages or translators or that type of thing. I am not sure what I should be doing at this point. And I don't know if what I am doing will put them at a disadvantage in other classes." This type of request for explicit, administrative policy statements is uncharacteristic for faculty who usually resist externally imposed demands, policies, or restrictions on their classrooms. And yet, the uncertainty created by the unfamiliar classroom situation seems to have created a desire for concrete policies.

The faculty involved in the course-long project illustrated this uncertainty with regard to language use. All three participants initially indicated a lack of willingness to incorporate multiple languages in their courses. Approximately two weeks into the course, however, two instructors changed their opinion on this, one stating, "They seem to do better with the concepts if they can write and talk and do some prewriting activities in their own languages." The other instructor tried a number of options, ultimately settling on an English-only approach. "For a while I let them talk to each other or do their initial writing tasks in Arabic, but things started getting out of control. I couldn't respond to their work in ways that were helpful to them, and when they would start talking to each other in class in Arabic, it was really distracting for me and for the other students."

Curricular and Pedagogical Adjustments

A second important aspect of the study was the degree to which faculty either did implement, or would consider implementing, pedagogical adjustments in their courses in order to accommodate the increased presence of international students. In the survey and interviews, responses to the question of pedagogical adjustments for L2 writers were mixed. On the one hand, all the faculty indicated willingness to work with international students in order to help them succeed. In particular, they all discussed spending additional time outside class—both in office hours and in responding to papers—in order to help students achieve their writing goals. When discussing adjusting pedagogical practices inside the classroom, however, the results became a little less clear. First, many faculty weren't sure what kinds of pedagogical practices might be helpful for international students in the composition classroom. As one respondent stated, "I'd be happy to do anything to work with students and help them do better, but I don't know what to do differently. I don't know what they need—it seems like they need more of everything, so I spend more time with them outside of class."

Not only were faculty unsure of pedagogical techniques and practices that could benefit international students in their classrooms, but many also equated adjusting pedagogical techniques with lowering classroom standards. One of the consistent themes throughout the survey and interviews was the concern that any changes to the curriculum or pedagogy associated with the Eng 100–200 sequence could be seen as lowering standards. One faculty member stated, "College level work and writing should be challenging and enriching. We should be pushing our students—all of them—not providing easy ways for them to get by." And another remarked, "Expecting that our courses be taught substantially differently to serve international students is not doing a service to our traditional students." The underlying beliefs represented in these comments, that making course material accessible to a variety of students is both lowering standards and harming the education of "traditional" students, could be seen throughout interview responses and represent an important tension faculty feel. As one put it, "I simply don't know how to teach all of my students and maintain high standards at the same time."

In the long-term study, pedagogical and curricular adjustments took on an important role throughout the semester. At the beginning of the course, all three faculty members indicated a willingness to make adjustments, if necessary, but a desire, much like their colleagues, "not to dumb down" the course content. The issue that the three instructors were most concerned with at the beginning of the semester was a cultural one: would students from different cultural and educational backgrounds be able and willing to engage with the themes of the courses. The Eng 100 course, having a writing-about-writing theme, seemed, at first, to be culturally neutral. But, soon after beginning the course, the faculty began to recognize the ways the US-dominant cultural references in most of the readings were serving as a barrier to international student understanding. Almost immediately one of the instructors asked, "Do I take time in class explaining cultural references, or do I abandon these readings for others that may be more appropriate for students from different cultures?" The faculty member teaching the theme-based Eng 200 class had the same questions. The course theme, based on a particular genre of music, was one that was unfamiliar to virtually all the international students in the course. Although the instructor had taught this theme many times in the past, the change in student population caused him to immediately rethink the role of the culture and music and the ways students from different cultures would react to and interact with the music in the course.

The emergence of this issue so early in the semester had an important impact on all three faculty members. One stated, "I've been teaching these readings for four years, and I've never before realized how much I assume my students know when they read them. I've never had to make it transparent before." And another noted, "I'm not willing to change the theme. It is part of the course and students can learn a lot from engaging with it. But I do need to think about how to make it more global. . . . A global perspective will be good for all of the students." Working in a class comprised predominately of international students opened up the space for these faculty members to question previously uncontested curricular choices. They also began to consider how to provide both cultural and linguistic inroads to difficult readings. In trying to look at the materials of the course through the eyes of their international students, they were able to see more clearly the ways cultural knowledge as well as disciplinary-specific terms might need to be unpacked and explicated. One of the faculty members began offering reading guides and questions to accompany all the readings. In describing this pedagogical shift, she noted, "I was worried it would be perceived as simplistic by the American students. But actually it helped them to read more closely and to pay attention to vocabulary in ways that they hadn't done in the past."

In fact, as the semester went on, there were very few areas of each of the courses that were not adjusted to meet the needs of the different student population. All three faculty members began incorporating more scaffolding into their instruction—linking shorter writing assignments to longer ones and building on students' vocabulary from one assignment to the next. They all began allowing more drafts of papers than they had in the past, and all three commented that they were spending far more time responding to papers than they had in previous semesters. Two of the faculty also began incorporating language lessons in ways they had not done before. "I generally don't focus on language," one stated. "I'm interested in the rhetorical situation and how students are communicating with their audience and working toward their purpose. But in this class I have to focus on language, on grammar, or the students won't be able to reach their audience. I've always been taught not to focus on grammar, but with these students it has to be there."

When asked if these changes represented a lowering of standards, responses were mixed. One said, "I'm definitely requiring less reading. That's lowering standards, content-wise. But I think all the students are reading more closely. Maybe the standards are lower, but I'm not sure what else I could do. I have to work with the students I have." Another respondent said definitively: no. "If anything the students have done more work. And the projects at the end of the semester have been the same I have always required, I just gave them more support along the way so they could get there. Are the projects perfect? Are they all As? No. But they've done good work."

Faculty Professional Identities

Perhaps the most interesting aspect of working with faculty as they taught for the first time in a multilingual classroom was seeing the ways in which the challenge of teaching a new student population interacted with the instructors' own professional identities. An important part of professional identity in working in the composition classroom is termed *self-efficacy*, which refers to teachers' own beliefs about their level of preparedness for instruction in particular settings (Bandura 1993; Sanchez and Borg 2014). Levels of perceived self-efficacy are generally higher among those teachers who have had more experience and have gone through extensive training programs. The faculty in these writing courses, however, despite having many years of experience and training in teaching writing at the university level, consistently displayed low levels of perceived self-efficacy in relation to teaching L2 writers. This perceived low level of self-efficacy manifested itself in a myriad of ways. In broader faculty interviews, requests for direct and specific policy statements from administrators seemed to be directly linked to a perceived notion that the faculty themselves weren't sure how to handle the use of multiple languages in the classroom. In addition, resistance to the incorporation of different pedagogical practices was a result not only of a desire to maintain high standards but also of an insufficient understanding of appropriate pedagogical practices for multilingual writers. Throughout the course-long research study, as faculty reflected on their teaching, they continually referred to their previous experience or their own training as writing teachers but inevitably concluded it came up short. "I'm trained in rhetoric and composition. I know what I'm supposed to be doing. But it doesn't seem to work with these students. They need something more."

This feeling of being inadequately prepared for the teaching situation in front of them led to a great deal of frustration among the faculty members in the study, but it also forced them to reevaluate every aspect of their approach to teaching, a task they found both stimulating and incredibly difficult. The diverse student population required them to rethink their approach to instruction, and though this reexamination was both time consuming and challenging, all three faculty thought they became better instructors by going through the process. As one faculty commented, "I'm being clearer in my teaching. I'm slowing down and giving more details. I'm providing more help along the way. I think all of my students are benefitting from it." The experience of working in a culturally and linguistically diverse classroom provided faculty the space and the impetus for instructional reflection, ultimately leading to changes in instructional practices that could help all students.

Implications for Faculty Development

This research has had important implications for faculty development in teaching multilingual writers in the composition classroom at the University of Dayton. First, it became clear that faculty development is both necessary and desired. Although faculty workloads across the university are increasing, there is still a strong desire to do good work with and for their students, but this desire is accompanied by the recognition that their own educational backgrounds and previous teaching experiences have not prepared them well for the multilingual classroom. Second, the research indicates that development opportunities could best be handled incrementally and that they must begin with faculty beliefs about language, L2 writers, and L2 teaching. Rather than simply giving faculty tips and suggestions about best practices, engaging them in a discussion about their own beliefs about international students in the university environment allows faculty to reflect on their own notions of good teaching and opens up spaces for new approaches to be considered. Finally, the writing program committed to developing varying types of programming so faculty members with different needs could participate in different types of faculty development.

These principles—that faculty both need and want development opportunities, that development is best handled incrementally, and that any faculty development should be begin with faculty beliefs about language and international students—led to the creation of three types of faculty-development activities for working with multilingual writers. The first type was an intensive, week-long seminar during the summer, wherein faculty members read articles on L2 writing, engaged in discussions of pedagogical approaches, and redesigned courses with principles of cultural and linguistic inclusivity in mind. Faculty read articles from L2 writing, composition, and second language acquisition research, and each day of the seminar was spent discussing common concerns in L2-writing teaching and research, including beliefs about language use, standards, developing assignments, responding to writing, plagiarism, and assessment. Throughout the course of the week, faculty were given the opportunity to examine their own readings and assignments through the lens of the international student and make changes or adjustments when they felt it might be necessary. This type of intense faculty development is not something all faculty would be interested in, but for those who are teaching newly diverse classes, it can allow them to consider the type of pedagogical adjustments that might be necessary even before they are teaching in a multilingual setting. Faculty who participated in this seminar received a stipend, and they then became resources for other faculty who have questions about working with L2 writers. Providing a stipend for participating in this type of work was an important aspect of the faculty-development approach, both because it provided a financial incentive for faculty to attend and because it showed a commitment on the part of the college to the improvement of education for diverse student populations.

Not all faculty could participate in this kind of intensive seminar, however, so the writing program and the College of Arts and Sciences also support shorter faculty-development workshops each semester, many of which respond to specific issues surrounding working with international students in the composition classroom. These workshops include lunch, sometimes provide a stipend to attendees, and address specific issues related to teaching in the L2 writing classroom. Because they happen on a rotating schedule, faculty can attend when they are able and generally take with them some actionable items to incorporate in their own writing classrooms. Workshop topics have included building community in intercultural classrooms, developing effective peer-review processes in intercultural classrooms, developing and scaffolding assignments for L2 writers, feedback in L2 writing, and understanding cultural backgrounds of international students.

Finally, the writing program worked with the broader university to provide online resources for the faculty, so even if they are unable to attend the seminars or workshops, they have access to readings, materials, and information they can use in their own classrooms. As the writing classroom continues to become more diverse, the need for all faculty to explore new approaches to reach students will become all the more apparent. Through greater understanding of faculty and student needs, and increased faculty development, we can continue to develop classroom spaces appropriate for all learners.

Note

1. I am using the term *international students* in this study to refer to students from outside the United States who are also multilingual/L2 (second language) users of English. Although I recognize not all international students are L2, and that not all L2 students are international, in the context for this study (the increased internationalization of a US university), the students are both multilingual and international, and both these factors play an important role in faculty response.

References

Andrade, Maureen Snow. 2006. "International Students in English-Speaking Universities: Adjustment Factors." *Journal of Research in International Education* 5 (2): 131–54. https://doi.org/10.1177/1475240906065589.

Andrade, Maureen Snow. 2010. "Increasing Accountability: Faculty Perspectives on the English Language Competence of Nonnative English Speakers." *Journal of Studies in International Education* 14 (3): 221–39. https://doi.org/10.1177/1028315308331295.

Bandura, Anthony. 1993. "Perceived Self-Efficacy in Cognitive Development and Functioning." *Educational Psychologist* 28 (2): 117–48. https://doi.org/10.1207/s15326985ep2802_3.

Barker, Michelle Carmel, Raymond Thomas Hibbins, and Peter Robert Woods. 2013. "Bringing Forth the Graduate as a Global Citizen." In *International Students Negotiating Higher Education*, edited by Silvia Sovic and Margo Blythman, 142–54. London: Routledge.

Bevis, Teresa Brawner, and Christopher J. Lucas. 2007. *International Students in American Colleges and Universities*. New York: Palgrave Macmillan. https://doi.org/10.1057/9780230609754.

Canagarajah, A. Suresh. 2006. "The Place of World Englishes in Composition: Pluralization Continued." *College Composition and Communication* 57 (4): 586–619.

Clerehan, Rosemary. 2007. "Designs for Supporting International Education: Identities of Participation." *International Journal of Learning* 13 (9): 187–93. https://doi.org/10.18848/1447-9494/CGP/v13i09/45047.

Deil-Amen, Regina. 2015. "The 'Traditional' College Student: A Smaller and Smaller Minority and Its Implications for Diversity and Access Institutions." In *Remaking College: The Changing Ecology of Higher Education*, edited by Michael Stevens and Michael Kirst, 98–117. Stanford, CA: Stanford University Press.

Donahue, Christiane. 2009. "'Internationalization' and Composition Studies: Reorienting the Discourse." *College Composition and Communication* 61 (2): 212–43.

Ferris, Diana, Jeffrey Brown, Hsiang Sean Liu, and Maria Eugenia Arnaudo Stine. 2011. "Responding to L2 Students in College Writing Classes: Teacher Perspectives." *TESOL Quarterly* 45 (2): 207–34. https://doi.org/10.5054/tq.2011.247706.

Grayson, J. Paul. 2008. "The Experiences and Outcomes of Domestic and International Students at Four Canadian Universities." *Higher Education Research & Development* 27 (3): 215–30. https://doi.org/10.1080/07294360802183788.

Haan, Jennifer, Colleen Gallagher, and Lisa Varandani. 2017. "Working with Linguistically Diverse Classes across the Disciplines: Faculty Beliefs." *Journal of Scholarship of Teaching and Learning* 17 (1): 35–51.

Haan, Jennifer, and Karen Mallett. 2015. "English Language Literacy and the Prediction of Academic Success in and beyond the Pathway Program." In *Literacy in Practice: Writing in Private, Public, and Working Lives*, edited by Patrick Thomas and Pamela Takayoshi, 134–47. New York: Routledge.

Horner, Bruce, Min-Zhan Lu, Jacqueline Jones Royster, and John Trimbur. 2011. "Language Difference in Writing: Toward a Translingual Approach." *College English* 73 (3): 299–317.

Janopoulos, Michael. 1992. "University Faculty Tolerance of NS and NNS Writing Errors: A Comparison." *Journal of Second Language Writing* 1 (2): 109–21. https://doi.org/10.1016/1060-3743(92)90011-D.

Jordan, Jay. 2009. "Second Language Users and Emerging English Designs." *College Composition and Communication* 61 (2): W310–W329.

Jordan, Jay. 2012. *Redesigning Composition for Multilingual Realities*. Urbana, IL: NCTE.

Kingston, Emma, and Heather Forland. 2008. "Bridging the Gap in the Expectations between International Students and Academic Staff." *Journal of Studies in International Education* 12 (2): 204–21. https://doi.org/10.1177/1028315307307654.

Knight, Jane. 2004. "Internationalization Remodeled: Definitions, Approaches, and Rationales." *Journal of Studies in International Education* 8 (1): 5–31. https://doi.org/10.1177/1028315303260832.

Leask, Betty. 2009. "Using Formal and Informal Curricula to Improve Interactions between Home and International Students." *Journal of Studies in International Education* 13 (2): 205–21. https://doi.org/10.1177/1028315308329786.

Leki, Ilona. 2007. *Undergraduates in a Second Language: Challenges and Complexities of Academic Literacy Development*. New York: Routledge.

Lindsey, Peggy, and Deborah Crusan. 2011. "How Faculty Attitudes and Expectations Toward Student Nationality Affect Writing Assessment." *Across the Disciplines* 8 (4). https://wac.colostate.edu/atd/ell/lindsey-crusan.cfm.

Maringe, Felix. 2011. "Higher Education Transitions: From International to Global Institutions." In *Moving Towards Internationalisation of the Curriculum for Global Citizenship in Higher Education*, edited by Valerie Clifford and Catherine Montgomery, 27–46. Oxford: Oxford Brookes University.

Matsuda, Paul Kei, Maria Fruit, and Tamara Lee Burton Lamm. 2006. "Second Language Writers and Writing Program Administrators." *WPA: Writing Program Administration* 30 (1–2): 11–14.

Murphy, Christina, Lory Hawkes, and Joe Law. 2002. "How International Students Can Benefit from a Web-Based College Orientation." *New Directions for Higher Education* 117:37–44. https://doi.org/10.1002/he.45.

Robertson, Margaret, Martin Line, Susan Jones, and Sharon Thomas. 2000. "International Students, Learning Environments and Perceptions: A Case Study Using the Delphi Technique." *Higher Education Research & Development* 19 (1): 89–102. https://doi.org/10.1080/07294360050020499.

Ryan, Janette. 2013. *Cross-Cultural Teaching and Learning for Home and International Students: Internationalisation of Pedagogy and Curriculum in Higher Education*. London: Routledge.

Sanchez, Hugo Santiago, and Simon Borg. 2014. "Insights into L2 Teachers' Pedagogical Content Knowledge: A Cognitive Perspective on Their Grammar Explanations." *System* 44 (1): 45–53. https://doi.org/10.1016/j.system.2014.02.005.

Schaub, Mark. 2003. "Beyond These Shores: An Argument for Internationalizing Composition." *Pedagogy: Critical Approaches to Literature, Language, Composition, and Culture* 3 (1): 85–98. https://doi.org/10.1215/15314200-3-1-85.

Tardy, Christine. 2009. *Building Genre Knowledge.* West Lafayette, IN: Parlor.

Tardy, Christine. 2011. "Enacting and Transforming Local Language Policies." *College Composition and Communication* 62 (4): 634–61.

Trice, Andrea G. 2003. "Faculty Perceptions of Graduate International Students: The Benefits and Challenges." *Journal of Studies in International Education* 7 (4): 379–403. https://doi.org/10.1177/1028315303257120.

You, Xiaoye, and Xiaoqiong You. 2013. "American Content Teachers' Literacy Brokerage in Multilingual University Classrooms." *Journal of Second Language Writing* 22 (3): 260–76. https://doi.org/10.1016/j.jslw.2013.02.004.

Zamel, Vivian. 2004. "Strangers in Academia: The Experiences of Faculty and ESL Students across the Curriculum." In *Crossing the Curriculum: Multilingual Learners in College Classrooms,* edited by Vivian Zamel and Ruth Spack, 3–17. Mahwah, NJ: Lawrence Erlbaum.

13

INTERNATIONALIZATION FROM THE BOTTOM UP
Writing Faculty's Response to the Presence of Multilingual Writers

Carolina Pelaez-Morales

INTRODUCTION

The internationalization of US campuses requires an examination of not just academic and social challenges L2 students face but also of ways in which their presence is being used as an opportunity for pedagogical and institutional reform. Most academic institutions enrolling large numbers of international students have responded to these students' presence by offering composition sections for international students. For instance, the eight institutions enrolling the largest numbers of international students in the United States in 2014–2015 (IIE 2014–2015) offer ESL writing sections: International Writing Workshop I & II (New York University n.d.), Introduction to College Writing in a Second Language (University of Southern California n.d.), University Writing for International Students (Columbia University n.d.), First-Year Composition for Multilingual Writers (Arizona State University 2016), English as Second Language 111, 112, or 115 (University of Illinois at Urbana-Champaign n.d.), First-Year Writing for Multilingual Writers (Northeastern University n.d.), English 106I: First-Year Composition for International students (Purdue University n.d.), English Composition 2i (University of California, Los Angeles n.d.).

While setting up L2-specific writing courses is an important response to the presence of L2 learners, doing so is not always feasible, especially at institutions where these students constitute a very small percentage of the student population. At these institutions, composition courses likely enroll no more than a handful L2 students per section, and these courses are likely be taught by faculty members with no expertise in L2 writing. Although these circumstances are not uncommon across US campuses, little is known about how faculty members at these institutions

DOI: 10.7330/9781607326762.c013

are addressing this shift in student population in spite of the fact that out of the 1,485 US institutions surveyed by the Institute of International Education (IIE), about 774, or 52 percent, enrolled 150 international students or fewer in 2014–2015 (IIE 2014–2015). Therefore, it is important to understand faculty perspectives on international students and what pedagogical strategies they use in their classes at institutions with low, but steady, L2 enrollment.

This case study of seven writing faculty members examines their response to the presence of multilingual writers (MLWs) in their mainstream composition classes at Columbus State University (CSU), a midsize public university typically enrolling 150–175 L2 students per academic year, under 2 percent of the student population. Much like at other institutions, CSU has a low L2 student enrollment that has progressively increased since the institution began internationalizing in the early 2000s. The presence of small numbers of international students in first-year composition courses at CSU provides an opportunity for research on faculty perspectives in composition programs with low L2 enrollment and no specific program for multilingual writers. This research contributes to efforts to understand how faculty in different types of institutional contexts are addressing shifts in L2 student populations (Ferris et al. 2011, Matsuda et al. 2013), and it is consistent with efforts by our profession to address the growing presence of MLWs in composition classrooms (CCCC 2001).

INSTITUTIONAL CONTEXT

Columbus State University (CSU) is a regional academic institution with about eight thousand students, 80–85 percent of whom are undergraduates. Over 80 percent of the students at CSU are residents of Georgia (CSU 2015: "Enrollment by Ethnic Origin"), many of whom are nontraditional, first-generation college students from diverse socioeconomic backgrounds. Of the 8,440 students enrolled in fall of 2015, 36 percent were African American, 53 percent Caucasian, 5 percent Hispanic, 2 percent Asian, two or more races 2 percent, and 2 percent international (CSU 2015: "Enrollment by Place of Residence").

CSU demonstrates its commitment to internationalization in a number of ways. Internationalization efforts are coordinated by the Office of Admissions, the English Language Center, and the Center for International Education (CIE), which handles the majority of internationalization programming. Notable programs by CIE include an international learning community (ILC) program, allowing faculty to integrate international content into their classes (CIE 2008–2009), an Internationalization Plan (CIE 2012), an International Studies Certificate (CIE 2013–2014), and study-abroad programs that have attracted students and faculty alike. CIE also offers programming and support for international students, including orientations, a host-family program, an international friendship program, international student field trips, tax workshops, opportunities for cross-cultural discussions, and so forth (CIE 2014–2015). As this list demonstrates, most services for international students provide assistance with cultural and pragmatic issues. While there have been multiple internationalization efforts at CSU, in the remainder of this chapter, I focus on CSU's internationalization as it relates to international students only.

L2 STUDENT POPULATION

The majority of L2 learners at CSU are traditional international students who are in the United States to complete a degree and who enroll in regular courses with the help of an advisor. International students are admitted as international freshmen, international transfer, international graduate, and English Language Institute (ELI) students. All international students except those enrolling in the ELI are required to demonstrate sufficient language proficiency via test scores. For instance, a 79 minimum TOEFL score is required for admission (Columbus State University n.d.).

In the fall of 2010, 114 international students enrolled in academic programs and ELI at CSU (CIE 2010–2011). By fall 2015, that number had grown modestly to 123 (CIE 2014–2015). That year, international students came from thirty-five different countries with the majority of them sending one to five students. According to the director of CSU's Graduate and International Recruitment, while traditionally CSU has attracted students from South Korea, Germany, Canada, and Colombia, in an effort to make its campus more diverse, CSU has increased the representation of multiple countries, while capping enrollments for others (pers. comm., March 11, 2016).

CSU also has a population of international students who through memos of understanding (MOUs) come to the United States for a semester or two, and many of these students voluntarily enroll in first-year writing courses to improve their writing in English. CIE just developed an initiative that might increase the number of these students at CSU. Starting in fall 2015, the American Cross-Cultural Experience Initiative allows "English proficient students at [partner universities to] enroll in full-time study in regularly offered academic courses for one or two semesters" (CIE 2014–2015, 14). This program, as well as CSU's interest in establishing a bridge program (CIE 2012) further emphasizes the need to strengthen the academic side of CSU's internationalization plan.

CSU is committed to increasing the number of international students to the national average by 2017–2018 (CIE 2012, 10), an effort that since 2012 has been supported by recruitment trips, virtual fairs, and the use of educational consultants in Southeast Asia, the Middle East, Central and South America, Brazil, and Japan. The director for Graduate and International and International Recruitment told me that enrollment growth has not corresponded with these recruitment emphases (pers. comm., March 11, 2016), and this is not uncommon at academic institutions that do not have an established international reputation but are still looking to internationalize their campuses.

In spite of slight increases in international student enrollment and plans to continue increasing the number of L2 students at CSU, this growth has not been seen as sufficient grounds for curricular changes across academic units. In the English department in particular there are currently no plans to offer ESL writing courses or specific resources for L2 writers or those who work with them. This situation is likely common at institutions where the number of L2 students is not substantial enough to create and maintain an L2 writing program. For instance, while I am an L2 specialist and I have over seven years of experience teaching L2 writers, I was not hired to teach courses for international students or to administer an L2 writing program. However, I have become a source of support for faculty members in my department. That informal role motivated me to conduct the case study I describe in the next section of this chapter as a means of exploring the tension between institutional efforts to internationalize and faculty members' perceptions of their role in that process.

STUDY DESCRIPTION

This case study of seven writing faculty members examines their responses to the presence of small numbers of multilingual writers in their composition classes. This study addresses the faculty members' preparation, experience, and perceptions of their work with MLWs, with a focus on their views on adequate pedagogical and institutional responses to these students' small, but regular, presence in writing classrooms at CSU. A case study was chosen as the methodology because it allows for an in-depth description of the institutional context and the participants' experiences and beliefs (Lincoln and Guba 1985), which are important components of comprehensive internationalization (Bartell 2003). Although I am aware that different terms exist, for simplicity, I use the term *multilingual writer* (MLW) to refer to international students in composition classes at CSU, although I use the term *L2 student* when referring to these students generally.

I conducted a two-part investigation consisting of an anonymous survey of faculty members in the English department and a voluntary focus group. The survey, completed by seventeen out of twenty-four faculty members, collected information on the participants' perceptions of their work with both native and nonnative English speakers in their composition classrooms. At the end of the survey, faculty were invited to participate in a focus group, which took place a semester later and primarily focused on the participants' perceptions of their work with MLWs. The research findings and conclusions I report here are based on the seven faculty members who volunteered for the focus group.

FINDINGS

This section provides evidence that supports two arguments: first, that activities taking place outside the classroom, including student conferences and student referrals to the writing center, can no longer be the primary pedagogical response to the presence of multilingual writers in composition classrooms; and second, that faculty members as well as writing program administrators are key players in the sustainability of internationalization efforts, and without them, internationalization efforts can fall short. This section starts with contextual information and is followed by a discussion on participants' perceptions of their work with MLWs. Suggestions about how writing faculty can work with L2 students and on how administrators can support internationalization efforts are provided toward the end of the chapter. These suggestions are particularly relevant to institutions that do not offer writing sections for L2 students.

Contextual Information: Teachers' Preparation and Experience

There are two required composition courses at CSU: ENGL 1101 and ENGL 1102. Although in 2014 one section of ENGL 1101 was designated as having seats reserved for MLW students, the course did not enroll enough international students. For that reason, this designation has not been used since, and there are no plans to offer L2 writing sections in the future. The lack of writing sections for MLWs is justified by three reasons of significance to the local context: the low number of L2 students, the need to offer enough composition sections to satisfy student demand, and the inability to hire additional lecturers. Many institutions across the United States will find themselves in the same position as CSU: wanting to serve the L2 students they enroll regardless of number but having to factor in administrative concerns, including scheduling and funding.

CSU's first-year writing program outlines objectives all CSU students should meet in ENGL 1101 and ENGL 1102, but faculty members can make independent decisions on how to help students reach those objectives. As is the case at most nonresearch institutions, all faculty members in the department regularly teach first-year writing courses, which constitute the majority of their teaching load per semester regardless of area of specialization.

As a group, the participants were experienced educators holding an array of credentials. Five of the participants were full-time faculty (four tenure or tenure track, one full-time lecturer) while two were part-time lecturers. Five of the seven held PhDs and had more than ten years of composition teaching experience, while the two part-time faculty had postgraduate degrees and had been teaching composition for under eight years. In spite of extensive composition teaching experience, the majority of them did not have formal training in L1 or L2 composition. One participant specialized in composition and rhetoric, two in education, while the rest had degrees in literature.

While none of the participants had a degree or specialization in L2 writing, all of them had had L2 learners in their classes. The survey asked participants to report how many MLWs they had in the fall of 2014 by choosing one of the following options: one to two, two to three, three to four, five to six, or more than seven MLWs. Two participants reported having one or two MLWs, two said they had either three or four, and one person had five or six. While these numbers do not appear significant, they are noticeable in composition classes at CSU, which have traditionally enrolled almost exclusively native English speakers.

Perceptions of the Work with Multilingual Writers in the Classroom

All seven participants had positive views of their work with MLWs, particularly regarding the degree to which these students contribute to diversity in the composition classroom. This impression is consistent with reports from faculty members outside English departments (Daniels 2013). When asked what the most common advantages to having MLWs in their

Table 13.1. Faculty perceptions of advantages of having L2 writers in class.

Contributions to Diversity
Multilingual students bring <u>different cultural perspectives</u> into class discussions and into their writings.
I enjoy having a <u>diversity of perspectives</u> in the classroom.
Speakers of other languages bring <u>different perspectives</u> to class discussions and projects.
Advantages revolve around the <u>diversity of perspectives</u> during discussions.
An advantage is the <u>contribution</u> multilingual students can make.
Strong Work Ethic
[They] help set a *high standard for effort*.
Both
Overall, the <u>diversity</u> and *work ethic* they provide enhance composition classrooms.

composition classrooms were, participants alluded to their contributions to different perspectives. The following excerpts reveal two themes: the importance of diversity, as seen in the underlined phrases, and MLWs' characteristics as hard workers, as seen in phrases in italics in table 13.1.

In composition classes, the diversity L2 students bring can challenge domestic students' perceptions of what is rhetorically persuasive as well as provide them with examples of how culture and experiences shape viewpoints—all important elements of critical thinking and writing (Arkoudis et al. 2013). Faculty also see MLWs' predisposition toward academic work as positive, which is further illustrated by a comment by the only participant with a specialization in composition and rhetoric. I use underlining to draw attention to descriptions of MLWs' personal characteristics as assets.

> Last semester, I tried a much different kind of final project with my two sections of composition. The format of it did not have to be a paper . . . but there was a script for it, so there was writing that I kind of sneaked into it. . . . The peer groups were not evaluating each other's products. They were meeting to talk about their process, so they were basically getting together to keep each other on track about how their process of developing the projects was coming along . . . <u>the L2 students were in fact the stronger members of many of those groups because what comes through when you're focusing on process is how hard they're working</u>. . . . The L1 students were not putting in enough effort or the kind of effort that I was expecting the project to require, <u>and L2 students were</u>—without my having planned to be that way—because <u>they [had] to plan their time very carefully.</u> And <u>they pay very close attention to instructions</u> in ways that not all the rest of students do.

Table 13.2. Faculty perceptions of L2 writers' metalinguistic knowledge.

L2 students have a better concept of grammar.
They don't have a good concept of structure and how to develop content.
I just started noticing *their grammar was actually much better in their papers* than my L1 students.
Did extremely well on grammar tests.
She had difficulty on her papers.
She knew the rules
but in [her] essays, she would have . . . errors.
If you learned English as 2nd language, [you] have to concentrate on grammar to some extent.
[*Article*] might be a foreign term to an L1; it is not a foreign term to an L2.

As this excerpt shows, MLWs can exceed teachers' expectations and set high academic standards when assignments acknowledge process and/or effort. However, like other writers, MLWs are required to produce writing in other classes, and these classes might have a different structure from English courses. In classes across the curriculum, for instance, there might not be an emphasis on process or on multiple drafts (Hyland 2013). Therefore, writing faculty must make MLWs aware of differences they may encounter in other courses and in writing in other disciplines.

Participants believe MLWs have good command of grammar and metalinguistic vocabulary, especially in isolation. The following excerpts from the focus group reveal two themes: L2 students' metalinguistic knowledge, as seen in the underlined phrases, and their ability to apply that knowledge, as seen in phrases in italics in table 13.2.

Participants in this study saw the need to help MLWs develop strategies to transfer their grammar knowledge and use it in the context of their writing, as the comments show. As these excerpts also show, participants draw comparisons between L1 and L2 learners, highlighting the latter group's command of grammar.

Overall, the strengths of MLWs faculty noted seemed to relate to general classroom practices such as class discussions, to L2 students' characteristics as students, or to their metalinguistic knowledge. As Jay Jordan reminds us, however, "Many teachers [might] wonder what positive effect, if any, L2 users have on their own and other students' performance on specific writing tasks" (Jordan 2009, 321). In this sense, the challenge for composition faculty is how to continue tapping into the

Table 13.3. Faculty perceptions of disadvantages of multilingual writers in composition classrooms.

If they do struggle with language acquisition issues, their peers don't know how to review their texts without focusing solely on errors.

The disadvantage is that I feel that *I don't have time to focus solely on their needs*.

They *struggle to keep up and sometimes are afraid to ask questions*, or when they do need extra help, *they hold the rest of the class up*, which can be frustrating for other students.

One thing I struggle with is how to *grade their work* and *being fair to both L1 and L2 students*. You know that there are going to be some language issues, but I feel like I *haven't had training on how to properly assess multilingual writers*.

---

resources MLWs contribute to their classes while finding writing-specific practices equally beneficial to all writers.

Perceptions of Adequate Pedagogical Strategies

Although participants indicated that they recognized advantages to having MLWs in their classes and acknowledged those students' strengths, they found it difficult to articulate specific pedagogical strategies they use with these learners. The following comments reflect pragmatic concerns in enacting pedagogical practices in mixed composition classrooms. All, except the last comment, are in response to the survey question, "What are the most common disadvantages, if any, in having MLWs in your composition classrooms?" The underlined sections in table 13.3 show pragmatic challenges for L1 students, while the italicized sections reflect concerns from the teachers' point of view.

Faculty members are aware of the pedagogical challenges in having multilingual writers in their classes, in particular lack of time and lack of L2 writing training, which go hand in hand. In other words, if faculty members do not know how to work with these writers, they might have to develop and test strategies in their classes, which requires an investment of time. Once these skills are developed, faculty will be better equipped to maximize their time in class, but because they receive no training for working with MLWs, each faculty member feels that they are on their own (Daniels 2013). Participants reported the following strategies when asked what, if anything, they did with multilingual writers in their classes. In table 13.4 I use underlining to highlight references to time demands and italics to refer to concessions faculty make.

Faculty members provided examples of adopting different strategies for working with L2 students. However, most of the strategies they adopt require them to schedule activities outside class, which is consistent with

Table 13.4. Faculty strategies with multilingual writers in composition classes.

In some ways, I treat all students the same. . . . But I am more likely to <u>request individual conferences</u> with my multilingual students throughout the semester. I also *do not count as much off if their papers do not meet the minimum word-count.*
<u>I meet with them outside of class to discuss their rough drafts in advance. I meet with them more one-on-one.</u>
<u>Working with the students individually.</u>

other studies (Matsuda et al. 2013). While of course all instructors need to be available to students outside of class, using individual conferences as the sole or primary way of assisting L2 learners can lead to teacher burnout. Instead, one implication of these findings is that instructors would benefit from professional development that would help them create in-class activities and assignments that tap into the explicit or implicit linguistic resources and the cultural knowledge L2 learners bring into the composition classroom and could reduce the need for as much out-of-class conferencing.

Maximizing the use of class time is particularly important for contingent faculty. At CSU, for instance, part-time faculty are only compensated by credit hour, and the number of hours they can teach is capped to reduce the cost associated with health benefits. These faculty members are not compensated for additional time spent with their students, yet they are essential to the functioning of our department: close to half our faculty are part time, and this situation is all too common across US institutions. In fact, as different professional organizations show, the number of contingent faculty has increased across institutions in the United States (CCCC 2016), and part-time instructors now constitute over 50 percent of all faculty appointments (AAUP 2016).

Table 13.5 includes excerpts that refer to strategies faculty use for peer review in their mixed composition classes.

These excerpts show that in creating and implementing pedagogical strategies, faculty must be mindful of students' cultural, linguistic, and educational backgrounds but also their personal characteristics. The idea of cultural sensitivity is best exemplified by a comment by a participant who at the time of the study was the WPA and who alludes to the ethnocentric views that permeate composition classrooms. In table 13.6 I use underlining to point at these views and italics to highlight the way they challenge multilingual writers.

In this excerpt, the faculty member highlights two significant pedagogical concerns: students' background knowledge and the need to

Table 13.5. Faculty strategies for peer review in mixed composition classes.

I try to a pair a stronger L1 writer with an ESL speaker when doing peer review.
I will try to pair a multilingual learner with a student who is a good writer for writing workshops and peer review session. . . . sometimes the L2 writers [who] have language acquisition issues are embarrassed or are very reluctant [to do peer review], so you have to be conscious in trying to find somebody who listens.

Table 13.6. Faculty comments regarding ethnocentric views.

I think a lot of *our composition courses stress so much on things that are hard for L2s*: one is the authority of the American voice . . . but also this emphasis on contemporary writing and this emphasis on culture, and pop culture. . . . If you have twenty native speakers and three nonnative speakers, you can assume that they know who Beyoncé is. You can assume these cultural references are shorthand and *you can move through* . . . a lot of the readings that are assigned across sections are based on this premise, but I think *it can be a real barrier to L2 learners who just don't have that understanding of recent American history.*

provide that background information in class. In particular, she points out that both L1 and L2 writers likely understand current, highly publicized, pop-culture references—in this case, they would know who Beyoncé is—and therefore, she does not have to explain this in class and she can simply "move through." However, other cultural references, including those to recent US history, will likely challenge L2 learners, who might not have that kind of knowledge. MLWs at institutions with low L2 enrollment will be at a disadvantage in these cases because faculty could assume (accurately or inaccurately) that the majority of students in the teaching context would have that knowledge, which might restrict the amount of background information they feel they need to provide. In this sense, the excerpt highlights the role of culture in shaping the curriculum, but it adds a layer of complexity in that it distinguishes different types of cultural knowledge MLWs might or might not share with L1 writers.

There are two implications of these findings. First, faculty can use contemporary topics in their composition classes, including those highly publicized in the media, but they should not assume cultural artifacts or rhetorical traditions, including an emphasis on voice, are shared by students regardless of their backgrounds. Particularly at institutions such as CSU that enroll a low number of MLWs from different countries, but also students from diverse socioeconomic backgrounds, blanket generalizations about culture and academic backgrounds can be counterproductive because they can shape pedagogical practices and inadvertently put learners at a disadvantage. Second, to help MLWs succeed in composition classrooms, faculty must provide background information on contemporary texts, background of the kind they typically provide when they assign academic or scholarly texts. Doing so will be helpful to L1 and L2 writers alike in that it can equip MLWs with the knowledge to understand class materials while helping close potential gaps in knowledge L1 writers might have.

Faculty should acknowledge that there are different rhetorical traditions (Kubota and Lehner 2004; Leki 1991), including those that see the suppression of individual voice as a rhetorical choice (Mott-Smith 2013), and that while culture is mediated by individual users (Atkinson and Sohn 2013), it is also socially constructed (Atkinson 1999). Doing so does not necessarily presuppose knowledge of different languages or cultures on the part of faculty. However, as our classrooms become more diverse, knowledge of different rhetorical traditions will be an important element in composition pedagogy, especially in light of institutions' interest in helping students become global citizens (Stearns 2009).

Institutional Support

Overall, the study participants perceived more direct support from departmental administrators, such as the director of first-year composition, than from other administrators. These comments reflect a degree of frustration in not being provided with the right resources to support MLWs, frustration countered by a sense of duty to help their students.

Participants believed student recruitment and faculty support should go hand in hand. For instance, at CSU, there has been an influx of international students who enroll at CSU for a semester or two, and while they are not required to take specific courses, as mentioned previously, they frequently enroll in courses offered by the English department. During our focus group, a participant who had had no training in L2 writing but had been teaching composition for over twenty years commented on this situation. In table 13.7, I use underlining to highlight references to academics, and I use italics to refer to the personal cost to both the student and the instructor.

This comment shows the faculty member's frustration with lack of a placement system and the disadvantages for instructors and students alike. As discussed earlier, CSU is currently implementing an initiative that will bring international undergraduate students to CSU temporarily. To contribute to the success of this initiative, CSU will have to continue strengthening the academic side of internationalization efforts. Writing faculty and the writing program are particularly important in this process because students enroll in composition courses early

Table 13.7. Faculty perceptions of institutional support for multilingual writers.

Last term, there were visiting Korean students who came [for] just one semester. And I had a young woman didn't really understand spoken English at all who was placed into an honors section of a composition class. . . . To me [this] is the biggest disadvantage. If the students are placed completely out of their depth, *they will be frustrated; the instructor would be frustrated. It makes coming to class scary for the student.*

Table 13.8. Faculty perceptions of institutional support structures.

Class sizes need to be smaller . . . and if we are going to have a larger L2 population, the people who are teaching them need to have some more training than we already have.

More support [is needed]. I had an L2 student who had difficulty in class [and] I began looking to see what was available to help. *The writing center offered some support,* but they weren't equipped there either. It was beyond my frame of knowledge in terms of how to teach the student. *We'll do the best we can, but I felt as if I had shortchanged him.*

[When] . . . I have a whole bunch of L2 students, I try to get them into the office either individually or in groups or something . . . [I try] . . . to close gaps especially *if there's nothing else available, as far as writing center, services,* etc.

in their academic careers and because many international students might believe composition classes can help them increase their English-language proficiency.

When asked what they thought would be an adequate institutional response if multilingual writers were to increase at CSU, the majority of respondents expressed dissatisfaction with current academic support structures. Three themes are seen in table 13.8: the need for training (underlined sections), the need for support (italics), and faculty members' personal reactions (both underlining and italics).

As these excerpts illustrate, writing faculty at CSU have developed strategies to account for lack of professional-development opportunities and support, which demonstrates their willingness and interest in helping L2 students succeed. It is important to capitalize on faculty members' willingness to help L2 learners, but these efforts must be supported from the top down. As expressed by participants, some examples on how to help faculty include more faculty training, more specific academic support services, and better infrastructure, including smaller class sizes. Faculty members cannot be expected to do more with fewer resources because this can lead to significant frustration, as the excerpts show, but more important, because there are missed opportunities to capitalize on the diversity L2 students bring to the classroom. Neither institutions nor individual faculty are to blame for lack of an academic infrastructure, but both are responsible to provide the academic support L2 students need.

SUGGESTIONS

Based on my research with English faculty members at CSU, I offer the following suggestions for faculty who find they are teaching writing classes with both L1 and L2 students and who are looking for strategies to help them work more effectively within an unfamiliar environment they may feel unprepared for. I also offer suggestions for administrators who wish to support internationalization efforts and the success of international students. These suggestions might be particularly helpful in institutions like CSU, where the numbers of international students, while growing, are too small and are likely to remain too small to warrant separate L2 writing courses. As will be clear, many of these suggestions will also benefit all students, not just multilingual writers.

Suggestions for Faculty

- Multilingual writers can perform better in writing classes that emphasize the process rather than the product. They also do better in classes that consider or reward their effort and work ethic.
- Writing faculty resort to out-of-class conferences to help multilingual writers. While this strategy is useful, faculty should find ways to integrate these students into the composition classroom. Some activities could include pairing an L1 student with an L2 student, meeting with groups of L2 students at once rather than individually, and creating assignments that engage L1 and L2 students in discussions about rhetorical differences.
- Multilingual writers might perform better in courses that provide them with some opportunities to display their knowledge of grammar. While improving grammar is not the primary goal in a writing course, allowing L2 students to demonstrate their metalinguistic knowledge can help bolster their grades and perhaps also increase their confidence in writing.
- That multilingual writers have command of grammar or want more of it does not mean they are able to use structures successfully in writing. Therefore, writing instructors should provide them with opportunities to develop rhetorical flexibility and to apply their linguistic knowledge in the context of their writing. Doing so is especially important in light of the kinds of writing experiences some MLWs might have had, which may have included being taught writing as a formulaic process.
- Common composition pedagogical practices can be challenging for some multilingual writers. Therefore, writing faculty should recognize and acknowledge that classroom activities are products of cultural, educational, and linguistic contexts and critically assess their implementation. For instance, rather than assume all writers are familiar with peer review and see its value, faculty should model the process

and teach students specific techniques to provide useful comments. Structured peer-review activities can take some time to prepare, but they can also help alleviate the commenting load for faculty and provide a nuanced perspective of audience for students.

- In creating in-class assignments to use in mixed composition classrooms, faculty members should be mindful of how groups are formed. For instance, reviewing L2 learners' writing requires patience and cultural sensitivity. Therefore, in setting up peer-review activities, faculty might consider pairing an L2 student with a student who likes helping others or a student who has studied abroad. Other kinds of assignments will require different pairings. For instance, L1 students who have had little exposure to other cultures could work with MLWs for activities like small-group conversations or small-group projects. In composition classrooms, which typically enroll under twenty-five students, faculty will likely know their students well, and therefore, mindful pairing of students will not be time consuming.

- In mixed composition classes, faculty must provide multimodal support, such as providing instructions orally but also in writing. Preparing written instructions can take some time, but doing so can save faculty time in the long run. For instance, faculty will likely spend less time clarifying assignments via e-mail or during office hours, and they will be able to use these handouts when teaching the same courses in the future.

- Multilingual writers often struggle with writing fluency, and for that reason, like basic writers, they tend to produce shorter drafts. Therefore, writing faculty might choose to make concessions for length or to assign frequent short, low-stakes assignments.

- Faculty should be attuned to students' reactions and interactions with others in class; for instance, a multilingual writer might only take notes when something is written on the board or if they misunderstand questions. In this case, faculty can provide MLWs with additional support in the form of written materials or ask students to paraphrase instructions to ensure comprehension. These in-class observations and others can be used to fine-tune pedagogical choices that will benefit not only MLWs, but all students.

- Some multilingual writers might prefer not to reveal their identity in the classroom. It is important for teachers to respect the students' choices while still being mindful of symptoms in their writing that indicate they might need support.

Suggestions for Administrators

- Administrators should understand that support initiatives must go hand in hand with efforts to internationalize. Increasing recruitment of international students without providing adequate support for students and faculty can be counterproductive since faculty will be tasked with doing more without the tools to do so.

- Because not all faculty have the knowledge needed to work with multilingual writers, faculty support is essential to the success of internationalization initiatives. Support can take different forms depending on the size of the institution and the amount of resources the institution is willing and able to invest. Administrators at institutions with limited resources, such as CSU, can provide free or low-cost resources, including purchasing books on L2 writing pedagogy, subscribing to journals that publish L2 writing research (the *Journal of Second Language Writing* or *TESOL Quarterly*) or to journals with a pedagogical emphasis (*TESOL Journal* or the *Journal of Response to Student Writing*), encouraging their faculty to use listservs or to take advantage of institution-specific resources, such as collaborations with faculty in other departments. Other options include providing funding for faculty to attend workshops or conferences in L2 writing. The Symposium on Second Language Writing or CCCC are good options, but other small conferences, for instance TESOL regional conferences, now include sections on multilingual writing. Sending faculty to regional conferences is a cost-effective option for institutions that want to support faculty development but lack the resources to do so. While attending conferences requires a time investment on the part of faculty, doing so is a form of professional development. Administrators on their part can support faculty members' interest in improving pedagogical practices by recognizing and accepting pedagogically oriented research as valid scholarship that can count toward faculty promotion.

- A portion of international students' tuition should be allocated to support initiatives, including the customization of support services. For instance, while many institutions, CSU included, have writing centers, as participants expressed, often these centers do not offer specific resources to support multilingual writers. One way to customize support services would be to pair a writing center tutor with a faculty member to work together over the course of a semester to offer assistance to MLWs. While working cooperatively can require some time on the part of faculty and others, doing so is a way to ensure that academic services are used and that both faculty and students receive the support they need.

- Working with multilingual writers requires time, which should be reflected in class sizes. At the time this research was conducted, for instance, writing classes at CSU enrolled twenty-four students. However, professional organizations recommend that in order to provide adequate support for writing development, writing courses should not enroll more than twenty students, while "remedial" or developmental courses should be capped at fifteen (CCCC 1989). Ideally, at institutions where L2 writing sections are available, the cap should be similar to that of developmental courses. Administrators must make efforts to meet class-size suggestions set by professional organizations while still being mindful of their institutional context and resources.

- Administrators should recognize pedagogical innovations that are in line with institutional efforts to internationalize. Tangible incentives can be provided for faculty members integrating international students in their classes. For instance, there could be merit raises, pay differentials, and small classroom grants, but also at institutions with fewer resources, faculty could be recognized for their pedagogical efforts in other ways, such as by acknowledging this work in annual reviews.

CONCLUSION

With increased numbers of L2 learners enrolled in composition classes comes responsibility to adapt pedagogical and institutional practices. Much is known about the benefits of diversity, including the ability to prepare students for a competitive global market (Andrade and Evans 2009), but more research is needed on how to address the needs of a changing student population and on pedagogical practices that tap into linguistic, cultural, and educational diversity found in our classrooms. Writing-faculty members as well as writing program administrators are in a good position to contribute to this discussion because unlike faculty in other departments, they have contact with the majority of students.

This research demonstrates that, to some extent, faculty modify their teaching practices to address the needs of their MLWs, often relying on out-of-class activities. While this is a good start, much remains to be done. To address the needs of a changing student population, which involves an array of both L1 and L2 students with different education, linguistic, and cultural backgrounds, faculty will have to invest some time in planning classroom strategies that make use of student diversity, such as providing students opportunities to discuss rhetorical patterns of different languages or the role sources play in different cultures. Even if students themselves are not aware of rhetorical patterns in writing, they can speak about what they believe is persuasive and why, and in this sense, students themselves can become informants in our classes. Faculty can reduce the number of out-of-class activities, including student conferences, reinvest that time in class planning, and hence have the most impact on the majority of their students, not just those who seek additional help.

This research also supports the need for administrators to channel the financial resources that come from international students' tuition revenue toward professional development of faculty (Moriña, Cortes-Vega, and Molina 2015). If institutions invest in training their own faculty, these same faculty members will be in a better position to apply that knowledge in the future with new students. Faculty training is an especially viable option at institutions such as CSU that do not possess the infrastructure or resources to offer dedicated sections for international students but that would like to continue attracting diverse students.

Institutions such as CSU should also reinvest financial resources in customizing and strengthening academic support services to address the needs of L2 students. For instance, CSU offers both social and academic support services to L2 students. These services, however, are often not integrated into or coordinated with the curriculum, and typically there have been more social rather than academic support services. Participants in this research did not feel the academic support offered was sufficient, and they reported frustrations based on their lack of expertise in L2 writing. Therefore, it is important that all those responsible for working with L2 students collaborate with one another so they can provide coordinated support. This cooperation is in contrast to creating student services and expecting students to use them or to outsourcing the work with L2 students to units on campus, such as the international student office or the writing center.

Last, this research demonstrates that administrators are in a good position to bridge institutional policies and faculty members' practices. Participants in this research, for instance, reported that they developed strategies to work with MLWs, which demonstrates their commitment to their students. However, they also reported a degree of professional isolation. Like faculty in other contexts, they might feel that "internationalization . . . has happened *to* [them]" (Daniels 2013, 242; emphasis in original) and that they are expected to provide pedagogical provisions without support. One way writing program administrators can support faculty is by communicating their needs to institutional administrators and by involving them in decision-making practices, especially those regarding student enrollment. In other words, rather than deciding to increase international student enrollment, there should be a discussion of the infrastructure needed in order to do so, and faculty are an important voice in this process.

To date, academic institutions have responded to the presence of multilingual writers using two models: by creating separate sections for L2 learners and by placing L1 and L2 learners in the same composition classrooms. In this chapter, I have argued that the primary pedagogical response to the presence of L2 writers in regular composition classrooms, even at institutions with low L2 enrollment, can no longer be limited to working with students individually and outside class and that the internationalization of US campuses is incomplete without faculty support and administrators' mediating role in that process. As this research demonstrates, faculty are aware of the positive ways in which L2 students contribute to the classroom (e.g., diversity of perspectives, serving as examples to other students). However, they also feel a sense of frustration in having to execute internationalization efforts without time, resources, or preparation. As my findings demonstrate, faculty must be provided with tools to enable them to work in an increasingly multicultural, multilingual composition classroom, and in this sense, writing program administrators are in a unique position to support internationalization efforts through the implicit and explicit support they can provide their faculty. All in all, as this research demonstrates, the internationalization of US campuses requires mindful and explicit allocation of resources toward academic support, including professional development of its faculty, as well as consideration of the way international students' presence in the academic community can be used as an opportunity for pedagogical and institutional reform.

References

AAUP. 2016. "Background Facts on Contingent Faculty." *American Association of University Professors.* Accessed April 2016. https://www.aaup.org/issues/contingency/background-facts.

Andrade, Maureen S., and Norman W. Evans, eds. 2009. *International Students: Strengthening a Critical Resource.* Lanham, MD: Rowan & Littlefield Education.

Arizona State University. 2016. "First Year Composition Courses: ENGL 107–108." Department of English. Accessed May 25, 2016. https://english.clas.asu.edu/admission/first-year-composition-courses.

Arkoudis, Sophie, Kim Watty, Chi Baik, Xin Yu, Helen Borland, Shanton Chang, Ian Lang, Josephine Lang, and Amanda Pearce. 2013. "Finding Common Ground: Enhancing Interaction between Domestic and International Students in Higher Education." *Teaching in Higher Education* 18 (3): 222–35. https://doi.org/10.1080/13562517.2012.719156.

Atkinson, Dwight. 1999. "TESOL and Culture." *TESOL Quarterly* 33 (4): 625–54. https://doi.org/10.2307/3587880.

Atkinson, Dwight, and Jija Sohn. 2013. "Culture from the Bottom Up." *TESOL Quarterly* 47 (4): 669–93. https://doi.org/10.1002/tesq.104.

Bartell, Marvin. 2003. "Internationalization of Universities: A University Culture-Based Framework." *Higher Education* 45 (1): 43–70. https://doi.org/10.1023/A:1021225514599.

CCCC. 1989. "Principles for the Postsecondary Teaching of Writing." *Conference on College Composition and Communication.* Accessed 20 May 2016. http://www.ncte.org/cccc/resources/positions/postsecondarywriting#principle9.

CCCC. 2001. "Statement on Second Language Writing and Writers." *Conference on College Composition and Communication.* Accessed 20 May 2016. http://www.ncte.org/cccc/resources/positions/secondlangwriting.

CCCC. 2016. "Statement on Working Conditions for Non-Tenure-Track Faculty." *Conference on College Composition and Communication.* Accessed 20 May 2016. http://www.ncte.org/cccc/resources/positions/working-conditions-ntt.

CIE (Center for International Education). 2008–2009. *Annual Report 2008–2009*. Accessed February 15, 2016. https://cie.columbusstate.edu/docs/_pdfs/CIE%20 Annual%20Report%202008-2009.pdf.

CIE (Center for International Education). 2010–2011. *Annual Report 2010–2011*. Accessed February 15, 2016. https://cie.columbusstate.edu/annual_reports/CIE%20 ANNUAL%20REPORT%202010-11.pdf.

CIE (Center for International Education). 2012. *Internationalization Plan 2012*. Accessed February 15, 2016. https://cie/Campus%20Internationalization%20Plan_2012_Final .pdf.

CIE (Center for International Education). 2013–2014. *Annual Report 2013–2014*. Accessed February 15, 2016. https://cie.columbusstate.edu/annual_reports/ciean nualreport201314.pdf.

CIE (Center for International Education). 2014–2015. *Annual Report 2014–2015*. Accessed February 15, 2016. https://cie.columbusstate.edu/annual_reports/2014 -2015cieannualreport.pdf.

Columbia University. n.d. "University Writing for International Students." http://www .college.columbia.edu/core/node/3291.

Columbus State University. n.d. "International Student Admissions." Accessed January 27, 2016. https://admissions.columbusstate.edu/international/.

CSU (Office of Institutional Research and Effectiveness). 2015. "CSU Facts & Figures 2015 Student Information." *Columbus State University*. Accessed 15 February 2016. https://ir.columbusstate.edu/reports/facts15/facts-student.php.

Daniels, Jeannie. 2013. "Internationalization, Higher Education and Educators' Perceptions of their Practices." *Teaching in Higher Education* 18 (3): 236–48. https://doi.org/10.1080/13562517.2012.719158.

Ferris, Dana, Jeffrey Brown, Hsiang Liu, and Maria Eugenia Arnaudo Stine. 2011. "Responding to L2 Students in College Writing Classes: Teacher Perspectives." *TESOL Quarterly* 45 (2): 207–34. https://doi.org/10.5054/tq.2011.247706.

Hyland, Ken. 2013. "Faculty Feedback: Perceptions and Practices in L2 Disciplinary Writing." *Journal of Second Language Writing* 22 (3): 240–53. https://doi.org/10.1016/j .jslw.2013.03.003.

IIE (Institute of International Education). 2014–2015. "International Students: All Institutions." *Open Doors*. Accessed April 25, 2016. https://www.iie.org/Research-and -Publications/Open-Doors/Data/International-Students/All-Institutions/2014-15.

Jordan, Jay. 2009. "Second Language Users and Emerging English Designs." *College Composition and Communication* 61 (2): 310–29.

Kubota, Ryuko, and Al Lehner. 2004. "Toward Critical Contrastive Rhetoric." *Journal of Second Language Writing* 13 (1): 7–27. https://doi.org/10.1016/j.jslw.2004.04.003.

Leki, Ilona. 1991. "Twenty-Five Years of Contrastive Rhetoric: Text Analysis and Writing Pedagogies." *TESOL Quarterly* 25 (1): 123–43. https://doi.org/10.2307/3587031.

Lincoln, Yvonna S., and Egon G. Guba. 1985. *Naturalistic Inquiry*. Newbury Park, CA: SAGE.

Matsuda, Paul K., Tanita Saenkhum, and Steven Accardi. 2013. "Writing Teachers' Perceptions of the Presence and Needs of Second Language Writers: An Institutional Case Study." *Journal of Second Language Writing* 22 (1): 68–86. https://doi.org/10 .1016/j.jslw.2012.10.001.

Moriña, Anabel, Dolores M. Cortes-Vega, and Victor M. Molina. 2015. "Faculty Training: An Unavoidable Requirement for Approaching More Inclusive University Classrooms." *Teaching in Higher Education* 20 (8): 795–806. https://doi.org/10.1080/1 3562517.2015.1085855.

Mott-Smith, Jennifer A. 2013. "Viewing Student Behavior through the Lenses of Culture and Globalization: Two Narratives from a US College Writing Class." *Teaching in Higher Education* 18 (3): 249–59. https://doi.org/10.1080/13562517.2012.725222.

New York University College of Arts and Science. n.d. "Expository Writing Program." Accessed May 25, 2016. http://cas.nyu.edu/ewp.html.

Northeastern University Writing Program. n.d. "First-Year Writing." Accessed May 25, 2016. http://www.northeastern.edu/writing/first-year-writing/.

Purdue University. n.d. "Course Information." Accessed May 25, 2016. http://icap.rheto rike.org/courseinfo.

Stearns, Peter N. 2009. *Educating Global Citizens in Colleges and Universities.* New York: Taylor & Francis.

University of California, Los Angeles Writing Programs. n.d. "Undergraduate: Requirements for First-year Students." Accessed May 25, 2016. http://wp.ucla.edu /wp/students/undergraduate/.

University of Illinois at Urbana-Champaign College of Liberal Arts and Sciences. n.d. "Composition I." Accessed May 25, 2016. http://www.las.illinois.edu/students/re quirements/comp/.

University of Southern California Dornsife College of Letters, Arts and Sciences. n.d. "Courses." Accessed 25 May 2016. https://dornsife.usc.edu/the-writing-program /courses/.

PART V

Conclusion

14

INFUSING MULTILINGUAL WRITERS
A Heuristic for Moving Forward

Libby Miles

This chapter begins with a conundrum shared by many: how do we become a more diverse institution in spite of the geographic, demographic, and economic limitations particular to midsized public institutions in New England? In January of 2015, I moved to Vermont. At the time, my new university had many things to be proud of, accumulating accolades such as *Travel + Leisure*'s Best College Town. We like our winters and our accolades, but there is always one area in which we fall short: "Interacting with Diverse Others" on the National Survey of Student Engagement (NSSE), which surveys student perceptions of their learning and experiences. In all other NSSE categories, we either match or exceed comparable or aspirant institutions, but "Interacting with Diverse Others" eludes and rankles. Clearly, in order for our students to interact with diverse others, we need to have diverse others at our institution.

For a university in a predominantly white state, in a predominantly white region, known for rather extreme winter temperatures, recruiting and retaining a diverse student body has been a challenge. Attempts to address our diversity deficiency have been ongoing for several decades, including a long-standing two-course diversity university-wide requirement. Thus, that lone red triangle in our NSSE report, indicating "below comparable institutions," stung. By 2010, when our percentage of white, non-Hispanic students still hovered at a whopping 87 percent, goaded by NSSE reports, declining US demographics, and increasing financial pressures, we began recruiting students from abroad. Thus, the 2013 strategic plan for my current institution—like so many other institutions—included a mandate for Enrollment Management to increase the university's international student population from its current 1 percent to 5–7 percent over the next three years.

DOI: 10.7330/9781607326762.c014

The initiative succeeded wildly: by 2015, when I arrived, we were rather rapidly approaching 7 percent. Missing, however, was consideration of how to support international students once they matriculated. As a result, instructors were reeling: who are these new students, and how do we teach them? From the rollout of the land grant, to the GI Bill, to open admissions, to so-called digital natives, it's an age-old story in writing studies: when any new population gains access to US higher education, faculty ask (sometimes with a note of rising panic), "How do we teach these new students?" Susan Miller-Cochran (2010) asks us to consider the WPA's responsibility toward international students; in this piece, I extend Miller-Cochran's concerns to also include our responsibilities toward our writing instructors and even to the institution itself.

The question then becomes *how*. How to do it? How to create an environment in which we attend to the needs of *all* students and *all* faculty in our programs, mindful of the goals and values of our institution? As WPAs we are often very good at gathering information and getting guidance from other WPAs; knowing what to design after gathering information and guidance, however, is a more difficult challenge. I am reminded of a story in which Richard Miller (1999) offers his graduate students several scenarios typical in the life cycle of a WPA. He asks them, "Given what you do know, how would you choose to respond?" (11). One student answers each scenario with a cheeky "need more information" (11). In response, Miller notes that "we are all regularly called upon to act in the absence of such information for the simple reason that collecting all the relevant data and interpreting it in the fullness of time is a luxury extended to no social agent at work in the world" (11). "So," Miller repeats, "how do you choose?" (13). With more information or without, the question of *how* still lingers, for all of us.

Having found myself as a WPA at a new institution faced with the need to make timely yet informed decisions, Miller's question resonates. Truly, myriad resources exist to help new and seasoned WPAs gather information and perspectives: the CWPA workshop, CompPile bibliographies, the *WPA Journal,* and scholarly collections. Such resources provide us with information but also with frameworks and philosophical approaches for approaching what to do with information. They show us the choices others have made; they articulate critiques and additional questions; they offer cautionary tales and salutary visions. With all those resources, WPAs nonetheless are still left with the question of *how* to choose.

Answering this *how* question for myself, articulating my own procedural knowledge, must acknowledge my participatory feminist administrative philosophy, which values local solutions and contextual explorations (for a brief overview of the principles underlying feminist writing program administration, see Goodburn and Leverenz 1998, 277). It requires designing a process consistent with the principles of feminist administration and developing capacity for practical wisdom. In the pages that follow, then, I offer a process for WPAs to respond to administrative exigencies. To wit, I explore a process through which we can begin to sort through how to best (1) support our new international students and (2) support their instructors while (3) developing a university culture enhanced by the differing perspectives, assumptions, backgrounds, and values a truly diverse campus affords.

In spite of professional hesitation, I turned to tagmemics. Often the butt of scholarly jokes (Sirc 1997) and lambasted as overly cognitivist, Richard Young, Alton Becker, and Kenneth Pike's tagmemics calls for a systematic inquiry, a purposeful shifting of perspectives, an unveiling of that which is already "partially known" (Young, Becker, and Pike 1970, 92), a generative process yielding "fruitful questions" (120). Attempts to rescue and revive interest in tagmemics over the past several decades have largely failed (see Kinney 1978; Kneupper 1980; Vitanza 1979; Lindemann 1995). Maybe it's the name. In any case, I am unlikely to announce in a public gathering that I use tagmemics on the job.

Tagmemics, like any heuristic, must be situated and adapted, so it focused my purposeful attention through multiple angles, strategies, and alternatives within the context of my material and time constraints as WPA. Tagmemics requires that users "vary [their] assumptions" (Young, Becker, and Pike 1970, 128). As Young, Becker, and Pike suggest, this purposeful shifting of perspectives does not provide the answers but rather "gives us some assurance that we are thinking well, that we have not overlooked important data" or perspectives (130). A process for thinking well, for including as many perspectives as possible, was exactly what I needed. It seemed, then, to be an excellent option for quickly gathering the relevant data in a way consistent with the principles of feminist administration. But getting more information wasn't quite enough; I also needed a tool for guiding and shaping the information into a responsive, local plan of action. Unexpectedly, tagmemics guided the transition from gathering information to making an informed choice—the elusive *how* of choosing.

The tagmemic process begins simply with a particle, a wave, and a field. In *particle*, we view the issue as a delimited and static entity, a mindful exploration of this present moment. Who are our students? Who are our instructors? How are they like and unlike others in this institution? *Wave* asks us to put that particle in motion, in dynamic exploration of what has come before and what is likely to come afterwards. What paths do our students and instructors take to reach us? Where to next? *Field* puts our wave in conversation with other waves, exploring networks of influence and mutual interdependence.

That process alone is highly generative. However, the rest of the matrix more fully addresses Miller-Cochran's concerns. Tagmemics then offers three additional lenses: *contrast* (What are the similarities? What are the distinctions?), *variation* (What are the far boundaries? What is the range and variety within our populations? How far can we go before it is no longer recognizable?), and *distribution* (What are the relationships with other systems?). Each connects to particle, wave, and field for a nine-cell matrix. An overwhelmed WPA can thus break an issue down to manageable pieces, which will be put back together later with additional specificity and complexity. At first, it feels like an invention technique designed mostly to generate a lot of text, a copia of information; later, however, solutions begin to emerge as connections and subtleties are explored.

	Particle	Wave	Field
Contrast	Describing and defining the individual	Describing and defining the group to which the individuals belong	Describing and defining the larger network to which the group belongs
Variation	Difference and diversity of individuals that fit the definition generated above	Difference and diversity of groups that fit the definition generated above	Difference and diversity of networks that fit the definition generated above
Distribution	Commonalities, affinities, and relationships with other individuals who do not fit the definition generated above	Commonalities, affinities, and relationships with other groups who do not fit the definition generated above	Commonalities, affinities, and relationships with other networks that do not fit the definition generated above

As with any heuristic, tagmemics' value shines when applied contextually, when used as a guide for situationally appropriate adaptations. In my case, as illustrated in what follows, it prompted an exploration back into L2 scholarship and also to offices and services throughout campus. It identified and clarified the complexities of my students and instructors; the possible avenues for professional development; and the personal, scholarly, and institutional networks needed to enact diversity infusion at my campus. It helped me move from "need more information" to the *how* of choosing.

A PARTICLE VIEW: INDIVIDUAL STUDENTS AND INSTRUCTORS

We begin at the particle level, with individual students struggling with the individual writing projects their individual writing instructors are assigning. The particle column in the matrix questions who our students and instructors are with questions like these:

> *Student Focus (particle/contrast):* Who are our multilingual students here at the University of Vermont? What paths do they take to reach us?

> *Student Focus (particle/variation):* To what extent are our multilingual students international, and to what extent are they domestic? If international, how long have they been in the United States? If domestic, what challenges might they face?

> *Student Focus (particle/distribution):* What other students have commonalities with our multilingual students that are worth exploring? What material conditions are needed for their success?

As Elena Lawrick (2013) and others have noted, multilingual students can enter our institutions through many avenues, yet we often lack tracking mechanisms to capture their data as a cohort. Further, not all students choose to identify themselves with our labels—whether ESL or multilingual or ELL (see Ortmeier-Hooper 2008). This is just as true at UVM. In general, however, our multilingual students tend to fall into the following clusters:

- Predominantly Chinese students from our home-grown global gateways program (GGP). Students whose TOEFL scores fall marginally below our cutoff for regular admissions may spend from one to three terms in this prematriculation program. During that time, they live in separate GGP housing, have separate GGP courses (including ESOL courses on academic writing and US academic culture), and they begin their acculturation to Vermont life. It is a partial acculturation, to be sure, because many of them rarely use English outside class. When they do matriculate, they transfer in as sophomores, so their GGP credits ultimately count toward graduation.
- Predominantly Chinese and Nigerian students through the US-Sino Pathway Program (USSP), offered through another institution. Chinese and Nigerian students take their prematriculation experience at a campus in their home country and then transfer directly to UVM as sophomores after a summer bridge elsewhere in New England.
- International admits through traditional channels. Because of our location (less than an hour from the Quebec border), the majority of these are French-speaking, yet bilingual, Canadians.
- International exchange students, in very small numbers.
- US citizens who speak other languages at home. This is the most difficult population to identify, as is the case everywhere. It includes

US citizens outside the fifty states, such as Spanish-speaking Puerto Ricans. It also includes those students who may have taken a year of high school in the United States and therefore apply as domestic students (with no TOEFL requirement). Given Burlington's status as a resettlement community, it also includes refugees (and their children) from Bhutan, Burundi, Congo, Iraq, Rwanda, Somalia, Sudan, Tibet, and Vietnam.

Note that many of our international students join us as transfer students. Many domestic transfer students find challenges with orientation, housing, advising, socialization, and adjusting to a new environment. Our international students must layer those difficulties with the challenge of being multilingual learners in a predominantly white, US setting. They seem doubly disadvantaged in this system.

What about the instructors who teach our foundational writing courses? The particle view leads to questions like these:

Faculty Focus (particle/contrast): Who are the instructors teaching our international students? And what paths have they taken to be where they are now?

Faculty Focus (particle/variation): What differences, abilities, and experiences present in our staff?

Faculty Focus (particle/distribution): Who else on campus might enrich our community (ESL faculty, writing centers, or instructional librarians)? What material conditions are necessary for our instructors to succeed?

My department values its full-time, non-tenure-track faculty and has not become overreliant on contingent labor. All of our lecturers regularly rotate through first-year writing, but first-year writing never constitutes more than half their teaching load. Often, in fact, first-year writing constitutes only one quarter of their teaching load for the year, and they teach a balance of literature-focused and writing-focused courses; this is well in line with best practices advocated by the Conference on College Composition and Communication and the Council of Writing Program Administrators. Most of our fulltime lecturers are publishing writers in their own right, both scholarly and creative works. Some are "trailing partners"; others are UVM-grown; still others enjoy this beautiful place and like the work (remember those Best College Town accolades?). They have a wide range of expertise and experience, although rarely with multilingual writers. I am fortunate to work with them, and they teach approximately half our English 1 sections.

The other half of our classes are taught by graduate teaching assistants, here for a two-year masters in literature. The department has twelve GTA lines, and each GTA teaches three sections per year for two years. Often, they bring prior experience working with multilingual populations; one or two per year have lived and/or taught abroad at some point. Thus, we have two very different instructor populations, both of whom are vital and valued.

Who we select to teach our classes reflects our model of teaching, learning, and writing. Upon my arrival at UVM, I was immediately urged to offload the international students to the newly burgeoning ESOL faculty—a tempting expeditious solution to a complicated problem. ESOL faculty would develop and teach a different course as an English 1 equivalent. I resisted.

Tagmemics aided my resistance to the simple solution. The contrast row of the grid encourages users to create an expansive definition of the entity in question. The variation row, then, demands attention to the full range of diversity and possibility within that definition. Having internalized an expansive definition of *first-year writer* that included all the permutations of our populations on campus, it seemed antithetical to exclude a wide swathe of our population from the environment I was designing.

Scholarship on L2 writing bears out my resistance as well. Various studies have found that writing programs and ESL programs tend to promote different models of teaching, learning, and writing, and this bifurcation too often results in unhelpful clashes and contradictions between the writing faculty and the ESOL faculty (see especially Atkinson and Ramanathan 1995; Zamel 1995). Too often, one group assumes language and knowledge are mutually constitutive and grow together in richness and complexity, while the other assumes language skills come first, before knowledge—that language is a building block that must be put in place before thinking and learning about content can happen. As a writing program administrator attempting to address Miller-Cochran's (2010) call for responsibility, I needed to create an environment in which the first assumption is primary: that language and knowledge are mutually constitutive and grow together in richness and complexity over time.

In addition, outsourcing writing instruction for international students would not help the university reach its goal of providing opportunities for all of us to learn from difference, for faculty and students alike to "interact with diverse others." Nor would it further my goal of developing a teaching community in which instructors invested in an ongoing collaboration to revise our shared, living curriculum.

That same desire, however, also triggered the distribution cell in our tagmemics grid into action. How might we build the English Department's capacity to better respond to our changing student body?

One solution was to expand our circle, to invite ESOL faculty to join with us in this collaboration. That led to a second expansion: our teaching librarians. With that, we increased our English 1 teaching community by two: one ESOL lecturer and one instructional librarian, both of whom had prior experience teaching college composition.

A WAVE VIEW: THE CLASS

Viewing particles together now as a wave leads to considering the classes we offer, with questions like these:

Class Focus (wave/contrast): What is the class, specifically at the University of Vermont? What options are available? What other options might we consider?

Class Focus (wave/variation): How much consistency and variation is there from section to section? How do the variations present? How might we change the existing course to better serve the needs of all students?

Class Focus (wave/distribution): What are the mechanisms for infusing multilingual professional development into the curricula? What material conditions are needed to ensure success? How do we guide the right individuals (teachers and students) to the right classes?

All students at the University of Vermont, multilingual or not, take one of three paths to fulfill the university's foundational writing and information literacy (FWIL) requirement: students in the College of Arts and Sciences take a first-year seminar taught by faculty in the disciplines; students in the Honors College take a first-year sequence taught by honors faculty from different disciplines; and all other students take English 1, whose instructors are described above. Although the College of Arts and Sciences comprises the largest college in the university, the majority of UVM students do fulfill their FWIL requirement through English 1. This is even more the case for our multilingual writers, who typically transfer in as sophomores from the GGP or USPP disproportionately into the College of Business or the College of Engineering and Mathematical Sciences. With neither type of first-year seminar available to sophomores, the majority of our international students are routed to English 1. One choice became clear: the greatest amount of good would result from focusing only on English 1 at this time.

Our English 1 ostensibly has a shared curriculum, a living document designed and revised through a collaborative process with the entire English 1 teaching staff. I say ostensibly because ownership of and participation in the shared curriculum are not, shall we say, universally

shared. There are, of course, slight variations in emphasis and pedagogy—and those are to be celebrated and enhanced. However, there
are other sections that bear no resemblance to the shared curriculum.
When considering options for revising English 1 to be more appropriate for multilingual writers, it became clear that we first needed to build
a sense of community, a collaborative experience in a shared environment. This approach was consistent with my feminist administrative aims.

Thus, another choice became clear: the way forward was to invite participation in English 1 community building and to broaden the range
of available options within the "official" curriculum so more instructors
could see themselves in the course design. Ultimately, a working group
would create sequences and materials more appropriate for all students—our multilingual writers as well as all others.

The tagmemic questions listed above include considering alternatives.
Our current (non)model would be considered "sink or swim," a terribly
accurate term introduced by Steve Simpson at a recent WPA Institute
(see also Roy 1988; Silva 1994). Other possible program designs include
offering ESL sections alongside traditional ones (see especially Braine
1996); cross-cultural sections that are purposefully mixed (see Matsuda
and Silva 1999; Ortmeier-Hooper 2008); or lab-enhanced courses (see
Shuck 2006). Each has its own benefits and drawbacks. What is important, L2 scholarship tells us (Costino and Hyon 2007; Silva 1994, 1997;
others), is to offer students a choice, to give them agency in determining whether they wish to enroll in a special section or mainstream themselves in traditional sections. Within my first three months on the job, I
had to ask which of these options, or what combination of these options,
made sense for the University of Vermont to pursue at that moment in
time, given current capabilities, conditions, and constraints.

In addition, I had to ask what sort of scaffolding might be added to
our official curriculum, those extra steps of learning we may take for
granted with our mainstream NES students? Scholarship offers many
suggestions for teaching or tutoring multilingual writers. For example,

- ensure assignment prompts aren't dependent on culture-specific background knowledge, compose assignment sheets in clear language, and
  distribute them in multiple formats (Harklau 1994; Leki 1992; Reid
  and Kroll 1995);
- speak more slowly, wait with patience for responses, allow more time
  in discussion, check to ensure students are understanding (Harklau
  1994; Leki 1992; Rafoth and Bruce 2009);
- restate main ideas, key themes, abstract concepts, and instructions in
  multiple ways using varied vocabulary (Leki 1992);

- scaffold smaller reading assignments and offer more time to complete longer ones (Leki 1992);
- assign a variety of types of texts to read, familiarizing students with a range of genres and rhetorical approaches, offering direct instruction on US academic rhetorical strategies and patterns (Benson et al. 1992);
- allow students to reflect on their cultural identities in relation to the class (Matsuda and Silva 1999).

In spite of these suggestions, it is crucial to heed the warnings offered by Dwight Atkinson and Vai Ramanathan: we do our students a disservice with the "uncritical application of L1 pedagogies" in a second language writing classroom (Atkinson and Ramanathan 1995, 539; see also Silva 1993). Indeed, I could see that our official curriculum was a pedagogy of read-draft-revise. Whereas this pedagogy would encourage variations in voice and "written accent" (see Canagarajah 2015; Marzluf 2006; Wetzl 2013), there was very little attention to invention or reflection. Most concerning to me was the absence of a final portfolio with one more round of revision and polishing at the end of the semester (see Song and August 2002 on the benefits of portfolios with L2 writers). The absence of a culminating portfolio gave me pause on behalf of all students. However, as I worked through the tagmemic grid, I became increasingly concerned about the lack of a final opportunity for our multilingual students to reflect, revise, and polish works of their choosing—a final chance to apply what they had learned throughout the semester with new insights and increase facility with their emerging written voices. In this case, it was clear that the change was necessary for our multilingual writers and that it would benefit all writers.

The remainder of the questions listed above could only be answered through the perspective of the field view, at the university level. Once there, the pieces began to connect, and the *how* of choosing fell into place.

A FIELD VIEW: THE UNIVERSITY

The field level of tagmemics demands attention to university-level structures, processes, and implications. As particles gather together in our classes to make waves, each wave connects in a field to the larger rhythm of the entire institution. Although it initially sounds the most abstract, for me, the field level quickly turned in the direction of bureaucratic problem solving and mechanical tweaks. Such tweaks are not trivial; on the contrary, it is the level at which much important and often hidden work gets done (see also Porter et al.'s [2000] notion of institutional critique). It is in the bureaucratic structures that enable and disable our actions that the truly available paths become apparent. More to the point, something needed to happen *soon*, and the field view helped me sort out the viable possibilities.

Institution Focus (field/contrast): How does the university currently function?

Institution Focus (field/variation): How much consistency and variation is there within those functions? What qualities do the variations present? What other avenues might be available?

Institution Focus (field/distribution): What are the mechanisms for allocating resources, space, bodies, and so forth? To which of these mechanisms can I gain access?

Field can also refer to our discipline: the scholarship of teaching and learning and administration, of L2 writing and writing studies, of rhetoric, and of higher education. The "CCCC Statement on Second Language Writing and Writers" offers sound advice for creating the appropriate material conditions for both students and faculty (Conference on College Composition and Communication 2014). Of their recommendations, smaller enrollment caps and teacher preparation rose to the top of my list.

At this point, I encountered a temporal contradiction: our long-term goal is to infuse multilingual writers (and those who teach them) throughout the institution, but in the short term we lack the development infrastructure to serve both students and faculty well (for a cautionary tale, see Hsieh 2007). If the exigence for this entire situation was the goal of infusing more domestic and international diversity into our campus, how could we work toward that goal rather than separating out multilingual writers in potentially Othered and exoticized classroom spaces? It became clear that resources for pilots are often available, whereas resources for departmental overhauls often are not. I had to make my peace with having to go through an intermediary step of parallel courses in order to reach our ultimate goal of choice and infusion. My short-term plan, then, would be to create a cadre of instructors with sufficient and appropriate professional development for working with multilingual writers. That cohort would work together to revise our English 1 curriculum with sequences, activities, practices, and policies appropriate for multilingual writers.

Pilots are fundable; pilots build capacity. The provost's office provided catering for a three-day workshop in January, as well as $1,000 in professional-development funds for each multilingual writing faculty fellow (cash stipends are not allowed). Provost approval hinged on two capacity-building principles: (1) that faculty fellows would actively create new materials that would be more appropriate for all students and (2) that faculty fellows would be better prepared for multilingual writers in any of their classes, whether writing or literature or film studies.

We also succeeded in reducing class enrollment to sixteen, down from twenty-two. Lower caps led to additional sections, which were funded and staffed by the university's director for global initiatives, the College of Arts and Sciences, and the English Department. The director of global initiatives (formerly a linguistics faculty member) and several members of the new ESOL faculty provided sessions during the three-day workshop. Prior to the January workshop, I was able to cohost with our writing-in-the-disciplines office a three-part reading group on multilingual learners, open to all faculty in the university. A professional-development support plan was taking shape.

But what to call the special sections? Kimberly A. Costino and Sunny Hyon argue that students have reasons for preferring some options, reporting a high degree of satisfaction with the choice they made, as long as they had a choice (Costino and Hyon 2007; see also Silva 1994, 1997). Others (Chiang and Schmida 1999; Lawrick 2013; Ortmeier-Hooper 2008) note that issues of linguistic identity formation are crucial to consider. That discussion is still very much underway, with *international* as a temporary placeholder during our pilot.

Student distribution became the next issue to tackle: how do we get the right students into these parallel international sections? At my new university, as at many institutions, there appear to be four mechanisms for making this happen:

- students enroll themselves because they see the title on the registration page, something like Written Expression, International section;
- advisors encourage/tell students which sections to take (as in, please register for Written Expression, International section or please register for any section between AA and FF);
- flyers around campus alert students to the special sections;
- restrictions are placed on an enrollment page so that the "wrong" students can't get in (this functions like prerequisites but instead might be tied to other attributes or prior courses).

None of these proved to be simple, however. The first option is the most transparent to students and offers an informed choice—an important goal of mine. However, the registrar's office informed me we could not have variable titles in English 1. I knew from my tagmemic exploration that variable title courses exist, even at the lowest level of our curriculum (English 5, for example). Armed with examples of wave/variation, I returned to the field of the registrar's office. Guided by tagmemics, we eventually realized we would need to change the catalog copy to allow for slight variations in the audience for the course—which would result in a different deep-level coding of the course-registration page. As with many important but nearly invisible bureaucratic mechanisms, the process would take a year. Although the transparency I sought was not in place for the spring 2016 pilot, it was by the following fall.

In the absence of clear labeling, how do we best advise students into this course? Then, how do students actually enroll in these sections? Is it possible to set up restrictions on some sections but not others? These puzzles were best solved in collaboration with the registrar's office and our Student Services Collaborative, a network of advisors from each college in the university. From the registrar's office, answers were usually no, regardless of the question; in contrast, from the Student Services Collaborative, answers were usually, "Okay, how do we do it anyway?" For the pilot, we settled on block scheduling as a short-term solution—not a happy solution but an expeditious and temporary one. On the field level, we are continually reminded of the distinction between what is and is not possible *now* versus what will and will not be possible in the future.

Interestingly, changing the deeper structure of the catalog description to allow for variation meant an alteration minimally visible to anyone looking at the course catalog (just a few tweaks in the words of the description, no substantive meaning changes) but a completely different architecture in the computer system underneath. Changing the deep structure of ENGS1 to allow for slightly variable titles (and therefore slightly variable student audiences) opened the door for and allowed for other useful variations—transfer or upper-division students, for example. In actuality, it also opened the door for thematic variations within our shared curriculum, and time will tell whether this evolves. This bureaucratic tweak may, in fact, further support the community-building collaborative evolution of a truly shared curriculum.

One more interesting twist occurred. A number of students preferring mainstream sections managed to register themselves as a group into a popular GTA's section. They unwittingly created what Paul Kei Matsuda and Tony Silva have called "cross-cultural" sections, which purposefully blend international and domestic students (Matsuda and Silva 1999). We invited that GTA to join our pilot cohort, funded through my office. It is worth noting that funding an additional participant would not have been possible at my previous institution because of the budget structure. There, the structure was use it or lose it—so any moneys not spent by June 30 disappeared forever into a general surplus fund (this often led to a spending spree for toner and copier paper in late spring). At my new institution, moneys not spent in previous years can be requested for specific, justifiable purposes, such as compensating three additional multilingual writers faculty fellows at $1,000: the cross-cultural section, the section taught by a librarian, and the section taught by an ESOL faculty member.

CONCLUSION

In sum, this situation—first encountered my second day on the job—allowed me to put into action any previous theoretical training and practical experience I have gathered in feminist administration, institutional critique, and second language writing. Tagmemics helped guide my inquiry and shaped the social networks I needed to join or build.

As of this writing, our pilot is currently underway. Some of us are trying a true end-of-semester portfolio; all of us are seeking new model projects to include in our custom reader; we are experimenting with variations on the assignment sheets, fewer or different readings, and new reflective prompts. We post our new materials and in-class activities to a shared BlackBoard site, and we meet biweekly to discuss what we are doing and learning. We are finding that our changes, those adaptations we are developing, are good for all our students. In a time when all students are multilingual in different ways, when all our students bring multiliteracies to our campuses, when all our students present different learning preferences and abilities, these are necessary changes (see also Matsuda 2006). In this new environment, our L1 curriculum is enriched by L2 principles. At least at the curricular level, we are listening to and learning from our international writers.

References

Atkinson, Dwight, and Vai Ramanathan. 1995. "Cultures of Writing: An Ethnographic Comparison of L1 and L2 University Writing/Language Programs." *TESOL Quarterly* 29 (3): 539–68. https://doi.org/10.2307/3588074.

Benson, Beverly, Mary P. Deming, Debra Denzer, and Maria Valeri-Gold. 1992. "A Combined Basic Writing/English as a Second Language Class: Melting Pot or Mishmash?" *Journal of Basic Writing* 11 (1): 58–74.

Braine, George. 1996. "ESL Students in First-Year Writing Courses: ESL versus Mainstream Classes." *Journal of Second Language Writing* 5 (2): 91–107. https://doi.org /10.1016/S1060-3743(96)90020-X.

Canagarajah, A. Suresh. 2015. "'Blessed in My Own Way': Pedagogical Affordances for Dialogical Voice Construction in Multilingual Student Writing." *Journal of Second Language Writing* 27:122–39. https://doi.org/10.1016/j.jslw.2014.09.001.

Chiang, Yuet-Sim D., and Mary Schmida. 1999. "Language Identity and Language Ownership: Linguistic Conflicts of First-Year University Writing Students." In *Generation 1.5 Meets College Composition: Issues in the Teaching of Writing to U.S. Educated Learners of ESL*, edited by Linda Harklau, Kay M. Losey, and Meryl Siegal, 81–99. Mahwah, NJ: Lawrence Erlbaum.

Conference on College Composition and Communication. 2014. "CCCC Statement on Second Language Writing and Writers." www.ncte.org/cccc/resources/positions/sec ondlangwriting.

Costino, Kimberly A., and Sunny Hyon. 2007. "'A Class for Students Like Me': Reconsidering Relationships among Identity Labels, Residency, Status, and Students' Preferences for Mainstream or Multilingual Composition." *Journal of Second Language Writing* 16 (2): 63–81. https://doi.org/10.1016/j.jslw.2007.04.001.

Goodburn, Amy, and Carrie S. Leverenz. 1998. "Feminist Writing Program Administration: Resisting the Bureaucrat Within." In *Feminism and Composition Studies: In Other Words*, edited by Susan C. Jarratt and Lynn Worsham, 276–90. New York: Modern Language Association.

Harklau, Linda. 1994. "ESL versus Mainstream Classes: Contrasting L2 Learning Environments." *TESOL Quarterly* 28 (2): 241–72. https://doi.org/10.2307/3587433.

Hsieh, Min-Hua. 2007. "Challenges for International Students in Higher Education: One Student's Narrated Story of Invisibility and Struggle." *College Student Journal* 41 (2): 379–91.

Kinney, James. 1978. "Tagmemic Rhetoric: A Reconsideration." *College Composition and Communication* 29 (2): 141–45. https://doi.org/10.2307/357298.

Kneupper, Charles W. 1980. "Revising the Tagmemic Heuristic: Theoretical and Pedagogical Considerations." *College Composition and Communication* 31 (2): 160–68. https://doi.org/10.2307/356370.

Lawrick, Elena. 2013. "Students in the First-Year ESL Writing Program: Revisiting the Notion of 'Traditional' ESL." *WPA: Writing Program Administration* 36 (2): 27–59.

Leki, Ilona. 1992. *Understanding ESL Writers: A Guide for Teachers.* Portsmouth, NH: Boynton/Cook-Heinemann.

Lindemann, Erika. 1995. "Three Views of English 101." *College English* 57 (3): 287–302. https://doi.org/10.2307/378679.

Marzluf, Phillip P. 2006. "Diversity Writing: Natural Languages, Authentic Voices." *College Composition and Communication* 57 (3): 503–22.

Matsuda, Paul Kei. 2006. "The Myth of Linguistic Homogeneity in U.S. College Composition." *College English* 68 (6): 637–51. https://doi.org/10.2307/25472180.

Matsuda, Paul Kei, and Tony Silva. 1999. "Cross-Cultural Composition: Mediated Integration of US and International Students." *Composition Studies* 27 (1): 15–30.

Miller, Richard E. 1999. "Critique's the Easy Part: Choice and the Scale of Relative Oppression." In *Kitchen Cooks, Plate Twirlers and Troubadours: Writing Program Administrators Tell Their Stories*, edited by Diana George, 3–14. Portsmouth, NH: Boynton/Cook/Heinemann.

Miller-Cochran, Susan K. 2010. "Language Diversity and the Responsibility of the WPA." In *Cross-Language Relations in Composition*, edited by Bruce Horner, Min-Zahn Lu, and Paul Kei Matsuda, 212–20. Carbondale: Southern Illinois University Press.

Ortmeier-Hooper, Christina. 2008. "English May Be My Second Language, but I'm Not 'ESL.'" *College Composition and Communication* 59 (3): 389–419.

Porter, James E., Patricia A. Sullivan, Stuart Blythe, Jeffrey T. Grabill, and Libby Miles. 2000. "Institutional Critique: A Rhetorical Methodology for Change." *College Composition and Communication* 51 (4): 610–42.

Rafoth, Ben, and Shanti Bruce. 2009. *ESL Writers: A Guide for Writing Center Tutors.* 2nd ed. Portsmouth, NH: Boynton/Cook.

Reid, Joy, and Barbara Kroll. 1995. "Designing and Assessing Effective Classroom Writing Assignments for NES and ESL Students." *Journal of Second Language Writing* 4 (1): 17–41. https://doi.org/10.1016/1060-3743(95)90021-7.

Roy, Alice M. 1988. "ESL Concerns for Writing Program Administrators: Problems and Policies." *WPA: Writing Program Administration* 11 (3): 17–28.

Shuck, Gail. 2006. "Combating Monolingualism: A Novice Administrator's Challenge." *WPA: Writing Program Administration* 30 (1–2): 59–82.

Silva, Tony. 1993. "Toward an Understanding of the Distinct Nature of L2 Writing: The ESL Research and Its Implications." *TESOL Quarterly* 27 (4): 657–77. https://doi.org/10.2307/3587400.

Silva, Tony. 1994. "An Examination of Writing Program Administrators' Options for the Placement of ESL Students in First-Year Writing Classes." *WPA: Writing Program Administration* 18 (1–2): 37–43.

Silva, Tony. 1997. "On the Ethical Treatment of ESL Writers." *TESOL Quarterly* 31 (2): 359–63. https://doi.org/10.2307/3588052.

Sirc, Geoffrey. 1997. "Never Mind the Tagmemics, Where's the Sex Pistols?" *College Composition and Communication* 48 (1): 9–29.

Song, Bailin, and Bonne August. 2002. "Using Portfolios to Assess Writing of ESL Students: A Powerful Alternative?" *Journal of Second Language Writing* 11 (1): 49–72. https://doi.org/10.1016/S1060-3743(02)00053-X.

Vitanza, Victor J. 1979. "A Tagmemic Heuristic for the Whole Composition." *College Composition and Communication* 30 (3): 270–74.

Wetzl, Ana Marie. 2013. "World Englishes in the Mainstream Composition Course: Undergraduate Students Respond to WE Writing." *Research in the Teaching of English* 48 (2): 204–27.

Young, Richard, Alton Becker, and Kenneth Pike. 1970. *Rhetoric: Discovery and Change.* San Diego, CA: Harcourt.

Zamel, Vivian. 1995. "Strangers in Academia: The Experiences of Faculty and ESL Students across the Curriculum." *College Composition and Communication* 46 (4): 506–21.

ABOUT THE AUTHORS

SHIRLEY K ROSE is professor of English at Arizona State University, where she is director of ASU writing programs. Her experience as a writing program administrator includes six years as director of composition at Purdue, two years as director of graduate assistants at Eastern Michigan University, five years as director of composition faculty development at San Diego State University, and one year as graduate adviser for SDSU's Department of Rhetoric and Writing Studies, where she was a founding faculty member. She regularly teaches graduate seminars in writing program administration and in archival research methodologies. She has served on the Council of Writing Program Administrators as a member of the executive board and as president. She is the director of the WPA Consultant-Evaluator Service.

IRWIN WEISER is professor of English at Purdue University. He has served as department head, director of composition, and director of developmental writing and most recently as dean of the College of Liberal Arts. He teaches graduate courses in contemporary composition theory, a practicum in the teaching of composition, and seminars in writing across the curriculum, writing assessment, and composition research in the rhetoric and composition PhD program. He is active in the Council of Writing Program Administrators, including serving several terms on the editorial board of *WPA: The Journal of the Council of Writing Program Administrators* and a term on the executive board. He has also co-led the annual summer workshop for WPAs and the Research Institute, both held in conjunction with the annual WPA summer conference.

JONATHAN BENDA teaches writing at Northeastern University in Boston, Massachusetts. Prior to coming to Boston, he taught English at Tunghai University in Taiwan for fifteen years. He received a PhD in composition and cultural rhetoric from Syracuse University. He has published articles in *Intercultural Communication Studies, Concentric: Literary and Cultural Studies,* and *Writing & Pedagogy.* His research interests include intercultural communication, second language writing, and Taiwan studies.

MICHAEL DEDEK is a lecturer of English at Northeastern University and Wentworth Institute of Technology. His research interests include college composition curricula and multilingual writing pedagogy. He recently completed a dissertation, "Practicing Change: Curriculum Innovation and Change in Writing Programs," which studied social processes of curriculum change in a first-year writing program at a university in the northeastern United States. He has given presentations at CCCC, including one that presented results from a case study of student experiences in a translingual writing course.

CHRISTIANE DONAHUE is associate professor of linguistics and director of the Institute for Writing and Rhetoric at Dartmouth College. She is the author of *Writing at the University: Comparative Analysis, France-United States* among several other books and articles and is a 2009 Fulbright Research Scholar for the project titled University Student Writing in Cross-National Perspective: Types, Difficulties, and Interventions. Donahue's areas of expertise include writing research methods, international writing studies, discourse analysis, and knowledge transfer. She teaches first-year writing and linguistics topics courses in the United States and abroad. She is a member of several European research groups.

CHRIS W. GALLAGHER is associate dean of teaching, learning, and experiential education and professor of English at Northeastern University. His books include *Radical Departures: Composition and Progressive Pedagogy* (NCTE, 2002), *Reclaiming Assessment: A Better Alternative to the Accountability Agenda* (Heinemann 2007), *Teaching Writing that Matters* (with Amy Lee, Scholastic, 2008), and *Our Better Judgment: Teacher Leadership for Writing Assessment* (with Eric Turley, NCTE, 2012). His articles on writing pedagogy, writing assessment, and educational reform have appeared in a variety of journals in rhetoric and composition as well as education.

KRISTI GIRDHARRY completed her PhD in English at Northeastern University in 2016 where she worked closely with multilingual students as an instructor, writing consultant, and co-researcher on the Multilingual Writers Project. Learning from her work with this project, she also used a mixed-methods approach in her dissertation to understand the complexities of story sharing and writing that was collected by a digital archive following the Boston Marathon bombings in 2013. She continues to explore her interests in pedagogy, writing, and digital literacies and identities as an assistant professor of English at Johnson & Wales University in Providence, Rhode Island.

TAREZ SAMRA GRABAN is associate professor of English at Florida State University. From 2002 to 2007 she taught academic writing and oral English proficiency to international graduate students and multilingual learners at Purdue University. From 2007 to 2012 she coordinated Multilingual FYC at Indiana University, training graduate TAs and forming partnerships with second language studies, English-language instruction, and the university libraries. She also conducted faculty seminars and workshops on teaching L2/multilingual writing. Since 2012, she has worked with composition instructors and writing center tutors at Florida State University on developing and sustaining a teaching practice informed by a multilingual paradigm.

JENNIFER E. HAAN is an associate professor in the English department at the University of Dayton, where she teaches courses in L2 writing, TESOL, linguistics, and rhetoric and composition. Her research focuses primarily on language-supported internationalization in higher education, including the incorporation of linguistically responsive instruction both in writing courses and across the curriculum. Her recent publications have examined literacy practices of undergraduate L2 writers, approaches to genre instruction for graduate L2 writers, and faculty perspectives on incorporating linguistically responsive pedagogical practices in the context of university internationalization. In addition to her teaching and research, she regularly provides workshops and seminars for faculty teaching in culturally and linguistically diverse university classrooms.

PAULA HARRINGTON has been the director of Colby College's Farnham Writers' Center since 2008. Like her coauthor Stacey Sheriff, she is an administrator-teacher-scholar who teaches peer-review pedagogy and writing as well as directing the writers' center. She holds a BA in English from Columbia University and a PhD in English from the University of California, Davis, where she also taught in the composition program. In 2013, she was a Fulbright Scholar in Paris, researching French stereotypes in the work of Mark Twain. That research resulted in a cross-cultural study, *Mark Twain & the French: The Making of a New American Identity*, coauthored with Professor Ronald Jenn of the University of Lille and forthcoming in spring 2017 from University of Missouri Press.

YU-KYUNG KANG is an assistant professor of English at Gonzaga University. She researches and publishes on transnational literacy, multilingual writing, and writing center practice and theory. In her current position, in addition to teaching and research, she is involved in collaborating with composition and writing concentration faculty and building relationships with campus programs and units such as TESOL, the English Language Center, and Global Engagement—as well as bolstering writing center tutor training and faculty development for working with multilingual writers.

NEAL LERNER is associate professor of English and writing program director at Northeastern University. His book *The Idea of a Writing Laboratory* won the 2011 NCTE David H. Russell Award for Distinguished Research in the Teaching of English. His is also the coauthor with Jennifer Craig and Mya Poe of *Learning to Communicate as a Scientist and Engineer: Case Studies from MIT,* winner of the 2012 CCCC Advancement of Knowledge Award, and coauthor with Paula Gillespie of *The Longman Guide to Peer Tutoring, 2nd ed.* With Michele Eodice and Anne Ellen Geller, he is the coauthor of *The Meaningful Writing Project: Learning, Teaching, and Writing in Higher Education* (Utah State University Press, 2016).

DAVID S. MARTINS is associate professor and founding director of the university writing program at Rochester Institute of Technology. He has served as a fellow of the SUNY Collaborative Online International Learning (COIL) Institute. His digital essay "Transnational Writing Programs and Emerging Models for Writing, Teaching, and Learning" (*Kairos*) explores the changing infrastructures for transnational writing programs. The collection *Transnational Writing Program Administration* (USUP) he edited endeavors to help writing program administrators engage critically with the key aspects of writing program administration that reveal its transnationality. In addition to focusing on program administration, his research addresses the pedagogies and outcomes of globally networked learning environments.

PAUL KEI MATSUDA is professor of English and director of second language writing at Arizona State University. He is also concurrent professor of applied linguistics at Nanjing University and Zhengzhou University, China. Founding chair of the Symposium on Second Language Writing, and the editor of the Parlor Press Series on Second Language Writing, and former president of the American Association for Applied Linguistics, Paul has published widely on issues related to the internationalization of writing programs and writing instruction. A sought-after speaker, he has been invited to speak at various institutions and conferences in over twenty-five countries and throughout the United States.

HEIDI A. MCKEE is the Roger and Joyce Howe Professor of Written Communication and associate professor of English at Miami University. She is director of the Howe Writing Initiative, which involves the writing center, the WAC program, and the business communication program in the Farmer School of Business. She has coauthored and coedited a number of books, including *Digital Writing Research: Technologies, Methodologies, and Ethical Issues* (2007); *The Ethics of Internet Research: A Rhetorical, Case-Based Process* (2009); *Technological Ecologies and Sustainability* (2009); and *Digital Writing Assessment and Evaluation* (2013). Her most recent book project with James Porter is *Professional Communication in a Digital Age: A Rhetorical, Ethical Approach.*

LIBBY MILES, associate professor of English at the University of Vermont, serves as the director of Foundational Writing and Information Literacy. Her published work focuses on institutional change through a variety of mechanisms, such as administrative issues in higher education, curricular design in writing majors, and classroom practices. She has published in *CCC, JAC, College English,* and *WPA,* among others. With Jose A. Amador and C.B. Peters, she coauthored *The Practice of Problem-Based Learning* (2006), and her various works have earned the CCCC Berlin and Braddock awards, as well as a Best Article in *WPA* award. She has served on executive committees for CCCC and CWPA, as well as a host of local, regional, and national committees. For this piece, she is grateful to Zoe McDonald's excellent research assistance.

SUSAN MILLER-COCHRAN is professor of English and director of the writing program at the University of Arizona, where her research focuses on the intersections of technology, multilingual writing, and writing program administration. Her work has appeared in *College Composition and Communication, Composition Studies, Computers and Composition,*

Enculturation, and *Teaching English in the Two-Year College,* and she is also an editor of *Rhetorically Rethinking Usability* (Hampton Press, 2009) and *Strategies for Teaching First-Year Composition* (NCTE, 2002). In addition, she is a coauthor of *An Insider's Guide to Academic Writing* (2016), *The Cengage Guide to Research* (Cengage, 2017), and *Keys for Writers* (Cengage, 2014). Before joining the faculty at the University of Arizona, she was the director of first-year writing at North Carolina State University (2007–2015) and also a faculty member at Mesa Community College (AZ). She currently serves as president of the Council of Writing Program Administrators.

MATT NOONAN is an associate teaching professor in the writing program at Northeastern University, where he teaches first-year and advanced writing-in-the-disciplines courses. He is coauthor of "Becoming Global: Learning to 'Do' Translingualism," forthcoming in *Crossing Divides: Exploring Translingual Writing Pedagogies and Programs.*

KATHERINE DAILY O'MEARA is assistant professor of rhetoric and composition and director of composition at Emporia State University. She specializes in writing program administration, second language writing, institutional ethnography, and writing-teacher training and support. Kat is a faculty mentor and past chair of the Writing Program Administrators Graduate Organization (WPA-GO) and an active member of the Council of Writing Program Administrators (CWPA).

CAROLINA PELAEZ-MORALES is assistant professor of TESOL and composition at Columbus State University, where she teaches first-year writing and TESOL courses and coordinates a TESOL certificate and an ESOL endorsement program. Her research interests include second language writing development in different educational contexts, academic support of L2 students, and bilingualism. She has published articles, chapters, and book reviews in *Language and Education Journal, INTESOL Journal, Preparing Teachers to Work with English Language Learners in Mainstream Classrooms,* and *Critical Inquiry in Language Studies.* Her most recent coauthored publication, *Graduate Studies in Second Language Writing,* was published by Parlor Press in 2016.

STACEY SHERIFF joined Colby College in 2012 as the inaugural director of the Colby Writing Program. She holds bachelor of arts degrees in English and environmental studies from Dartmouth College and a PhD in English, specializing in rhetoric and composition, from Pennsylvania State University. At Colby, Stacey is an administrator-teacher-scholar who wears many hats, from first-year writing to assessment to faculty development. Her research interests include small-college WPAs and inclusive pedagogy, histories of rhetoric, Progressive Era activism, and writing studies.

GAIL SHUCK is associate professor of English and coordinator of English-language support programs at Boise State University, where she has directed the first-year ESL writing sequence, taught courses in applied linguistics, sociolinguistics, and second language writing, and developed resources and programs for multilingual Boise State students since 2001. Her research investigates the ways teaching practices and institutional structures operate from default assumptions about language users—specifically, multilingual students as "deviations" from a monolingual norm.

CHRISTINE M. TARDY is professor of English applied linguistics at the University of Arizona, where she also serves as the writing program's associate director for second language writing. Her primary areas of research include second language writing, genre theory and pedagogy, English for academic purposes/writing in the disciplines, and policies and politics of English. She has published widely in journals such as *Written Communication, Research in the Teaching of English, College Composition and Communication, English for Specific Purposes,* and *Discourse & Society.* Her recent books include *Beyond Convention: Genre Innovation in Academic Writing* (University of Michigan Press) and *Ethnographic Perspectives* *on Academic Writing* (Oxford University Press, with Brian Paltridge and Sue Starfield). She served as coeditor of the *Journal of Second Language Writing* from 2011 through 2016.

STANLEY VAN HORN is the director of the English Language Center at the Rochester Institute of Technology, Rochester, New York. Research interests include intercultural communication, discourse analysis, and professional and academic genres in English. He has developed and coordinated specialized academic English courses for business, administration, science, and law. Stanley received his doctorate in linguistics from the University of Illinois, Urbana-Champaign (Urbana). He serves on the editorial advisory board of the journal *World Englishes*.

DANIEL WILBER is a lecturer at Ithaca College and an assistant researcher at Boise State University. He has an MA in rhetoric and composition and has taught language learners for nine years in the United States and abroad in South Korea and Turkey. His research explores linguistic diversity more broadly and considers how institutions can locate and seize opportunities to develop policies, support programs, curricular designs, and placement procedures that serve not only international students but also US-resident multilingual students, who are often much less visible in institutional policies and practices.

MARGARET K. WILLARD-TRAUB is associate professor of composition and rhetoric at the University of Michigan–Dearborn, where she served as director of the writing program and writing center from 2006 to 2012 and as member of the campus-wide task force charged with overseeing general education reform. Her research interests include transnational and cross-cultural teaching and learning, reflective approaches to higher education and writing program administration, feminist rhetoric, scholarly memoir, and large-scale writing assessment. She teaches introductory and advanced courses in writing and rhetoric and women's and gender studies. Her work has appeared in *College English, Assessing Writing, Feminist Studies, Rhetoric Review,* and *Pedagogy,* as well as in a number of collected editions. She currently is working on a book-length project that examines twenty-first-century higher education trends and practices through a feminist, rhetorical lens.